SOURCES AND DOCUMENTS IN THE
HISTORY OF ART SERIES

H. W. Janson, *Editor*

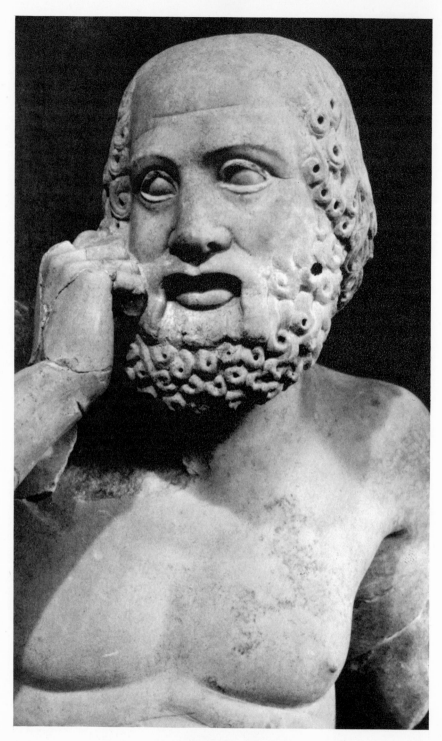

"Old Seer," east pediment, temple of Zeus at Olympia

The Art of Greece

1400-31 B.C.

SOURCES and DOCUMENTS

J. J. POLLITT

Yale University

PRENTICE-HALL, INC.

Englewood Cliffs, New Jersey

PRENTICE-HALL INTERNATIONAL, INC., *London*
PRENTICE-HALL OF AUSTRALIA, PTY., LTD., *Sydney*
PRENTICE-HALL OF CANADA, LTD., *Toronto*
PRENTICE-HALL OF INDIA (PRIVATE) LTD., *New Delhi*
PRENTICE-HALL OF JAPAN, INC., *Tokyo*

709.38   P775ag   1965   FV
POLLITT
THE ART OF GREECE, 1400-31 B. C.:
SOURCES AND DOCUMENTS
                                    3.95

Preface

This volume is designed to make the major literary sources for the history of Greek art available to the student who is not a specialist in the Classical languages. The chronological framework of the book has been arranged by subject matter rather than by the date of the authors whose writings are used, and hence it can be read as a consecutive history. Passages which deal with more than one epoch are assembled in the final chapter.

With the exception of most of the material on architecture and of a few passages of general interest which do not deal with specific artists, the texts used in the present collection may be found in Overbeck's *Die Antiken Schriftquellen zur Geschichte der bildenden Künste bei den Griechen* (Leipzig, 1868).[1]

In translating the passages collected in this volume I have sometimes added short explanatory phrases that are not in the original texts in order to make the meaning clear. The explanatory phrases are placed in brackets [ ]. Parenthetical remarks which are part of the original appear in parentheses ( ). In cases where the reading of a text is doubtful or the meaning of a word is unclear, I have tried to indicate the nature of the problem in the footnotes.

The problem of transliterating Greek names and words for the English speaking reader is always a difficult one, since some modern writers use the conventional Latinized forms which have become part of our academic tradition (e.g., "Phaeacia, Ajax, Dipoenus") while others prefer a more direct adaptation of the Greek spelling (e.g., "Phaiakia, Aias, Dipoinos"). In the present volume I have used the un-Latinized forms except in cases where the traditional Latinization has become so familiar that to change it would only seem pedantic (hence, for example, "Thucydides" is used rather than "Thoukydides"). In one case I have used alternate spellings to distinguish between two artists: the name of the famous artist-wizard of early Greece has been spelled "Daedalus" while the obscure fourth century sculptor from Sikyon of the same name has been spelled "Daidalos."

In cases where Roman authors use Latin names to refer to Greek

---

1. Photomechanical reprint (Hildesheim, 1959). In some cases the texts used by Overbeck have been superseded by later edition.

deities (e.g. "Diana" for "Artemis" or "Venus" for "Aphrodite"), I have always used the Greek name in the translation.

The bibliography given in the footnotes is intended to aid the reader in correlating the literary or epigraphical sources with extant monuments of ancient art and to call attention to useful studies which might help to clarify particularly difficult passages. It is not intended to be exhaustive. For the most part I have chosen to refer to the photographs provided in well-known and easily accessible volumes such as the second edition of Richter's *Sculpture and Sculptors of the Greeks,* Picard's *Manuel d'Archeologie Greque: La Sculpture,* etc.

Biographical information on the authors used in this volume is detailed in the appendix.

J. J. POLLITT

INDEX OF ABBREVIATIONS FOR PERIODICALS

A.J.A.   American Journal of Archaeology.

Abh. Sächs. Akad. Wissenschaften zu Leipzig.   Abhandlungen der Sächsischen Akademie der Wissenschaften, Philologisch-Historische Klasse, Leipzig.

Abhandl. d. Sachs. Ges. d. Wiss., Phil.-Hist. Kl.   Abhandlungen der Sächsischen Gesellschaft der Wissenschaften, Philologisch-Historische Klasse, Leipzig.

Ath. Mitt.   Mitteilungen des Deutschen Archaeologischen Instituts, Athenische Abteilung.

J.H.S.   Journal of Hellenic Studies.

Riv. del R. Inst. d'Arch. e Storia d. Arte.   Rivista del Reale Istituto d'Archeologia e Storia dell'Arte.

Contents

Introduction

THE NATURE OF THE SOURCES

The study of Greek art through ancient literary sources is complicated by a number of factors which cannot be said to apply to the study of any other period. First there is the fact that most of the authors who provide significant information lived *much later than the artists about whom they write*. The Elder Pliny, for example, who is our most comprehensive source for the history of Greek painting and sculpture of the Classical period (the fifth and fourth centuries B.C.), wrote in the mid first century A.D. Not only is the distance between Pliny and Pheidias about 500 years, but, as a Roman, Pliny spoke a different language and belonged to a society far different from that of the artists who were his subject. The fact is that there are scarcely any "contemporary sources" in the extant literature on ancient art; there is no ancient writer who wrote on Pheidias or Zeuxis, as Vasari wrote on Michelangelo, through a direct knowledge of the artist's personality, aims, and products. The only contemporary references of any length that exist today for the art of the Classical period are inscriptions, some of which are presented in the present volume, but these, it will be seen, are the most impersonal documents imaginable.

Another factor which complicates the study of the literary sources for ancient art is that, with the exception of Vitruvius' *De Architectura* and the rhetorical descriptions of works of art which became fashionable in late antiquity, there are *no writings which deal intentionally, directly and exclusively with art as such*. Many of the passages which will be found in this volume are in the nature of parenthetical remarks made by writers like Herodotus or Aristotle, who, in pursuing another subject, fund their attention momentarily arrested by the example of a particular monument or a particular artist. Even the all-important sections on art given in books XXXIII-XXXVI of Pliny's *Natural History* are really digressions from more basic subjects.[1] Nor can Pausanias'

1. The basic subject of Books XXXIII and XXXIV, for example, is metals; sculpture in metal is treated as a special aspect of this general subject. The ostensible subject of Book XXXV is types of earth and minerals, although, since painters used many types of minerals as pigments, most of the book deals with painting. Book XXXVI deals with the different types of stone.

meticulous and invaluable description of Greece in the second century A.D., any more than the modern *Guide Bleu* to Greece, be said to
deal primarily with art. In every case the information is there, but the
modern scholar is required to select and arrange it in order to achieve
a cohesive picture of ancient art. Hence in the present volume the
reader will often find himself confronted with a series of relatively
short passages extracted from larger works and juxtaposed for the purpose of unifying our knowledge of a particular artist or monument. It
is well to point out that the nature of our sources makes this arrangement necessary. There is no ancient document which, like Baldinucci's
Life of Bernini, can profitably be quoted without interruption and
in toto. If the average beginning student in the history of art were to
read through Pausanias without special instruction, he might well get
little out of it.

Granting all these qualifying factors, however, there are certain
reasons why the writings of late authors like Pliny and Pausanias have
a better claim to be considered "sources and documents" for the art
of their early predecessors than does, say, a modern Englishman's critical
evaluation of Masaccio. One reason is the *continuity of tradition* in
ancient writings on art and the other is the relatively *objective, unoriginal nature* of many of our sources. Pausanias, for example, carefully
describes the art which he saw but almost never ventures any farther
into the field of subjective evaluation than to say that a particular
work is "worth seeing." Whatever historical information Pausanias
gives about the works of art which he encountered is derived from inscriptions which he saw, earlier writers he had read, or word of mouth
information given to him by his guides and informants. He never tried
to be original or to provide for his own age a new assessment of the
art which he described.

The traditional and unoriginal nature of Pliny's chapters on art
is even more marked. As Pliny himself boasts at the beginning of the
Natural History, the information in his work had been culled from
2,000 earlier sources. The picture of Greek art which Pliny presents
is consequently an elaborate *mélange* of biographical, historical and
critical information derived from earlier sources which were characterized by diverse aims and interests. Fortunately we know what some of
these sources were, since Pliny mentions them both in the text of the
Natural History and in a book-by-book bibliographical index. These
indices are especially important because they indicate that most of his
sources for the history of art were Greek writers and that some of these
writers were also practicing artists. Among the sources listed in the
index to book XXXIV who are said to have written on sculpture, for
example, we meet the following names: "Menaichmos, who wrote on

sculpture in metal;[2] Xenokrates, who wrote on the same subject; Antigonos, who wrote on the same subject; Douris, who wrote on the same subject; Heliodoros, who wrote on Athenian dedications; Pasiteles, who wrote on marvellous works . . . ." Of the writers mentioned, Menaichmos, Xenokrates, Antigonos, and Pasiteles are known to have been practicing sculptors. The date of Menaichmos[3] and the nature of his writings are uncertain, but in the case of the other three writers there is enough information preserved to enable us to formulate some idea of their contribution to Pliny.

Xenokrates[4] was active in the early third century B.C. Although he may have been an Athenian by birth, he belonged to the sculptural school of Sikyon, and was a pupil of Euthykrates, the son of Lysippos, or of Tisikrates, a pupil of Euthykrates. In either case, he was a direct artistic descendant of Lysippos, the guiding genius of the Sikyonian school. Pliny not only tells us that Xenokrates wrote *volumina* on sculpture, but also refers to a statement made by Xenokrates (and Antigonos) in praise of the painter Parrhasios' ability as a draughtsman; hence it is clear that he wrote about painting as well as sculpture. It has long been felt by modern scholars that Xenokrates must have been the source of an evolutionary system of art history, characterized by a distinct Sikyonian bias, which is imbedded in both Pliny's history of sculpture and his history of painting.[5] In this evolutionary system both painting and sculpture, after an early period of *rudis antiquitas,* gradually progressed toward a stage of perfection which was reached in the early Hellenistic period. Significant contributions or inventions which are ascribed respectively to five famous sculptors and five famous painters are thought to make distinct stages in this progression. In the history of sculpture which appears in book XXXIV, 54-65, of the *Natural History,* for example, the art is said to have been "opened up" (*aperuisse*) by Pheidias and to have been "refined" (*erudisse*) by Polykleitos. Myron is then said to have been "more precise in the application of *symmetria*"

2. "Sculpture in metal"—the word used here is *toreutikē,* the Greek term for "chasing" or "engraving" with a punch, burin, etc. It is applied to sculpture in gold and ivory as well as bronze. On the background of the term see p. 43.

3. See pp. 33-34.

4. For the literary testimonia on Xenokrates cf. p. 159 and p. 197. Three statue bases signed by a sculptor named Xenokrates and dating from the early third century B.C. have been found (two from Oropos, one from Elateia). Cf. Loewy, *Inschriften griechischer Bildhauer* (Leipzig, 1883), nos. 125, a, b, c. On one of these (Loewy 135a = *Inscriptiones Graecae* VII, 336), he refers to himself as an Athenian.

5. On the significance of Xenokrates cf. B. Schweitzer's invaluable article, "Xenokrates von Athen," *Schriften der Königsberger Gelehrter Gesellschaft,* 1932, pp. 1-52. On the sources of Pliny in general see A. Kalkmann, *Die Quellen der Kunstgeschichte des Plinius,* Berlin, 1898. Still the best source in English is E. Sellers' introduction to Sellers, Jex-Blake, *The Elder Pliny's Chapters on the History of Art* (London, 1896).

(*et in symmetria diligentior*) and to have made other improvements in the art. In the next stage the sculptor Pythagoras is credited with surpassing Myron (*vicit eum*) in the rendering of naturalistic details such as veins, hair, etc.; and finally Lysippos is said to have made the greatest contribution to the art (*statuariae arte plurimum traditur contulisse*) by improving on the achievements of all his predecessors. A similar evolutionary scheme, though perhaps less clearly presented, appears in the history of painting given in book XXXV of the *Natural History*. Apollodoros is said to have begun the great era of Greek painting by developing the technique of "shading" or what the Greeks called *skiagraphia*. These innovations in the use of light and shade were further developed by Zeuxis. Parrhasios was then the first to introduce *symmetria* into painting, to perfect the rendering of the hair, the details of the face, etc., and to insist on clarity in draughtsmanship. In the next stage Euphranor "made symmetry his own" (*usurpasse symmetrian*), and finally Apelles brought all these qualities together (*picturae plura solis prope quam ceteri omnes contulit*). In each case, it will be noted, the sequence culminates with a great master of the Sikyonian school who was an immediate predecessor of Xenokrates. The criteria used to evaluate the artists in question are in many cases technical achievements—the use of proportion, control of detail, mastery of draughtsmanship and shading—which would be better understood by professional painters and sculptors than by laymen. The subject-matter of their statues and paintings seems, on the other hand, not to have been a primary concern. Basically what was handed down to Pliny from Xenokrates was the outlook of a practicing artist in the late fourth and early third centuries B.C. It is by preserving such material that Pliny can have some claim to being a significant document for the history of Greek art.

Of Antigonos, another of the sculptor-authors mentioned by Pliny, less is known. He is said by Pliny to have worked on the monuments set up by the Attalid kings of Pergamon after their victory over the Gauls in the latter part of the third century B.C.[6] and is probably identical with Antigonos of Karystos, a versatile writer of the period who dabbled in biography, philosophy, and epigraphy as well as art history.[7] Since Pliny attributes the opinion that the painter Parrhasios was a draughtsman to Xenokrates and Antigonos jointly, it is usually assumed that Antigonos must have undertaken to expand and elaborate upon Xenokrates' treatise. Possibly he added certain new standards of judgment to Xenokrates' system, such as the representation of char-

---

6. See p. 200.
7. For a convenient summary see Sellers, *op. cit.*, pp. xxxvi-xlv, which is based on H. v. Wilamowitz-Moellendorff, *Antigonos von Karystos, Philologische Untersuchungen,* IV, Berlin, 1881.

acter and emotion—*ēthos* and *pathos*—which is ascribed, in particular, to the fourth century painter Aristeides.[8]

Pasiteles, another of Pliny's sources, was a native of one of the Greek cities of south Italy and obtained Roman citizenship in 89/88 B.C. He wrote five volumes on art, the subject of which is variously given by Pliny as *Marvellous Works* (*Mirabilia Opera*) or *Famous Works Throughout the World* (*Nobilia Opera in Toto Orbe*). Although we have no extant works of art which can positively be said to represent Pasiteles' own style, statues executed by members of his school are known and these suggest that Pasiteles was one of the guiding spirits of the neoclassic movement in late Hellenistic art.[9]

In the case of Xenokrates, Antigonos, and Pasiteles, then, we see that Pliny derived information from sources which were not only close to but in fact part of the history of Greek art.

The same conditions also apply, at least in part, to the two other brief histories of Greek art that are preserved in Roman literature—those given by Quintilian, *Institutio Oratoria* XII, 10, 3-9, and by Cicero, *Brutus,* 70.[10] The purpose of both these histories is to provide a series of stylistic comparisons between important rhetoricians and important artists. Quintilian's history, which is the more extensive of the two, clearly amalgamates several critical attitudes. Part of what he says about painting—as, for example, when he praises Zeuxis for his mastery of light and shade and Parrhasios for his draughtsmanship—seems to be derived from Xenokrates. His praise of Apelles' *ingenium et gratia,* on the other hand, may be derived from the painter's own writings; [11] while the other *diversae virtutes* which he ascribes to various painters seem to stress qualities which would have been emphasized in treatises on rhetorical style.[12] Quintilian's history of sculpture, however, seems to follow a unified scheme of development which is derived neither from Xenokrates, nor from rhetorical criticism. In this scheme sculpture initially evolves from a state of "hardness" which characterizes the early fifth century toward a state of "softness" which is reached in the statues of Myron around the middle of the fifth century B.C. This development is followed by a stage in which Polykleitos is said to have attained perfection in representing human beauty and Pheidias is credited with having given form to the sublime qualities of the gods. In doing so, Quintilian says, Pheidias "added something to traditional

---

8. On Aristeides see p. 174. On *ēthos* in general see Chapter 6, p. 229.
9. On Pasiteles see pp. 206-207.
10. See Chapter 6, pp. 219-221.
11. On Apelles and his writings see p. 164.
12. The concept of a *virtus,* or in Greek, *aretē,* of rhetorical style, i.e. "an essential excellence," seems to have originated in the literary criticism of the Peripatetic school, perhaps with Theophrastos. Cf. Cicero, *Orator,* 75 ff.; J. Stroux, *De Theophrasti Virtutibus Dicendi,* Leipzig, 1912.

religion." After Pheidias a decline sets in. Praxiteles and Lysippos mastered realism in sculpture, but Demetrios is blamed for having carried realism so far that he was "fonder of similitude than of beauty." Thus the high point of Greek sculpture comes, not, as in Xenokrates' system, with Lysippos in the late fourth century, but rather with Pheidias in the Classical period. And the characteristic feature of this high point is not the mastery of different technical aspects of sculpture but rather the possession of a kind of "spiritual intuition"—which the Greeks came to call *phantasia*—through which the sublime qualities of the gods could be perceived.[13]

The origin of this *phantasia* theory is not certain, but it has been ascribed to the philosophical school which is usually called the "Middle Stoa." The thought of the chief figures of this school, Panaitios (c. 185-109 B.C.) and Poseidonios (c. 135-50 B.C.), is characterized by a fusion of Platonic idealism and Stoic psychology, both of which seem to characterize the *phantasia* theory.[14] It was also characterized by a respect, even nostalgia, for the civilization of Greece in the fifth century B.C., i.e. the age of Pheidias and Polykleitos, and thus in many ways provided an intellectual background for the classicism which pervaded the late Hellenistic period. It is at least possible that this classicistic view of the history of sculpture was promulgated in the *quinque volumina* of the sculptor Pasiteles, since his date and artistic predilections seem to have been in harmony with it.[15]

The original Greek source which lies behind our extant Roman sources in this case is perhaps more truly a document for the neo-Attic phase of Greek art than for the Classical phase which it ostensibly discussed. Be that as it may, the value of our extant sources as documents for the history of Greek art seems once again to be supported by the continuity of tradition in ancient writings on art.

CLASSIFICATION OF SOURCES

The different types of writers on Greek art and the critical attitudes which they expressed have already been touched upon in the

13. For some of the important passages connected with this theory see Chapter 6, pp. 221-222.
14. On this question see the second appendix to Schweitzer's "Xenokrates von Athen"; see also Schweitzer's "Der bildende Künstler und der Begriff des Kunstlerischen in der Antike," *Neue Heidelberger Jahrbücher*, N.F., 1925, especially pp. 107 ff. and his "Mimesis und Phantasia," *Philologus*, 89, 1934, pp. 286-300.
15. Pasiteles was known to Cicero, the earliest Roman proponent of the theory, and Cicero himself studied briefly with Poseidonios (in 78 B.C.). Cf. *De Natura Deorum* I, iii, 6; *De Finibus* I, ii, 6; Plutarch, *Life of Cicero*, IV, 4.

preceding discussions. They may be summarized in four basic categories. The best preserved and hence most prominent group might be called *compilers of tradition;* it consists of writers who collected from disparate sources biographical, technical and anecdotal information about art and artists. Sometimes these collections were supplemented by a certain amount of first hand observation, as was the case with Pausanias, while at other times, they were almost wholly traditional, as is the case with Pliny. Such compilations can be traced back at least as far as the early Hellenistic period when Douris of Samos (c. 340-260 B.C.), one of the sources cited by Pliny in his index to book XXXIV of the *Natural History,* wrote a volume *On Painting.* Douris' life and writings had many facets.[16] We know that he was at one time the tyrant of Samos, that he won a prize as a boxer in the Olympic games, and that he was a pupil of Theophrastos, Aristotle's successor as head of the Peripatetic school. His writings included historical chronicles, literary criticism, essays and biographies, and seem to have been characterized by an interest in unusual personalities [17] and sensational anecdotes. In view of his background Douris is thought to be responsible for much of the anecdotal detail about the lives of artists which appear in Pliny. Pliny directly cites him as the source for the story that Lysippos had no teacher, but entered upon a career as a sculptor after having heard the painter Eupompos declare that nature itself, rather than any human teacher, was his model. Other anecdotes in Pliny such as the story of the painting contest between Zeuxis and Parrhasios or the story of how Protogenes finally perfected one of his paintings by throwing a wet sponge at it seem to bear Douris' stamp.[18] The critical attitude which lies behind these stories is one which might be called *popular criticism,* since it is characterized by ideas about art which are more characteristic of the layman than of either the practicing artist or the experienced connoisseur. The most abiding ideas of this popular criticism are an unquestioning acceptance of naturalism as the goal of art—i.e., the purpose of art is to imitate the external world and the best work of art is that which imitates it most convincingly—and an interest in the role of chance and the miraculous in art.

Another group of ancient writers on art might be called the *literary analogists;* to it belong the rhetoricians and poets who looked to the visual arts as a source for stylistic analogies with literature or sometimes even as a direct source for literary inspiration. The short histories of

16. Cf. Kalkmann, *op. cit.,* pp. 144 ff.; Sellers, Jex-Blake, *op. cit.,* pp. xxvi ff.

17. In this regard he may have been influenced by his teacher Theophrastos, whose *Characters* was the first work to make the study of personality a subject in itself.

18. All these anecdotes appear in the present volume; see pp. 143-144, 155, and 177.

art given by Quintilian and Cicero, for example, are primarily intended to serve as analogies to the stylistic development of Greek and Roman rhetoric. Dionysios of Halikarnassos (late first century B.C.), in writing on the different styles of Greek rhetoric, likewise draws analogies between the style of particular rhetoricians on the one hand and particular painters or sculptors on the other.[19] It has been suggested that these analogies may be traced back to a comparative canon of artists and rhetoricians which was formulated in the second century B.C.[20] The works of painters and sculptors also served as the subject matter for short poems and rhetorical descriptive exercises and in this sense they may be said to have had an influence on the actual content of ancient poetry and rhetoric. The tradition of writing short poems about works of art originated in the custom of inscribing metrical epigrams on the bases of statues. Many of the poems from the *Greek Anthology* which are quoted in this volume were presumably written for such a purpose. In time, however, the epigram became a formal genre, and many were written without any intention of ever having them inscribed on a stone base. There are, for example, over thirty epigrams extant about the famous Heifer by the sculptor Myron. Rhetorical descriptions of works of art, which in Greek were called *ekphraseis* (singular *ekphrasis*) appear to have come into vogue during the Roman period. A good example is Lucian's description of Zeuxis' *Centaur Family* (see pp. 156-158).

While it is clear that the literary analogists were primarily interested in their own disciplines rather than in the visual arts, they must be given credit for recognizing the importance of "personal styles" in the history of ancient art. They were aware that great artists, like great rhetoricians, had certain *virtutes* which distinguished them from other artists. The primary interest of the literary analogists was not so much in the ethical value of art nor in the evolution of artistic technique as in those obvious but sometimes difficult to define personal mannerisms which made each artist unique.

The third significant group of writers on ancient art might be called the *moral aestheticians,* and would include Plato, Aristotle and the other Greek philosophers who judged art chiefly by its capacity to influence man's moral awareness and behavior. Plato's condemnation of painting in the tenth book of the *Republic* is based on the belief that art encouraged men to indulge their natural tendency to be deceived and hence made it more difficult for them to perceive a higher undistorted reality. Aristotle, unlike Plato, does not reject the value of all painting, but he does recommend in the *Politics* that the youth of a city be allowed to see only those paintings which will have an en-

19. See Chapter 6, pp. 219-224.
20. Cf. C. Robert, *op. cit.,* pp. 53 and 73 ff.

nobling effect.[21] Even the authors of the late Hellenistic *phantasia* theory discussed above, while taking a more positive and reverent view of art, proposed that the greatest artistic creations were those which could convey spiritually uplifting qualities. The ultimate artistic experience in this view was a kind of mystical communion; it is best expressed by Dio Chrysostom when he says that even the most wretched man upon viewing Pheidias' Zeus at Olympia forgot his worldly afflictions and found peace.[22]

The fourth and final important group of ancient writers on art consisted of the artists themselves. Treatises by practicing architects go at least as far back as the middle of the sixth century B.C. when Theodoros and Rhoikos wrote on the Heraion at Samos and Chersiphron and Metagenes wrote on the temple of Artemis at Ephesos.[23] Technical manuals on sculpture were written at least as early as the second half of the fifth century B.C. when Polykleitos wrote his famous *Canon,* and in the fourth century there was apparently a rash of treatises by well-known painters.[24] The common element in all such writings seems to have been a preoccupation with problems of form and the technical procedures by which form is produced. Polykleitos' *Canon,* judging by what evidence is available, was essentially a highly technical manual of proportions. Its ultimate purpose was, in all probability, to define what perfect beauty in the human figure was, but it proceeded to this goal not by analyzing and praising known works of sculpture but rather by presenting a complex series of measurements through which the commensurability (*symmetria*) of all the parts of a statue was to be effected. The *Canon* was perhaps only an unusually complex and philosophical representative of a tradition of sculptors' workshop manuals which dated back (like architectural manuals) to the sixth century B.C. We know that at least one of his prominent predecessors, Pythagoras of Rhegion, "aimed at *rhythmos* and *symmetria.*" [25] The preservation of such workshop manuals throughout the fifth and fourth centuries B.C. would account for the relatively unified and steady development of Greek sculpture during this period. Each new generation of sculptors began with a clear conception of the standards of the preceding one, and made innovations on the basis of its own taste and convictions. According

21. For the relevant passages from Plato and Aristotle see Chapter 6, pp. 230-232 ff.

22. See p. 73.

23. See pp. 36, 37-38, and 232.

24. In the index and text of book XXXV of the *Natural History* Pliny mentions writings by Apelles, Melanthios, Asklepiodoros, Euphranor and Parrhasios; and the names of other painters who wrote on art are known. Cf. H. L. Urlichs, *Über Griechische Kunstschriftsteller,* Würzburg, 1887.

25. *Rhythmos* = compositional patterns. See p. 56 and p. 62.

xviii The Art of Greece

to Cicero (*Brutus*, 296), Lysippos used to say that the *Doryphoros* of Polykleitos was his model; Pliny, on the other hand, notes that Lysippos modified the "square quality" which was a characteristic of statues by his predecessors by using a new and hitherto untried system of proportions (*N.H.* XXXIV, 65). This "square quality," moreover, is specifically ascribed to Polykleitos. Taken together, these two passages, rather than being contradictory, suggest what the effect of the theoretical treatises of one generation may have been on the art of the next: Lysippos admired the work of Polykleitos enough to make it a point of departure for his own experiment in proportion; he did not treat it as an immutable standard.

The interests and aims of the *professional critics,* as we might call Polykleitos and the other artists who wrote on art, seem to have been summed up [26] in Xenokrates' history of sculpture and painting, in which, it will be remembered, the artists in question were evaluated on the basis of their formal and technical achievements. As a practicing artist Xenokrates must have been familiar with the technical treatises of his predecessors, and it is not unlikely that he used them in formulating the critical bases of his history.

The existence of these professional treatises is of paramount importance in the study of the sources and documents for the history of Greek art, since they form the last link in the chain of tradition by which our extant sources are connected with the original spirit that characterized the art of the Classical period.

26. It would appear that the practice of writing workshop manuals and technical treatises on sculpture came to an end around the time of Xenokrates, that is, in the early third century B.C. This may be the explanation behind Pliny's enigmatic remark (*N.H.* XXXIV, 52) that the art of sculpture "came to a halt" (*cessavit deinde ars*) in the 121st Olympiad (295 B.C.) and that it was reborn in the 156th Olympiad (156 B.C.)—i.e. that an interest in Classical theories of proportion etc. died out shortly after the time of Lysippos but was revived by the classicistic artists of the neo-Attic period. Cf. O. J. Brendel, "Prolegomena to a book on Roman Art," *Memoirs of the American Academy at Rome,* XXI, 1953, p. 54, n. 111.

I

Ancient Memories
and
Primitive Beginnings

THE MEMORY OF MYCENAEAN GREECE

While the myths and sagas of Classical Greece preserved a sub-stantial amount of information about personalities and events of the Mycenaean age, the art of this period was almost totally forgotten. A few of the major Bronze Age sites were visited in the second century A.D. *by the traveller Pausanias who was impressed with the scale of their architecture.*

Pausanias II, 16, 5-7 (on the ruins of Mycenae): Parts of the fortification wall, however, still remain, and also the gate, on which lions stand. They say that these are the works of the Cyclopes, who made the wall for Proitos in Tiryns. Among the ruins of Mycenae there is a fountain called the *Persea* and also the underground chambers of the children of Atreus, where their treasured possessions were stored. There is a tomb of Atreus, and also the graves of those whom Aegisthus entertained and slew upon their return from Troy with Agamemnon. . . . Another tomb is that of Agamemnon, another that of Eurymedon the charioteer, another that of Pelops and Teledamos (the twin sons whom they say Kassandra bore and whom Aegisthus slew, while still babies, along with their parents), and still another is that of Electra. . . . Clytemnestra and Aegisthus were buried a short distance from the wall. They were not deemed worthy to rest within the wall, where Agamemnon lay along with those who were murdered with him.

Pausanias had a similar impression of the ruins of Tiryns, another great Bronze Age citadel south of Mycenae.

Pausanias II, 25, 8: The wall, the sole part of the ruins which still remains, is a work of the Cyclopes and is made of unwrought stones, each stone being so huge that the smallest of them could not be moved even in the slightest degree by a pair of mules. Smaller stones were inserted long ago, in such a way that there is a tight fit between each of them and the larger stones.

THE ORIGIN OF THE ARTS

The legends among the Classical Greeks about the origin of the arts were naturally connected with those areas where Bronze Age crafts-manship had reached a high level. One such area was the island of Rhodes.

Diodorus Siculus V, 55, 1-3: A people known as the Telechines was the first to settle the island called Rhodes. . . . [Tradition records] that they were the inventors of some of the arts and the introducers of other things that were useful for the life of men. They are said to have been the first to make images of the gods, and some of the ancient images are named after them. Among the Lindians, for example, there is a statue referred to as the Telechinian Apollo; among the Ialysians there is a Telechinian Hera and the nymphs, and among the Kameirians a Telechinian Hera. These men were also wizards and could summon clouds, storms, and hail whenever they wished, and in a like manner they could even bring forth snow. . . . It is also said that they could change their own shapes, and that they were jealous about giving instruction in their arts.

The great Bronze Age civilization of Crete, now referred to as "Minoan" civilization, was also recognized as an early center of artistic production. Tradition held that there was an early school of Cretan artisans, known as the Idaian Daktyls, who were eventually apotheosized.

As the stories about Daedalus, the Telechines, and the Idaian Daktyls make clear, an aura of magic and wizardry surrounded the careers of the earliest artists and their creations.

Diodorus Siculus V, 64, 3-5: The present settlers of Crete say that the earliest inhabitants to dwell there were those who are called the Eteocretans, an indigenous people, whose king, named Kres, was responsible for the discovery on this island of a great number of important skills which benefit the common life of men. Likewise a great number of the gods are reported by tradition to have come into being in this land, gods who, because of their benefactions directed to the common good, won the rank of the immortals. . . .

The first of such gods, about whom there is a record preserved for posterity, dwelt around Mt. Ida in Crete and were called the "Idaian Daktyls." . . . The Idaian Daktyls are said by tradition to have discovered the use of fire and also the nature of bronze and iron . . . and the technique by which they are worked.

DAEDALUS

The Greeks attributed many of the first great achievements in sculpture and architecture to a legendary artist named Daedalus. The legends about Daedalus fall into two principal categories: those con-

*necting him with Bronze Age Crete, and those connecting him with the
earliest phases of "Archaic" sculpture in post Bronze Age Greece.*

The name Daedalus *in Greek means something like "the cunning
worker" or perhaps simply "the skillful one." The later Greeks ascribed
to Daedalus almost any work of great merit which was produced in an
early period for which there were no historical records. Thus, the name
Daedalus is probably a personification of the artistic skill which was
to be found in many ancient images, especially wooden images, made
in the period before the Greeks developed the technique of working
stone. Pausanias, although he believed that an actual Daedalus once
existed, recognized the symbolic quality of the name:*

Pausanias IX, 3, 2: . . . men of old used to refer to wooden images as
daidala. It seems to me that they gave them this name even before
Daedalus, the son of Palamaon, was born in Athens; I suspect that he
received this surname later on from these *daidala* and was not given
the name at birth.

*Whether Daedalus was only a personification or whether he was
an actual person, stories of his career were already common in the
earliest recorded stage of Greek literature, as is attested by Homer.*

Homer, *Iliad,* **XVIII, 590-3:** Thereon the renowned mighty-armed god
contrived a dance floor like that which Daedalus once fashioned in wide
Knossos for the fair-haired Ariadne.

*The Cretan tradition is most completely preserved by Diodorus
Siculus:*

Diodorus IV, 76, 1 ff: Daedalus was an Athenian by birth, his name indicating that he was one of the Erechtheids, for he was the son of
Metion, who was the son of Eupalamos, who was the son of Erechtheus.
Surpassing all others in natural ability, he pursued with zeal the art of
building and also of fashioning statues and carving stone. He was the
discoverer of many devices which contributed to the development of
art, and he produced marvellous works in many parts of the inhabited
world. In the production of statues he so excelled all other men that
later generations preserved a story to the effect that the statues which
he created were exactly like living beings; for they say that they could
see, and walk, and preserved so completely the disposition of the entire
body that the statue which was produced by art seemed to be a living
being. Having been the first to render the eyes open and the legs separated as they are in walking, and also to render the arms and hands as

if stretched out, he was marvelled at, quite naturally, by other men. For the artists who preceded him used to make their statues with the eyes closed, and with the arms hanging straight down and attached to the ribs.

The story follows of how a nephew of Daedalus, named Talos, invented the potter's wheel and also the toothed saw. Daedalus was so jealous of these achievements that he slew his nephew and, after being tried and convicted of murder, fled to Crete, where he became a close friend of King Minos. Here Daedalus' skill as an artist resulted in further achievements and also further difficulties.

Diodorus IV, 77, 4:   According to a tradition which has been handed down, Pasiphaë, the wife of Minos, conceived a passion for a bull, and Daedalus, having made a structure in the shape of a cow, made it possible for Pasiphaë to gratify her desire. The story goes that before this time it had been the custom of Minos to dedicate each year the most beautiful of the newly born bulls to Poseidon and then to sacrifice it to the god. But at this time, a bull of surpassing beauty was born, and he sacrificed in its stead another victim from among the inferior bulls. Poseidon, being angry with Minos, forced his wife Pasiphaë to conceive a passion for the bull. By means of the ingenuity of Daedalus Pasiphaë had intercourse with the bull and gave birth to the creature known in myth as the Minotaur. This creature, they say, was a hybrid form, the upper part of its body as far as the shoulders being like a bull, and the remaining parts like a man. As a place in which this monster could subsist, it is said that Daedalus built the Labyrinth, with winding passageways which were very difficult to follow for those unacquainted with them.

After the Pasiphaë incident, Daedalus fell out of favor with King Minos and was forced to flee from Crete. He did so by inventing sets of wings for himself and for his son Icarus, with which they could fly to Sicily. Once again his ingenious device was successful, although during the flight Icarus flew too near to the sun, which melted the wax which held the wings to his body, and plunged into the sea. Daedalus, however, reached Sicily, where, while in the service of King Kokalos, he was responsible for several remarkable feats of engineering, including a reservoir and an underground steam bath. Cf. Diodorus IV, 78, 1-5.
Another legendary cycle, also preserved by Diodorus, connects the artistic activity of Daedalus, both as a sculptor and architect, with Egypt. Diodorus states that Daedalus modelled his Labyrinth in Crete on the tomb of an Egyptian king named Mendes or Marros, and then

comments on the general connections between the art of Daedalus and that of Egypt:

Diodorus I, 97, 1-6:   They say that Daedalus copied the maze-like plan of the labyrinth [in Egypt] which remains up to the present day and was built, as some say, either by Mendes, or, as others say, by King Marros, many years prior to the time of King Minos.[1] It is also a fact that the *rhythmos*[2] of the ancient statues of Egypt is the same as that of the statues made by Daedalus among the Greeks. The extremely beautiful propylon of the Hephaisteion in Memphis was also built by Daedalus, and having become an object of admiration, he won the right to set up a wood statue of himself, which he wrought with his own hands, in the aforementioned sanctuary; at length, because of his genius, he was honored with great fame, and, after having made many discoveries, he attained honors equal to those of the gods. For on one of the islands off Memphis there exists even today a sanctuary of Daedalus, which is honored by the local inhabitants.

During his travels in Greece, Pausanias saw a number of ancient images which he ascribed to Daedalus. The following passage is a typical example.

Pausanias IX, 40, 3:   Of the works of Daedalus, there are two in Boeotia —the Herakles in Thebes and the Trophonios in Lebadeia. There are two other wooden images in Crete, that of Britomartis in Olus and the Athena at Knossos. The Knossians also have the "Dance of Ariadne," of which Homer made mention in the *Iliad,* a relief executed in white stone.[3] And the Delians possess a wooden image of Aphrodite, not very large, which over the years has lost its right hand. It is finished at the bottom with a square base instead of feet. I believe that this is the statue which Ariadne received from Daedalus, and that, when she followed Theseus, she carried away the image from her home. And the Delians relate that, when Theseus got rid of her, he set up the image of the goddess to Apollo at Delos.

HOMER

Up to this point we have been looking at myths and traditions about early Greek art preserved in the writings of authors who wrote long after the periods which they were describing. The earliest sources

---

1. Cf. also Diodorus I, 61, where he adds that in his own day the Labyrinth of Minos was no longer visible.
2. For a discussion of *rhythmos* see Myron, pp. 62-63, and Pythagoras, p. 57.
3. This phrase normally signifies marble.

which contain descriptions of Greek art are, of course, the Iliad and the Odyssey of Homer. While the date of these epics is still subject to some debate, most scholars now feel that they were composed sometime in the latter half of the eighth century B.C. Thus even Homer lived about 500 years later than the Heroic Age which his epics purport to represent, although the oral tradition of heroic poetry of which his epics are the culmination may have already begun in the second millennium B.C. Homer's descriptions of art are thought to reflect partly the art of his own time and partly, through the conservative medium of the oral tradition, the art of the Mycenaean period. A famous example of the latter type of description is that of the wine cup used by Nestor in his tent on the shore of Ilium.

Iliad XI, 632-637:   . . . an exceedingly beautiful cup, which the old man had brought from home, studded with golden rivets. There were four handles on it, and around each two golden doves were represented as if feeding, while below there were two supports. Another man would have been hard pressed to lift the cup from the table when it was full, but old Nestor raised it without any trouble.

In the early excavations of Mycenae, Schliemann found a gold cup which bears a general similarity to the one described by Homer.[4]
Elsewhere the specific connections of Homer's descriptions of art are more difficult to establish. His various descriptions of houses and palaces, for example, combined memories of Mycenaean palaces (with their great central hearths), suggestions of architectural decoration in the Orient, and elements of the houses of his own time, especially those in Ionia. Some typical examples follow.

Odyssey IV, 71 (Telemachos' exclamation to Peisistratos on seeing the palace of Menelaos):   Take a look, son of Nestor, delight of my heart, at the gleam of bronze in the echoing halls, and of gold and electrum, of silver and ivory; the court of Zeus the Olympian must be like this inside.

Odyssey VII, 81 ff (The palace of Alkinoös in Phaiakia):   . . . But Odysseus came to the renowned palace of Alkinoös. And his heart was stirred with many thoughts as he stood there, before crossing the bronze threshold. For a shimmer as if of the sun or the moon played through the high-roofed palace of great-hearted Alkinoös. Bronze walls ran around at every point, from the threshold to the innermost recess, and there was also a cornice of dark enamel all around. Golden doors closed

4. Cf. S. Marinatos and M. Hirmer, *Crete and Mycenae*, London, 1960, pl. 188; H. L. Lorimer, *Homer and the Monuments*, London, 1950, pp. 328-335.

in the sturdy palace, and silver door-posts stood on the bronze threshold, with a silver lintel overhead, and a gold ring-handle. There were gold and silver dogs on either side, which Hephaistos had wrought with knowing ingenuity, serving as guards of the palace of great-hearted Alkinoös, immortals, and unaging all their days. Within there were arm chairs placed along the whole extent of the wall, from the threshold to the innermost recess, and on these were thrown light, finely woven covers, the work of women. There the leaders of the Phaiakians used to sit, as they drank and ate, for they had unending abundance. Golden youths stood on solidly built bases, holding gleaming torches in their hands, illuminating the palace at night for the banqueters.

Homer seems most interested in and makes most frequent reference to the art which the later Greeks were to call toreutikē, *the art of chasing metal, and inlaying precious metals with one another and with gems. His descriptions of gems and the like often suggest connections with the Near East, but whether these connections were Mycenaean or later is difficult to say.*

Odyssey XIX, 226 (Odysseus, disguised, describes to Penelope the brooch which he wore to Troy): . . . his brooch was of gold and had twin sockets for pins. It was skillfully worked on the front: a dog held a spotted fawn in his forepaws, clutching it as it gasped. And everyone marvelled at how, though being of gold, the dog clutched the fawn and throttled it.[5]

Iliad XXIII, 740 ff (One of the prizes which Achilles offers at the funeral games of Patroklos): The son of Peleus immediately set out other prizes for speed of foot, a silver krater, finely wrought. It held just six measures, but in beauty it surpassed all others on earth by far, since highly skilled Sidonians had wrought it well, and Phoenicians had carried it over the misty sea.

The most elaborate description of an object in Homer is the famous description of Achilles' shield, Iliad XVIII, 468 ff. Although some have seen in this description a reflection of the psychology of Greek art in the Geometric period, the description itself is part of a formal literary genre and does not describe a real object. The description of Agamemnon's armor in Iliad XI, 19 ff, however, may reflect objects which Homer had actually seen:

The son of Atreus shouted aloud and commanded the Argives to arm for battle. And he himself put on the gleaming bronze. First he

5. On the archaeological parallels for this brooch, see M. P. Nilsson, *Homer and Mycenae*, London, 1933, p. 123.

fastened the greaves on his ankles, beautiful greaves, fitted with silver clasps. After that he put on a breast plate over his chest, the one which Kinyras once gave him as a guest's gift; for the great rumor had reached Cyprus that the Achaeans were about to sail forth in ships to Troy. It was on account of this that he gave it to him, wishing the king well. On it there were ten bands of dark enamel, and twelve of gold and twenty of tin. And serpents of dark enamel stretched up toward the neck, three on each side, like the rainbows which the son of Kronos fixes into a cloud, a portent to mortal men. Then he threw his sword over his shoulders. The golden nails upon it glittered, while the scabbard around it was of silver and was equipped with golden swordstraps. After that he took up his shield, big enough to hide a man, intricately worked, mighty, a beautiful shield; around it there were ten circles of bronze, and on it were twenty raised bosses of white tin, in the middle of which was one of dark enamel. And wreathed around in the very center was the grim face of the Gorgon, glaring terribly, and around it were Terror and Fear.

The patron deities of the men who produced such objects were Hephaistos and Athena. The picture which Homer gives us of Hephaistos at work probably reflects, with epic exaggeration, the appearance of a successful artist's workshop in Homer's own day.

Iliad VIII, 372 ff: Silver-footed Thetis came to the house of Hephaistos, an imperishable starry house, outstanding among the immortal houses, wrought all of bronze, which the lame-footed god had made himself. She found him there sweating as he hovered around the bellows busily. He was engaged in making tripods, twenty in all, which were to stand along the wall of his well-constructed hall, and he set gold wheels beneath the stand of each, so that they might, moving by themselves, enter the divine assembly and again come back to the house—a marvellous thing to see. They were complete up to a point, but the skillfully wrought handles had not yet been placed upon them. These he was preparing, and he was also cutting the attaching bands.[6]

The role of Athena and Hephaistos as the inspirational force behind the Homeric artist is reflected in the following passage.

Odyssey VI, 232 ff (Athena sheds grace on Odysseus in Phaiakia): . . . just as when a man inlays silver with gold, a craftsman, whom Hephaistos and Pallas Athena have taught all manner of skills, and he fashions pleasing works of art.

6. For illustrations of similar tripods from the Geometric period, cf. J. Charbonneaux, *Greek Bronzes* (English translation, London and New York, 1962), p. 53, Fig. 7.

2

The
Archaic
Period

Up to this point our testimonies have dealt with artistic traditions which the Classical Greeks knew largely as hazy mythological records about a type of art which was no longer produced in their own time. Any systematic knowledge which our sources have of specific artists, their schools, and their technical innovations applies only to the artists who were active after the beginning of the sixth century B.C. The Geometric style (c. 900-725 B.C.) which was in its final stages in the late eighth century B.C. (Homer's own lifetime) was lost to the historical memory of the Classical Greeks. It was in this period, however, that the Greeks first developed their sensitivity to the importance of the proper disposition of commensurate and clearly definable parts in creating a work of art. Around 700 B.C. increasing Greek contacts with the Orient, especially with Syria and Phoenicia, led to the adoption into Greek art of many new figural motifs and to an increasing emphasis on narrative representation rather than ornamentation, although ornament always continued to be an important factor in Greek art. The "Orientalizing period" lasted roughly a century (c. 700-600 B.C.), during which time the influence of the figural styles of the Orient were fused with the basic Greek sensitivity to harmony and structure. The style which emerges from this fusion is now called "Archaic." No rigid date can be cited as the beginning of the Archaic period, since the Orientalizing and Archaic styles overlap and blend into one another. Perhaps 650 B.C., when the first works of monumental Greek sculpture begin to appear, is a reasonable date. The end of the period is normally placed at the time of the Persian Wars (480-479 B.C.) after which the "Classical" style develops. During the Archaic period the Greek artists achieved an independent and confident mastery in all the major categories of the visual arts—sculpture, painting, architecture.

The following passages illustrate the traditions about the early masters in these different categories.

SCULPTURE: EARLY DEVELOPMENTS AND THE SIXTH CENTURY B.C.

The Daedalidae

Whether Daedalus as a person existed or not, a group of sculptors from various parts of Greece, all of whom were apparently active in the first half of the sixth century B.C., were regarded as his disciples.

Dipoinos and Skyllis

Pliny, *N.H.* XXXVI, 9: The first to win fame in the carving of marble were Dipoinos and Skyllis, who were born on the island of Crete while the empire of the Medes still existed and before Cyrus began to rule as king in Persia, that is, in about the 50th Olympiad.[1] They betook themselves to Sikyon which was for a long period the home of all arts of this sort. The Sikyonians contracted with them to make images of the gods for the benefit of the city, but before the statues were finished the artists complained of unjust treatment and went off to Aitolia. Thereupon a famine invaded Sikyon and with it barrenness and dire mourning. To those who were seeking the remedy Pythian Apollo replied, "if Dipoinos and Skyllis finish the images of the gods," a prophecy which was brought to fulfillment with great expense and with much obsequious behavior. These images were of Apollo, Artemis, Herakles, and Athena, the last of which was later struck by lightning.

Works by Dipoinos and Skyllis were still visible in the second century A.D. *when Pausanias travelled through Greece.*

Pausanias II, 15, 1 (At Kleonai):   There is a sanctuary of Athena in which the image is the work of Skyllis and Dipoinos. Some say that they were pupils of Daedalus, while others maintain that Daedalus took a woman from Gortyna, and that Dipoinos and Skyllis were born to him by this woman.

Pausanias II, 22, 5 (At Argos):   After these things there is a temple of the Dioscuri. There are images of them and their children, Anaxis and Mnasinous, and along with them their mothers, Hilaeira and Phoibe, all the work of Dipoinos and Skyllis, made of ebony. Likewise most of the parts of their horses are made of ebony, although a few are made from ivory.

Clement of Alexandria, *Protrepticus* IV, 42:   There were two other sculptors, Cretans I believe, Dipoinos and Skyllis by name. These men made the images of the Dioscuri in Argos, the statue of Herakles in Tiryns, and the wooden image of Artemis *Mounichia* in Sikyon.

Endoios

Pausanias I, 26, 4 (on the Acropolis at Athens):   Endoios was an Athenian by birth and a pupil of Daedalus, who followed Daedalus to Crete when the latter was exiled because of the death of Talos. By him

---

1. The 50th Olympiad, that is, the 50th celebration of the quadrennial athletic festival held at Olympia, occurred in 580 B.C. Cyrus' rule as King of Persia began in 559 B.C.

there is a seated image of Athena, which has an inscription to the effect that Kallias dedicated it, and Endoios made it.[2]

Pausanias VII, 5, 9: There is at Erythrai a temple of Athena *Polias* with a wooden image of great size seated on a throne and holding a distaff in each hand, and also having a *polos*[3] on its head. That this is a work of Endoios we surmised from having observed,[4] among other things, the quality of its workmanship and also its similarity to the figures of the Graces and the Seasons, which stand in the open air before the entrance and are of white marble.

Smilis of Aegina

Pausanias VII, 4, 4 (on the cult image of Hera at Samos): Not the least significant among the points of evidence which one might cite for the fact that this is a very ancient sanctuary is to be found in the cult statue. For it is the work of an Aeginetan, Smilis the son of Eukleides. This Smilis was of the same period as Daedalus, but he never achieved an equal reputation.

Pausanias V, 17, 1: In the temple of Hera in Olympia there is a statue of Zeus, as well as the image of Hera seated on a throne. It [the Zeus statue] stands alongside and is bearded and equipped with a helmet on the head; these are simple[5] works. Next to them are statues of the Seasons seated on thrones made by Smilis the Aeginetan.

Klearchos of Rhegion

Pausanias III, 117, 6 (monuments in Sparta): On the right of the Brazen House[6] there is an image of Zeus the Highest, the oldest of all

---

2. An Archaic seated statue of Athena found on the Acropolis is frequently associated with the work of Endoios; cf. G. Richter, *The Sculpture and Sculptors of the Greeks* (revised edition, New Haven: 1950), Fig. 64 (hereafter cited as "Richter, *Sculpture and Sculptors*,2"); the inscribed signatures of this sculptor which have been found in Athens appear to date from around the third quarter of the sixth century B.C. The Kallias mentioned in the passage cited above seems to be Kallias the son of Phainippos, an Olympic victor in 564 B.C. and one of the major political opponents of the tyrant Peisistratos in the 540's and 530's B.C. A survey of the complex archaeological evidence connected with this sculptor suggests that his career spanned the period between c. 550 and 500 B.C., and that he was hence a generation or so younger than Dipoinos and Skyllis. For an excellent summary, see E. Raubitschek, *Dedications from the Athenian Acropolis* (Cambridge, Mass.: 1949), pp. 491-495 (hereafter cited as "Raubitschek, *Dedications*").

3. *Polos*: a cylindrical shaped headdress resembling a round basket. It acquired ritual significance in the cults of several goddesses.

4. Reading *eidontes* for *endon*. The text of this sentence is defective, and we give an approximate rendering.

5. Greek *hapla;* perhaps also "primitive, undeveloped."

6. A famous temple of Athena in Sparta, see p. 41.

those works which are in bronze. For it is not made of one piece [that is, cast], but after each of the parts was hammered individually, the parts were then fitted together with one another, and rivets hold them so that they do not come apart. They say that Klearchos, who was a citizen of Rhegion, made this image; some say that he was a pupil of Dipoinos and Skyllis and others that he was a pupil of Daedalus himself.

The technique of making statues by fastening together hammered sheets of metal around a core was known as sphyrelaton. *Some examples of this technique have been found at Dreros in Crete and are to be dated c. 650* B.C.[7] *This style went out of fashion after the technique of casting large-scale bronze statues was perfected, presumably by Theodoros of Samos* [8] *around the middle of the sixth century* B.C. *This would suggest a rather early date for Klearchos, perhaps late seventh or early sixth century* B.C. *In another passage, however, Pausanias himself mentions a Klearchos of Rhegion as the teacher of Pythagoras of Rhegion (VI, 4, 4), a sculptor who undoubtedly worked during the first half of the fifth century* B.C.[9] *The chronological difficulty may be resolved by the assumption that there was an elder and a younger Klearchos, or that Klearchos simply made repairs on the venerable statue of Zeus.*

The Pupils of Dipoinos and Skyllis

Pausanias V, 17, 1 ff: By these [the statues of the Seasons by Smilis; see above, page 15] stands an image of Themis, who was the mother of the Seasons, the work of Dorykleides, a Lakedaimonian by birth and a pupil of Dipoinos and Skyllis. The statues of the Hesperides, five in number, were made by Theokles, also a Lakedaimonian, whose father was Hegylos. He too is reputed to have been a pupil of Dipoinos and Skyllis. They say that the image of Athena, wearing a helmet and holding a spear and a shield, is the work of the Lakedaimonian Medon, and that this man was the brother of Dorykleides and was taught by the same teachers.

Pausanias VI, 19, 8 (about Olympia):   The third of the treasuries, and also the fourth, are votive monuments of the Epidamnians.[10] . . . It shows the celestial sphere held aloft by Atlas, and it shows Herakles and

7. Cf. Richter, *Sculpture and Sculptors,*[2] Fig. 14.
8. See p. 18.
9. For relevant passages see pp. 56-57.
10. There is a lacuna in the text, and it is hence not clear to which treasury or to what part of it the wooden sculptures which are described belonged. Presumably they were reliefs.

the tree which was to be found among the Hesperides, the apple tree, as well as the snake coiled around the apple tree. These are also of cedar wood, and are the works of Theokles and Hegylos. The writing on the celestial sphere says that he made it along with his son.

Pausanias II, 32, 5: Kallon [11] was a pupil of Tektaios and Angelion; these latter made the image of Apollo for the Delians. Angelion and Tektaios were taught by Dipoinos and Skyllis.

This image of Apollo is described by Plutarch.

Plutarch, *De Mus.*, 14: The arrangement of the image of him in Delos has a bow in his right hand, and in his left hand the Graces, each of which holds some musical instrument; one holds a lyre, another holds flutes, while the one which is placed in the middle holds a reed-pipe to her mouth.[12]

The Sculptor of the Megarian Treasury at Olympia

The name of the artist associated with this treasury is preserved in the manuscripts of Pausanias as "Dontas." Because this name is so unusual many modern scholars have felt that "Dontas" is a corruption of "Medon," a Spartan sculptor (mentioned above, p. 16) who appears to have been active toward the end of the sixth century B.C.

Pausanias VI, 19, 12: The Megarians, who lived on the border of Attica, constructed a treasury, and in this treasury they set up offerings, small figures of cedarwood adorned with gold, representing the battle of Herakles with Acheloös. Zeus is depicted there, and Deianeira, as well as Acheloös and Herakles, and also Ares who is giving aid to Acheloös; likewise an image of Athena, who was Herakles' ally, once stood there. But this is now set up next to the Hesperidai in the temple of Hera. In the pediment of the treasury the battle of the gods and giants is represented, and a shield is placed above the pediment, [with an inscription] stating that the Megarians set up the treasury [with the spoils taken] from the Corinthians. . . . The Megarians built the treasury in Olympia some years after the battle [with the Corinthians]. But it seems likely that they had offerings there dating from an earlier

11. For Kallon see p. 26.
12. Representations of what appears to be this statue are preserved on Athenian coinage. Cf. L. Lacroix, *Les Reproductions de Statues sur les Monnaies Greques,* Liège, 1949, p. 201; pl. XVII, nos. 1 and 2 (cited hereafter as Lacroix, *Reproductions*).

time which the Lakedaimonian Dontas, a pupil of Dipoinos and Skyllis, made.[13]

The Sculptors of the Aegean Islands

Theodoros and Rhoikos

Theodoros of Samos, sculptor, architect, and master of the minor arts, was the most famous artist of the sixth century B.C. *The literary sources for his career and lineage come from authors who, with the exception of Herodotus, lived at least 500 years after the artist's own time, and a certain lack of precise detail in their writings is understandable. Some, including Herodotus, refer to Theodoros as the son of Telekles and colleague of Rhoikos; others (Diodorus, Diogenes Laertius) refer to him as the son of Rhoikos. Some scholars in the nineteenth century sought to resolve the contradictory points within the literary sources by postulating the existence of an elder Theodoros, the architect of the Heraion of Samos, and a younger Theodoros, who made the famous ring of Polykrates.[14] It is more likely, however, that only one artist existed, who, toward the beginning of his career, worked with Rhoikos in the temple of Hera at Samos (c. 560 B.C.) and who, toward the end of his career, made the ring of Polykrates (c. 520 B.C.). Rhoikos was perhaps an older relative of Theodoros.*

One of the innovations of the school of Theodoros and Rhoikos appears to have been that of casting hollow bronze statues (as distinct from the earlier sphyrelata *of hammered metal sheets; see above, page 16).*

Pausanias VIII, 14, 8:   The first men who made use of molten bronze for casting images in moulds were the Samians Rhoikos, the son of Phileas, and Theodoros, the son of Telekles.

13. The pediment from this treasury representing the gods and giants is still preserved in the Museum at Olympia. It would appear to date from about 520 B.C. Cf. Richter, *Sculpture and Sculptors,*2 Fig. 383. The battle referred to in this passage probably occurred in 458 B.C. (cf. Thucydides, I, 103-105), and the shield seen by Pausanias was probably dedicated at this time, not, as Pausanias seems to have thought, the whole treasury. The actual date of the treasury, c. 520 B.C., is quite probably also the date of Dontas-Medon, and he may well have been the sculptor of the pediment.

14. Cf. Herodotus III, 41-42. Polykrates was the tyrant of Samos. During the heyday of his rule he was advised by Amasis, the King of Egypt, to give up his most prized possession, and thus avoid the possibility of the gods growing jealous of his fortune. Polykrates decided that his most precious possession was an emerald and gold ring which had been made for him by Theodoros. He proceeded to throw the ring into the sea, but it eventually came back to him in the belly of a fish. Polykrates interpreted the return of the ring as a mark of divine favor, although it actually signified that his ruin had already been decreed.

Pausanias later says, however:

Pausanias X, 38, 6: I have pointed out in the earlier sections of my work that the Samians Rhoikos, son of Phileas, and Theodoros, son of Telekles, were the discoverers of how to melt down bronze with controlled precision. These men were also the first to cast bronze. Of Theodoros I have not been able to discover any work still extant, at least among works made of bronze. But in the sanctuary of Ephesian Artemis, as you come to the building which has the paintings, there is an entablature above the altar of "Artemis of the First Throne," as she is called. There are a number of images set up on the entablature and among them is the figure of a woman which stands near the end; this is the work of Rhoikos, and the Ephesians call it "Night."

Another tradition states that Theodoros made the first self-portrait. Pliny's remark about the exactitude of the likeness is undoubtedly exaggerated.

Pliny, *N.H.* XXXIV, 83: Theodoros, who made the labyrinth, cast a bronze portrait of himself in Samos, which, besides its reputation as a marvellous likeness, was celebrated for its great subtlety of detail. The right hand holds a file, and the left held a little quadriga (now removed to Praeneste) in three fingers—this latter is on such a small scale that, marvellous to say, were it to be made into a drawing, the fly, another work which Theodoros made at the same time, would cover both the chariot and the charioteer with its wings.[15]

The following anecdote, although probably not literally true, may suggest that Theodoros was one of the earliest sculptors to be interested in the problem of proportions.

Diodorus Siculus I, 98, 5-9: Among the old sculptors who are particularly mentioned as having spent time among them [the Egyptians] are Theodoros and Telekles, the sons of Rhoikos, who made the statue of Pythian Apollo for the Samians. Of this image it is related that half of it was made by Telekles in Samos, while, at Ephesus, the other half was finished by his brother Theodoros, and that when the parts were fitted together with one another, they corresponded so well that they appeared to have been made by one person. This type of workmanship is not practiced at all among the Greeks, but among the Egyptians it is especially common. For among them the *symmetria* of statues is

15. The manuscripts offer several variations for the second sentence in this text, but the general idea is clear enough.

not calculated according to the appearances which are presented to the eyes, as they are among the Greeks; [16] but rather, when they have laid out the stones, and, after dividing them up, begin to work on them, at this point they select a module from the smallest parts which can be applied to the largest. Then dividing up the lay-out of the body into twenty-one parts, plus an additional one-quarter, they produce all the proportions of the living figure. Therefore, when the artists agree with one another about the size of a statue, they separate from each other, and execute the parts of the work for which the size has been agreed upon with such precision that their particular way of working is a cause for astonishment. The statue in Samos, in accordance with the technique of the Egyptians, is divided into two parts by a line which runs from the top of the head, through the middle of the figure to the groin, thus dividing the figure into two equal parts. They say that this statue is, for the most part, quite like those of the Egyptians, because it has the hands suspended at its sides, and the legs parted as if in walking.

The School of Chios

Pliny, *N.H*. XXXVI, 11-13: [Before the time of Dipoinos and Skyllis] the sculptor Melas already lived in Chios, and after him his son Mikkiades, and still later his grandson Archermos, whose sons Bupalos and Athenis were the most famous men in this craft in the time of the poet Hipponax; the last named can be dated with certainty in the 60th Olympiad [that is, 540-537 B.C.]. If one were to trace the lineage of their family all the way back to their grandfather, one would find that the beginning of their art coincided with the beginning of the Olympiads.[17] Hipponax's face was notorious for its ugliness. Consequently they exhibited a portrait of him, for the purpose of making fun of it, to circles of laughter-loving companions; whereupon the indignant Hipponax unleashed the bitterness of his satire to such a degree that, as some believe, he drove them to hang themselves. But this is false; for they made a number of works later on in the neighboring islands, as for example those in Delos; on the bases of these, moreover, they have added the following epigram: "Chios is valued not only for its vines but also for the works of the sons of Archermos." And the people of Iasos [18] show an Artemis which is the work of their hand. In Chios itself there

---

16. *Symmetria* means the "commensurability of parts." Diodorus' statement refers to Greek sculptors of the fourth century and later, not the artists of Archaic Greece.
17. 776 B.C. was the traditional date for the beginning of the Olympiads.
18. An Ionian city in Asia Minor south of Miletos.

is reported to be a face of Artemis which is their work; it is set on high and those entering the building find its expression sad, while those who are leaving find it cheerful. In Rome there are statues by them in the pediment [19] of the temple of Apollo on the Palatine and in almost all the other structures which the divine Augustus had built. Works by their father also exist both in Delos and on the island of Lesbos.

Early Sculpture in Terracotta

Pliny, N.H. XXXV, 151-152: . . . The modelling of portraits from clay was first invented at Corinth by Butades, a potter from Sikyon; it was really the achievement of his daughter, who was in love with a young man and, when that young man was leaving for a trip abroad, drew an outline of the shadow of his face which was cast from a lamp onto the wall. From this her father made a relief by impressing the outline in clay and fired it along with his other clay products so that it became hard. This relief, they say, was preserved in the sanctuary of the Nymphs, up until the time when Mummius sacked Corinth.[20] There are those who hold that the art of modelling was first invented in Samos by Theodoros and Rhoikos, well before the Bacchiadae were expelled from Corinth, but in fact Demaratus (who in Etruria begat Tarquinius, the king of the Roman people), when he was exiled from the same city, took with him Eucheir, Diopos, and Eugrammos, who were modellers in clay; from these men the art of modelling was imported into Italy.[21] It was Butades' invention either to add red earth or to model from red chalk, and he also first placed masks by the outermost tiles of tile-roofs; [22] at first he called these masks *prostypa,* but later he also made *ectypa.*[23] It was from these also that the pediments [24] of temples originated. It was on account of this artist that the *plastae* [25] got their name.

19. In the pediment—*in fastigio;* the phrase could also refer to the *akroteria* on the top of the gable of the temple.

20. The Roman general Mummius sacked Corinth in 146 B.C. No absolute date is given for Butades, but the character of the passage suggests that he was one of the foremost artists of the Proto-Corinthian and Corinthian periods, that is, of the seventh or early sixth centuries B.C.

21. The archaeological record supports the tradition of a strong influence from Corinth on the early ceramic art of the Etruscans, especially in the seventh century B.C.; the date usually accepted for the rule of the Roman King Tarquinius Priscus is 616-579 B.C. The expulsion of the Bacchiadai occurred c. 580 B.C.

22. That is, he made ornamental antefixes.

23. The Greek words *ectypa* and *prostypa* are usually taken as "high relief" and "low relief" respectively.

24. That is, the ornamentation of pediments with terracotta reliefs.

25. That is, "modellers."

Early Traditions about Portrait Sculpture

*In addition to the passages below, see the tradition of Theodoros'
self-portrait (page 19) and the portrait of Hipponax by the sons of
Archermos (page 20).*

Pliny, *N.H.* XXXIV, 16-17:   It was not customary to make effigies of
men unless, through some illustrious cause, they were worthy of having
their memory perpetuated; the first example was a victory in the sacred
contests, especially at Olympia, where it was the custom to dedicate
statues of all who had been victorious; and in the case of those who
had been winners there three times they moulded a likeness from the
actual features [26] of the person, which they call "icons." [27] The Athenians, I am inclined to believe, set up statues in public for the first time
in honor of the tyrant-slayers, Harmodios and Aristogeiton.[28]

Pausanias, VI, 18, 7:   The first portraits of athletes set up in Olympia
were those of Praxidamas the Aeginetan, who was the victor in boxing
in the 59th Olympiad [544 B.C.] and Rhexibios the Opuntian, who prevailed as a pankratiast [29] in the 61st Olympiad [536 B.C.]. These statues
stand not far from the column of Oinomaos and are made of wood,
that of Rhexibios of fig-wood and that of the Aeginetan, which is less
weathered than the other, of cypress.

Pausanias, VIII, 40, 1:   In the assembly-place in Phigalia there is a
statue of Arrhachion the pankratiast, which is archaic in several ways
and not the least of all in its format. The feet are not separated by
very much and the arms hang down by the sides as far as the buttocks.
The portrait is made of stone, and they say that an epigram was inscribed upon it, but this has disappeared with time. Two Olympic victories went to Arrhachion in the Olympiads which preceded the 54th
[564 B.C.] . . . .

Pausanias, VI, 15, 8:   Two victories went to the Spartan Eutelidas in
the boys' contests of the 38th Olympiad [628 B.C.],[30] one for wrestling
and one for the pentathlon. For this was the first and last time that

26. The Latin reads *ex membris* and appears to refer to the whole body.
27. Latin *iconica* from the Greek *eikōn*, a "likeness." Many scholars doubt
Pliny's contention that portraits of this sort were made in Archaic Greece.
28. The work of Antenor; see p. 33.
29. The *pankration* was an unusually rough event in the Olympic games which
combined boxing and wrestling simultaneously. It continued until one of the contestants either gave in or was unable to continue.
30. If Pausanias gives this date correctly, he contradicts his own statement,
quoted above, that the earliest portrait at Olympia was set up in 544 B.C.

boys were called to be contestants in the pentathlon. There is an ancient image of this Eutelidas, and on its base are letters which have been worn dim with time.

Herodotus I, 31 (Kleobis and Biton: an illustration given by Solon to Croesus of what sort of men could be considered truly happy): Kleobis and Biton. For the wealth which belonged to them (they were Argives by birth) was sufficient for their needs, and in addition to that they had great strength of body, as is shown by the fact that they were both prize-winning athletes. The following story is also told about them. There was a festival in honor of Hera at Argos, and their mother had to be transported to the sanctuary in an ox-cart; but the oxen did not arrive from the fields in time. Unable to wait because time was growing short, the young men put on the yoke themselves and drew the cart, with their mother riding along in it; after transporting her over a distance of forty-five stades, they arrived at the sanctuary. Having performed this feat, which was witnessed by everyone at the festival, their lives came to the best possible end, and in their case again the god showed how much better a thing it is to die than to live. For the Argive men, standing around the cart, commended the strength of the young men, and the Argive women congratulated the mother for being fortunate enough to have such sons. Then the mother, being overwhelmed both by the feat and the praises which it brought, stood before the image and prayed to the goddess to give Kleobis and Biton, her own children who had honored her so greatly, the best thing that can befall a man. Following her prayer they performed sacrifice and enjoyed the feast; afterwards the young men lay down to sleep in the sanctuary and never rose again—it was in this way that they met their death. The Argives made statues of them and set them up in Delphi because they were among the most virtuous of men.[31]

SCULPTURE: THE LATE ARCHAIC PHASE

The sculptors treated under this heading were primarily active during the last decade of the sixth century B.C. *and the first two decades of the fifth. Several of them lived through the Persian Wars, overlapped into the Early Classical period, and played a role in forming the new Classical style. They were also the teachers of the great sculptors of the Classical period, such as Myron, Polykleitos, and Pheidias.*

31. The statues of Kleobis and Biton have survived and are now in the Museum in Delphi. Cf. G. M. A. Richter, *Kouroi*,[2] London, 1960, Figs. 79-83.

Ageladas [32] of Argos

*Ageladas was probably the oldest of the sculptors in this group.
His earliest known work, the statue of the Olympic victor Anochos of
Tarentum, dates from around 520 B.C. Later tradition held that he was
the teacher of three great sculptors of the Classical period—Myron,
Pheidias, and Polykleitos. The last of these was also from Argos and
may have received his early training from the disciples of Ageladas;
otherwise there is probably no truth in the tradition. The ancient
sources give us no idea of the quality of his works, but they do give
some conception of their variety.*

STATUES OF ATHLETES:

Pausanias VI, 14, 11 (at Olympia):   . . . there is also a statue of Anochos
of Tarentum, the son of Adamatas, who was victorious in the single-
course and double-course foot race; it is the work of Ageladas of Argos.

Pausanias VI, 10, 6 (at Olympia):   Next to [the chariot of] Pantarkes
is the chariot of Kleosthenes, a man of Epidamnos. This is the work of
Ageladas; it stands behind the Zeus which was set up by the Greeks
from the spoils of the battle of Plataea. Kleosthenes was victorious in
the 66th Olympiad [516 B.C.], and he set up a statue of himself and his
charioteer along with the horses.

Pausanias VI, 8, 6 (at Olympia):   Not far from the statue of Promachos
a statue of Timasitheos, a Delphian by birth, is set up; it is the work
of Ageladas of Argos; this man [Timasitheos] won victories in the
Pankration, twice at Olympia and three times at Pytho.[33]

STATUES OF GODS:

Pausanias VI, 33, 2:   Every day they carry water from the spring to the
sanctuary of Zeus on Mt. Ithome. The image of Zeus is the work of
Ageladas and was originally made for the Messenian settlers in Naupaktos.[34] The priest, who is chosen each year, keeps the image in his
house.

32. The Latin version of the name is "Hagelades"; cf. Pliny, *N.H.* XXXIV, 49,
55, 57.
33. Herodotus V, 72, relates that Timasitheos was executed in Athens in 507
B.C. after participating with the Spartan King Kleomenes in an abortive *coup d'état.*
34. In 456 B.C. the Athenians enabled Messenian refugees, who were fleeing the
Spartans, to settle in Naupaktos. If Ageladas began his career around 520 B.C., it is
unlikely, although not impossible, that he was active at this time. On the other hand,
if the Zeus shown on the coins of Messenia (cf. Richter, *Sculpture and Sculptors,*2
Fig. 562; Lacroix, *Reproductions,* pl. XIX) is that of Ageladas, then he may have been
active as late as the second quarter of the fifth century, since the style of the statue
represented on the coins seems to be Early Classical.

Pausanias VII, 24, 4: There are other statues at Aigion[35] made of bronze, Zeus as a child and a Herakles, who has no beard yet either; these are the work of Ageladas of Argos.

Scholiast on Aristophanes, *Frogs*, line 504: Melite is a deme in Attica, in which Herakles celebrated the Lesser Mysteries. There is also a notable sanctuary of Herakles *Alexikakos*.[36] The image of Herakles is the work of Ageladas of Argos, who was the teacher of Pheidias.

A STATUE OF THE MUSES:

Anthologia Graeca II, 15, 35 (*Anthologia Planudea* IV, 220), by Antipater of Sidon:

> Muses three entwined here we stand,
>> One holds a flute
> Another in her hands the barbiton,
>> The third a lyre;
> The one by Aristokles holds the lyre;
>> By Ageladas
> The barbiton, and she of Kanachos
>> The hymning reeds.

A MILITARY VOTIVE:

Pausanias X, 10, 6 (at Delphi): The bronze horse of the Tarentines and the captive women are from the spoils taken from the Messapians, the barbarian neighbors of the Tarentines; these are works of Ageladas of Argos.

Kanachos of Sikyon

(In addition to the passages cited below, see Cicero's critical analysis of the style of Kanachos, Chapter 6, p. 221.)

Pliny, *N.H.* XXXIV, 75 (the statue of Apollo at Didyma): Kanachos made a nude Apollo, which bears the cognomen Philesios, in the sanctuary at Didyma,[37] made from bronze of the Aeginetan formula;[38] and with it a stag, which is suspended in its tracks in such a way that a string can be drawn underneath its feet, with the heel and toe alternately retaining their grip, for a "tooth" on each part is so geared that

35. A town in Achaia on the northern coast of the Peloponnesos.
36. *Alexikakos*—"Averter of evil."
37. Literally "in the *Didymaion*," the oracular sanctuary of Zeus and Apollo near Miletus in Asia Minor.
38. *Aeginetica aeris temperatura*. The Aeginetan workshops had a special formula for compounding bronze which was famous in antiquity; cf. Pliny, *N.H.* XXXIV, 10.

when one is dislodged by pressure the other in its turn springs into place.[39]

Pausanias IX, 10, 2 (the statue of Ismenian Apollo at Thebes): . . . there is a hill to the right of the gates which is sacred to Apollo. Both the hill and the god as well are called "Ismenian," since the river Ismenos flows right by it. . . . The image is equal in size to the one at Branchidai [40] and not very different in form. Whoever has seen one of these images and has learned who the artist was, requires no great skill to recognize, on beholding the other, that it is a work of Kanachos. They differ only in this way: the one at Branchidai is of bronze, while the Ismenian statue is of cedar-wood.

Pausanias II, 10, 4 (a cult statue of Aphrodite at Sikyon): Immediately after this there is a sanctuary of Aphrodite. The only people authorized to enter it are a priestess (for whom it is no longer legal to have intercourse with a man) and a virgin, who has charge of the sacrificial rites for a year and is given the name "the bath-bearer." The rest of the people are required to watch from the entrance and to make their prayers from there. The image, which is seated, was made by Kanachos of Sikyon, who made the statue of Apollo for the Milesians at Didyma and the Ismenian Apollo for the Thebans. It is made of gold and ivory and has a *polos* on its head; in one of the hands it holds a poppy and in the other an apple.

Kallon of Aegina

(See also Quintilian's criticism of the style of Kallon, Chapter 6, p. 220; for Kallon's teacher see p. 17 above.)

Pausanias II, 32, 5 (at Troizen): . . . on the Acropolis there is a temple of Athena, called *Sthenias*. The *xoanon* [41] of the goddess was

39. Reproductions of this statue on coins and in small bronzes and terracottas suggest that this stag was a small object placed in the Apollo's outstretched hand. Cf. *Enciclopedia dell'Arte Antica*, s.v. "Kanachos," and Lacroix, *Reproductions*, p. 221 ff. and plate XVIII. The statue was taken away to Ecbatana by the Persian King Darius (Herodotus VI, 19, and Pausanias I, 16, 3) but was later restored by the Hellenistic King Seleukos Nikator (312-281 B.C.).

40. Branchidai: another name for Didyma.

41. The word, which is derived from *xeo*, to "shave down," or "plane," usually refers to a wooden image; but this is not always true since Pausanias also used it to refer to chryselephantine statues such as Pheidias' Zeus at Olympia. The connection may be that wood and ivory were carved in a similar manner (marble, of course, is actually chiseled). *Xoanon* frequently connotes a rather primitive type of image to Pausanias. Like most of the Aeginetan sculptors, however, Kallon probably worked primarily in bronze. Pausanias saw a bronze tripod made by Kallon set up at Amyklai; cf. Pausanias III, 18, 8.

made by Kallon the Aeginetan. Kallon was the pupil of Tektaios and Angelion.

Kallon of Elis

(Possibly identical with Kallon of Aegina. Greek artists were itinerant.)

Pausanias V, 25, 2-4: It once happened that when the Messenians on the strait [42] in accordance with an old custom sent a chorus of thirty-five boys, and with them a trainer and a flute-player, to some local festival of the Rhegians, a disaster overtook them. Not one of those who were sent off returned again safely; but the ship which was carrying the boys vanished into the deep along with them. . . . At that time the Messenians mourned over the loss of the children, and in addition to the other ways which were devised to honor them, they set up bronze statues at Olympia, which included along with the children, the trainer and the flute-player. The ancient inscription made it clear that they were votives of the Messenians on the strait. At a later time, Hippias,[43] who is called the "wise man" by the Greeks, composed elegiac verses in honor of them. They are the works of Kallon of Elis.

Pausanias V, 27, 8 (a Hermes at Olympia): Not far from the offering of the people of Pheneos,[44] there is another image of Hermes, this one holding the *kerykeion*.[45] The inscription [46] says that it was set up by Glaukias, who was a Rhegian by descent, and that Kallon of Elis made it.

Hegias and/or Hegesias

The two names given separately by Pliny are usually thought to refer to the same artist. The rhetoricians of the Roman Empire looked upon the art of Hegesias and Kallon as a paradigm of a hard, linear style (see Chapter 6, p. 220). Thus, although the literary sources give us little specific information about Hegias/Hegesias, he must have been one of the best known of the Late Archaic sculptors. "Hegias" (if a very probable emendation of the text of Dio Chrysostom, Or. LV, 1, is correct) was apparently the teacher of Pheidias.

42. That is, Messina in Sicily.
43. The Sophist Hippias of Elis, active in the second half of the fifth century B.C.
44. The Hermes by Onatas. See p. 31.
45. The herald's wand which is characteristic of Hermes.
46. This inscription has been found at Olympia. E. Loewy, *Inschriften griechischer Bildhauer*, Leipzig, 1885, no. 33.

An inscribed statue base dating from around the second decade of the fifth century B.C. *and bearing the signature of Hegias, has been found on the Athenian Acropolis.*[47]

Pliny, N.H. XXXIV, 78:   The Athena and King Pyrrhos[48] of Hegias are praised, as are his boys, called *kelētizontes,*[49] and his Castor and Pollux, which stand before the temple of Jupiter the Thunderer;[50] by Hegesias there is a Herakles in the colony of Parium.[51]

Onatas of Aegina

The sculptural school of Aegina was one of the most active and prosperous of the Late Archaic period, and its products were apparently so distinctive in style that Pausanias was able to recognize them centuries afterwards (for the texts see Chapter 6, p. 225). Onatas would appear to have been the foremost sculptor in the school. The pedimental sculptures from the temple of Aphaia at Aegina were made at the time when Onatas' influence must have been at its high-point, and we may reasonably assume that they provide us with a fair idea of what his style was like.

Pausanias VIII, 42, 1 ff. (the "Black Demeter" of the Phigalians and other works):   The other of the mountains, Mt. Elaion, is about thirty stades from Phigalia, and there is a cave there sacred to Demeter, whom they call "the black." Now what the people of Thelpousa say about the mating of Poseidon and Demeter, that much the Phigalians tend to believe; but the Phigalians maintain that what was given birth to by Demeter was not a horse, but rather the deity who is given the name "Despoina"[52] by the Arcadians. They say that afterwards, feeling simultaneously anger against Poseidon and anguish over the rape of Persephone, she put on black raiment, and entering into this cave, remained hidden for a long time. During this time it is said that all the things which the earth nourishes were dying, and that the race of men was being destroyed even more so by hunger, but none of the other gods knew where Demeter was hidden, until Pan went to Arcadia, and in pursuing the hunt from one mountain to another, arrived at Mt. Elaion

47. See Raubitschek, *Dedications,* no. 94, pp. 101-102, 504-505.
48. Athena and Pyrrhos, the son of Achilles; not the Hellenistic King Pyrrhos.
49. *Kelētizontes:* "boys riding horses" or "doing acrobatics on horseback."
50. This temple was, of course, in Rome. The statue was undoubtedly carried off to Rome from its original location.
51. Parium: a Roman military colony founded by Augustus in Asia Minor, near the Hellespont.
52. Despoina—"the Mistress."

and spied on Demeter, noting what her bearing [53] was and what sort of raiment she was clothed in. It is said that Zeus learned of these things from Pan, and consequently the Fates were sent by him to Demeter, who, in turn, was persuaded by the Fates so that she put aside her anger and gave up grieving. As a result of these things, the Phigalians say, they declared this cave sacred to Demeter and set up a wooden image in it. The image, they say, was fashioned by them in the following way: it was seated on a rock, and was like a woman in all parts except the head; she had the head and hair of a horse, and images of serpents and other beasts grew out of the head; she was dressed in a tunic which reached to her feet; there was a dolphin in one of her hands and a dove in the other. Why they made the wooden image in this way should be clear to any man who is intelligent and capable of assessing traditions. They say that they named her "black" because the goddess wore black raiment. However, they neither remember who was responsible for fashioning the image nor what was the manner in which it caught fire. But when the ancient image was destroyed, the Phigalians not only did not provide the goddess with another image but they neglected her many festivals and sacrifices, until finally barrenness fell upon the land.

[The Phigalians consulted the oracle at Delphi about the cause of the blight, and were told that it would be alleviated if they restored to Demeter her former honors.]

When the Phigalians heard the oracular response that was brought back, they made the other offerings in such a way as to give Demeter even greater honor than she had had before, and they also persuaded Onatas the Aeginetan, the son of Mikon, to make the image of Demeter for them at as great a price as he asked. The people of Pergamon have a bronze Apollo by Onatas, and it is a great marvel among them both because of its size and its art. This artist then, discovering a picture or a copy of the ancient wooden image—but guided even more, as it is said, by visions which he had in dreams—made the image for the Phigalians in the generation after the invasion of Greece by the Medes. For this reckoning my evidence is as follows: at the time when Xerxes made his crossing into Europe, Gelon the son of Deinomenes was reigning as tyrant over the Syracusans and over the rest of the Sicilians as well. When Gelon died (478 B.C.) the rule passed on to Hieron, the brother of Gelon. When Hieron died (467/6 B.C.) before he could set up the offerings to Olympian Zeus which he had vowed for his victories in the horse races, Deinomenes the son of Hieron set them up on be-

---

53. Bearing—Greek *schēma,* possibly referring to the format which was later reproduced in Onatas' statue.

half of his father. These too are works of Onatas, and there are inscriptions at Olympia, one of which, the one over the offering, reads:

> In your holy games, Olympian Zeus, having been
> victorious/ Once in the four horse chariot,
> twice with a single horse,/ Hieron offered
> these gifts to you. His son set them up,/
> Deinomenes, as a memorial to his father.

The other inscription reads:

> The son of Mikon, Onatas fashioned me,
> Who has his home on the island of Aegina.

Thus the age of Onatas coincides with that of Hegias the Athenian and Ageladas the Argive.

It was mainly on account of this Demeter that I came to Phigalia. . . . But the image which was made by Onatas no longer existed in my time, and most of the Phigalians were not aware that it had ever existed at all. The oldest man of those whom I happened to converse with said that in the third generation prior to his own, rocks from the roof had fallen on the image; it was smashed by these, he said, and completely destroyed. And indeed, I could still see clearly the place in the roof where the rock had broken away.

Anthologia Graeca **II**, 14, 30 (*Anthologia Palatina* **IX**, 238) (epigram by Antipater of Sidon, perhaps connected with the statue of Apollo at Pergamon mentioned in the previous passage):

> Apollo is a hulking youth in this bronze by Onatas,
> A testimony of beauty for Leto and Zeus,
> Proclaiming that Zeus did not love her in vain, and
>   that, as the saying goes,
> The eyes and head of the son of Kronos are glorious;
> Not even to Hera is it hateful, this bronze which Onatas
>   cast and
> Which he modelled in this way with the help of Eilythia.

Pausanias V, 25, 12 (a statue of Herakles at Olympia): "The Thasians . . . set up a statue of Herakles at Olympia, the base as well as the image being of bronze. The height of the image is ten cubits; it has a club in the right hand and a bow in the left. . . . On the image at Olympia there is the following elegiac couplet:

> The son of Mikon, Onatas, fashioned me,
> The one who has his home in Aegina.

This Onatas, though the style of his statues is that of Aegina, I could class as inferior to none of the sculptors who are descendants of Daedalus and belong to the Attic school.[54]

Pausanias V, 27, 8 (a statue of Hermes at Olympia): The Hermes who carries a ram under his arm and has a leather cap perched on his head, and is also clad in a tunic and travelling cloak . . . has been given to the god by the Arcadians of Pheneos. Onatas the Aeginetan, and along with him Kalliteles, made it, according to the inscription. I assume that Kalliteles was either a pupil or a son of Onatas.

Pausanias X, 13, 10: The Tarentines sent another tithe to Delphi from the spoils of their war with the barbarian Peuktians. The offerings were the work of Onatas the Aeginetan. . . .[55] The statues represent foot-soldiers and horsemen, and also king Opis of the Iapygians who came as an ally of the Peuktians. This man is represented as having perished in battle, and over his prostrate body stand the hero Taras and Phalanthos, the Lakedaimonian, not far from whom is a dolphin. For they say that before he reached Italy, Phalanthos was shipwrecked in the Krisaian sea, and was carried to shore by a dolphin.

Pausanias V, 25, 8 (at Olympia): There are also offerings made by the whole Achaean race in common: [these are statues of] those who, after Hector offered to fight a Greek champion, in single combat, awaited the outcome of the lot for the contest.[56] They stand near the great temple armed with spears and shields. Opposite them on another base Nestor is represented, casting the lot of each into the helmet. Those who are drawing lots for the combat with Hector are eight in number—for the ninth, the one of Odysseus, was carried off to Rome, they say, by Nero—and of the eight, the only one with the name inscribed on it is that of Agamemnon. The inscription runs, moreover, from right to left. The figure whose shield-device is a rooster is Idomeneus, the descendant of Minos. Idomeneus' lineage stems from Helios the father of Pasiphaë, and they say that the rooster is sacred to Helios and announces when Helios is about to rise. . . . As to who the sculptor was, this is written on the shield:

54. "School—*ergastērion,* literally "workshop." Daedalus was an Athenian, and in this passage the "Daedalidae" and the sculptors of Attica are apparently synonymous. But elsewhere, as we have seen, Pausanias classifies non-Attic sculptors, such as Dipoinos and Skyllis, among the Daedalidae.

55. Omitted here is a phrase in the text which is problematic. As it stands it apparently refers to a co-worker named Kalynthos. No artist by that name is known, although an offering from the Athenias Acropolis was dedicated by a man who was named Kalynthos. Cf. Raubitschek, *Dedications,* no. 279, pp. 299-301, 509. Others have emended the text to read Kalliteles; or possibly Ageladas, who also worked on a Tarentine votive at Delphi.

56. Cf. *Iliad* VII, 54 ff.

Many other works, and this one too, are by skillful Onatas,
The Aeginetan, the son whom Mikon bore.

Glaukias of Aegina

Pausanias VI, 9, 4-9 (statues of victorious athletes at Olympia):   . . .
They say that the chariot was an offering of Gelon who was the tyrant
in Sicily. The inscription on it says that Gelon, the son of Deinomenes,
of Gela, set it up, and the time of this victory by Gelon was the 73rd
Olympiad. [488 B.C. Pausanias proceeds to offer reasons for his belief
that the Gelon who dedicated the chariot was not the Syracusan tyrant,
but his reasoning seems to be incorrect.] . . . Glaukias the Aeginetan
made the chariot and the statue of Gelon himself. . . . Next to the
chariot of Gelon is a statue of Philon, a work of the Aeginetan Glaukias.
For this Philon, Simonides the son of Leoprepes, composed a skillful
elegiac couplet:

> My fatherland is Corcyra, Philon is my name.
>   Of Glaukos I am
> The son and I won two Olympic victories in boxing.

Pausanias VI, 10, 1 ff: . . . After those which I have enumerated stands
Glaukos of Karystos. They say that he was originally from Anthedon in
Boeotia and was descended from the line of Glaukos, the sea-deity. This
Karystian was descended from Demylos, and they say that he started
out as a farmer. When one day the ploughshare fell off the plough,
he proceeded to fit it back on the plough using his fist instead of a
hammer. Demylos happened to witness the feat performed by his son
and as a result took him to Olympia to fight in the boxing matches.
There Glaukos, having no experience in the fine points of boxing, was
being wounded by his antagonists, and when he was boxing with the
last of them, it was expected that he would give in owing to the number
of his injuries. His father, they say, then shouted, "Son, the plough-
punch!" Then he dealt his antagonist an even more violent blow and
immediately won the victory. He is said to have won other victory
wreaths as well, twice at the Pythian games, and eight times at both
the Nemean and Isthmian games. The son of Glaukos set up this statue
of him, and Glaukias the Aeginetan made it. The statue represented
him as if he were shadow-boxing, because Glaukos was the smoothest
fighter of his day.[57]

(For another athlete statue by Glaukias, cf. Pausanias VI, 11, 9.)

---

57. The Greek literally says something like "because Glaukos was by nature the
most proficient of the men of his time in moving his hands in an orderly fashion."

Anaxagoras of Aegina

Pausanias V, 23, 1 ff (a statue of Zeus at Olympia): As you go by the entrance to the *Bouleuterion* there stands a statue of Zeus which has no inscription, and again, turning to the north, there is another image of Zeus. This one faces the rising sun; the Greeks who fought against Mardonios and the Medes at Plataea set it up. On the right side of the base, the names of the cities which took part in the action are inscribed. . . . This image which was set up at Olympia by the Greeks was the work of Anaxagoras of Aegina. Those who have written about Plataea have neglected to make mention of this artist in their accounts.

Pausanias' last remark may refer to Herodotus IX, 81, who, in discussing the spoils from the battle of Plataea notes:

. . . a tithe was taken for the god at Olympia, from which a bronze statue of Zeus, ten cubits high, was set up. . . .

Antenor of Athens

Antenor and Hegias seem to have been the foremost Athenian sculptors of the Late Archaic period. One of Antenor's works, a korē from the Acropolis of Athens, is still preserved.[58] *It is dated about 510-500* B.C. *His most famous works were the statues of the Tyrannicides, Harmodios and Aristogeiton, who slew Hipparchos, the brother of the tyrant Hippias, in 514* B.C.

Pausanias I, 8, 5 (part of his description of the Athenian agora): Not far away stand figures of Harmodios and Aristogeiton who slew Hipparchos. . . . Of these statues, one group is the work of Kritios, while Antenor made the other group. Xerxes, when he took Athens after the Athenians had evacuated it, carried off the latter group as spoils, but Antiochos later sent it back to the Athenians.[59]

Menaichmos and Soidas of Naupaktos

Pausanias VII, 18, 8: On the acropolis at Patras there is a sanctuary of Artemis *Laphria*. The name of the goddess is foreign, and the image

58. Richter, *Sculpture and Sculptors,*2 Fig. 273.
59. Pliny, *N.H.* XXXIV, 70, and Arrian III, 16, 7; VII, 19, 2, say that Alexander restored the statues to Athens. Valerius Maximus II, 10, ext. 1, says it was Seleukos. None of these writers mentions Antenor by name.

too was brought in from the outside. For Kalydon as well as the rest of Aitolia were abandoned in order that the Aitolian population could be incorporated into Nikopolis above Actium, and, as a result, the people of Patras got possession of the image of Artemis *Laphria*. As was the case with the population, so too most of the statues from Aitolia and Akarnania were taken to Nikopolis, but to the people of Patras, along with the other spoils from Kalydon, Augustus gave the image of *Laphria*, which was still receiving honors on the acropolis of Patras in my own day. . . . The image represents her as a huntress, and it is made of ivory and gold. It is the work of the Naupaktian sculptors, Menaichmos [60] and Soidas. The evidence indicates that these men were active not much later than the time of Kanachos of Sikyon and Kallon the Aeginetan.

PAINTING: EARLIEST DEVELOPMENTS AND THE SIXTH CENTURY

Pliny, *N.H.* XXXV, 15-16:   The question of the origins of painting is uncertain, nor does it belong within the scope of this work. The Egyptians affirm that it was invented among themselves six thousand years ago and that it later passed over to Greece—an empty claim, as is quite obvious. As for the Greeks, however, some say that it was invented in Sikyon, and others say among the Corinthians, but all assert that the first sort of painting involved tracing the shadow of a man with lines and that later a second, more difficult method employing single colors, and called "monochrome," was invented; the latter method exists even now. They say that the linear method was invented by Philokles the Egyptian or by Kleanthes of Corinth but that the first to make extensive use of it were Aridikes the Corinthian and Telephanes the Sikyonian; these men were still working without any color but were already adding lines here and there within the outline. For this reason it became the custom to add identifying inscriptions to the figures which they painted. The inventor of filling in these lines with the color of ground clay was, they maintain, Ekphantos of Corinth.[61]

Kleanthes of Corinth, who is mentioned by Pliny in the preceding passage, and his contemporaries, also executed some paintings in a sanctuary of Artemis in the area of Pisa near Olympia.

60. Pliny, *N.H.* XXXIV, 80, and in his index to book XXXIV mentions a sculptor named Menaichmos who *scripsit de sua arte*. If this Menaichmos is the same as the one referred to by Pausanias, he would be the earliest sculptor known to have written about his art.

61. The manuscripts offer a number of variant readings for this last sentence.

Strabo VIII, 343: In the sanctuary of [Artemis] *Alpheionia* there are paintings by Kleanthes and Aregon, who were Corinthians; by the former is the *Sack of Troy* and the *Birth of Athena;* by the latter *Artemis carried aloft on a Griffon; . . .*

Athenaeus VIII, 346 B-C: I am acquainted with the painting which is kept in the sanctuary of Artemis *Alpheiosa* in the area of Pisa. It is the work of Kleanthes the Corinthian. In it Poseidon is shown offering a tuna fish to Zeus, who is having birth pangs.[62]

Pliny, *N.H.* XXXV, 55-56: It is generally acknowledged that a picture by the painter Boularchos, which represented the battle of the Magnetes,[63] was acquired in exchange for its weight in gold by Candaules, also called Myrsilos, the King of Lydia and the last of the Herakleidai.[64] So great had the value of painting already become. This must have happened around the time of Romulus, for indeed Candaules died in the 18th Olympiad, or, as some maintain, in the same year as Romulus, when, unless I am mistaken, painting was already remarkable for the brilliance of its technique; in fact, for the perfection of it.[65] And, if one is obliged to accept this conclusion, it becomes evident at the same time that the basic developments were much earlier and that those who painted in monochrome, the date of whom has not been handed down, came somewhat earlier—such as Hygiaenon, Dinias, Charmadas, Eumaros of Athens, the artist who first distinguished the male sex from the female sex in painting,[66] and Kimon of Kleonai, who dared to represent all sorts of figures and further developed Eumaros' inventions. This Kimon invented *katagrapha,* that is to say three-quarter views; [67] he also disposed the countenances of his figures in various ways, showing them looking backward, upward, and downward; he made the distinction between the parts of the body more clear by articulating the joints; he emphasized the veins; and, beyond that, he depicted the creases and folds in the drapery.

62. Probably from the birth of Dionysos, who, after Semele gave birth to him prematurely, was sewed up in the thigh of Zeus and later reborn.
63. A tribe, possibly of Greeks, living in the mountains along the eastern border of Thessaly. The occasion of the battle is not known.
64. The Classical Greeks believed that the rulers of western Asia Minor in the eighth and seventh centuries B.C. were descendants of Herakles.
65. The 18th Olympiad—708-705 B.C. The traditional date for the death of Romulus was 717 B.C. Candaules, whose murder is described by Herodotus I, 8-12, is thought to have died in the 680's B.C.
66. The convention of representing the skin of men as dark and that of women as light existed in the Near East long before the rise of Classical Greece, and it is found on Greek vase painting from the seventh century B.C. onward.
67. "Three-quarter views"—Latin *obliquae imagines;* the phrase could also mean "profile portraits," but "three-quarter views" seems more in keeping with the inventions ascribed to Kimon.

The invention which Pliny ascribes to Kimon in the preceding passage—foreshortening, experimentation with different bodily poses, articulation of naturalistic detail—are all features which developed in Greek vase painting between c. 520 and 480 B.C. In spite of the fact that Pliny seems to visualize Kimon as being much earlier, this date appears to be confirmed by an epigram of Simonides (c. 556-468 B.C.) preserved in the **Palatine Anthology** IX, 758:

> Kimon painted the door on the right;
> The one on the right as you leave, Dionysios [68] painted.

ARCHITECTURE: EARLY DEVELOPMENTS

Theodoros and Rhoikos

See above, pp. 18-20.

The Temple of Hera at Samos [69]

Pliny, *N.H.* XXXIV, 83:   Theodorus, who made the labyrinth at Samos, also made a portrait of himself in bronze.

Herodotus III, 60 (for the rest of this passage see below, pp. 42-43):   [At Samos there exists] . . . the largest temple of all the temples which I have seen; the first architect of it was Rhoikos, the son of Phileas, a local man.

Pliny, *N.H.* XXXVI, 90:   Concerning the Cretan labyrinth enough has been said. The Samian [70] labyrinth, which was similar to this one, was more remarkable insofar as it had 150 columns, of which the drums, when they were suspended in the workshop, were so well balanced that they could be turned on their axes by a boy. The architects were local men, Zmilis,[71] Rhoikos, and Theodoros.

Vitruvius VII, praef. 12:   . . . Theodoros and Rhoikos published a volume on the Ionic temple of Hera [72] at Samos.

68. On Dionysios, see p. 109.
69. Several temples were built on this site. The remains of the one associated with Theodoros and Rhoikos date from about 560 B.C.
70. The text says Lemnian, not Samian, but since the architects were said to be *indignae* of the place where the labyrinth was built, since Theodoros and Rhoikos were Samian, and since no appropriate structure exists on Lemnos, most modern scholars feel that Pliny, or the later copyists of his manuscript, have made a mistake, and that the passage actually refers to the *Heraion* at Samos, which, with its forest of tall Ionic columns, would have seemed labyrinthine.
71. A name otherwise unknown. Possibly Smilis is meant.
72. For the context of this passage see Chapter 6, pp. 232-233.

Other Projects

Pausanias III, 12, 10 (in Sparta): There is another road leading out from the agora, on which a structure has been built for them which is called the *Skias*,[73] where even now they meet in public assembly. They say that this *Skias* is the work of Theodoros of Samos, who first discovered how to cast iron and mould images from it.

Diogenes Laertius II, 103: There were twenty men named Theodoros. The first was a Samian, the son of Rhoikos. It was he who advised the placing of a layer of ashes beneath the foundations of the temple in Ephesos.

Chersiphron and Metagenes

Pliny, *N.H.* XXXVI, 95-97 (the temple of Artemis at Ephesos): As a true testimony to the magnificence of Greece there is still extant the temple of Ephesian Artemis, which was worked on by all of Asia Minor over a period of 200 years.[74] It was constructed on marshy ground, so that it would be neither subject to earthquakes nor in danger of landslips; on the other hand in order that such a massive work would not be placed on shifting and unstable foundations, they were underlaid with a layer of packed charcoal, and after that with a layer of wooly sheepskins. The length of the temple as a whole is 425 feet and its width is 225 feet; its 127 columns were contributed by different kings and are 60 feet in height; thirty-six of these are carved in relief, one by Skopas.[75] The architect who was in charge of the work was Chersiphron. It was a remarkable achievement that he was able to raise the epistyle blocks of such a great work. He accomplished this with wicker baskets full of sand, which he heaped up in a sloping ramp which reached to the top of the column capitals, and by gradually emptying the lower baskets the work settled into place. But he encountered the greatest difficulty with the lintel which he was placing in position above the doors. For this was the greatest block, and it would not settle into its resting place; and in his anxiety the artist debated whether his final resolution should be for death. They say that with this thought in

73. The name is presumably connected with the Greek word *skia*, "shade."
74. The temple in question was built around 560 B.C. with the financial aid of the Lydian king Croesus. It was burned down in 356 B.C. and subsequently rebuilt. The time between these two building periods is about 200 years; Pliny seems to have viewed it as one long building period.
75. The foundations of this temple measure about 180 by 360 English feet. The column base supposedly carved by Skopas (see pp. 140-143) belonged to the fourth century rebuilding. Some identify it with a drum found at Ephesos and now in the British Museum. See Richter, *Sculpture and Sculptors*,[2] Fig. 705.

mind, worn out as he was, he saw in his sleep during the night the goddess for whom the temple was being built actually present before him and exhorting him to go on living: because she herself had put the stone in place; and in the light of the following day, it turned out to be so. The block appeared to have settled in place by its own weight. The other ornaments of the temple would occupy a good many volumes, since none of them is connected with prototypes in nature.

Vitruvius III, ii, 7:   The dipteral temple has eight columns at the ends, but has double rows of columns on the long sides,[76] like the Doric temple of Quirinus and the Ionic temple of Artemis of Ephesos, built by Chersiphron.

Vitruvius X, ii, 11-12:   It is not outside the scope of our subject to describe an ingenious procedure of Chersiphron's. For he, when he wished to transport the shafts of the columns from the quarries to the temple of Artemis at Ephesos, not having confidence in wagons because he feared that (on account of the size of the load and the softness of the roads in the level country) their wheels would be engulfed, devised the following procedure. He arranged and fastened together four beams of four-inch timber so that two of them served as cross beams which were as long as the column drums, and he inserted iron pivots into the ends of the column drums with lead, dovetailing them, and then fixed circular sockets into the wood in which the pivots could rotate. He also fastened pieces of wood as buffers onto the ends of the column drums. The pivots fastened into the sockets, however, were left completely free to turn. Thus, when the oxen were yoked to the frame and drew it, the drums turned like wheels by revolving endlessly on the pivots in the sockets.

When they had transported all the column drums and were taking up the problem of transporting the blocks of the epistyle, Metagenes, the son of Chersiphron, adapted the method of transporting the column drums to the problem of hauling the epistyle blocks. He made wheels about twelve feet in diameter, and fixed the ends of the epistyle blocks into the middle of the wheels. By the same method he connected pivots and sockets to the ends; [77] so, when the frames of four-inch beams were drawn by the oxen, the pivots which were fitted into the sockets moved the wheels, and the epistyle blocks, which were fixed into the wheels like axles by the same method as had been the case with the column drums, arrived at the building site without delay. A parallel for this

76. The text says literally that a "*dipteros* is octastyle in the *pronaos* and in the back," and that it has two rows of columns "around the sanctuary."

77. That is, the wheels which were fastened on the inside to the blocks were again fastened to a wooden frame on the outside.

will be seen in the way in which cylindrical rollers level the walkways in palaestras. Nor would this have been possible in the first place had not the two sites been near to one another—for it is not more than eight miles from the quarry to the sanctuary, and there is no hill but rather a level plain.

Bathykles of Magnesia

The passage which follows is Pausanias' description of the throne of "the Amyklaian god," later identified with Apollo, at Amyklai near Sparta. Fragments of the throne are preserved in the Museum in modern Sparta.[78] It combined elements of both the Ionic order (extremely rare in the Peloponnesos in the Archaic period) and the Doric order. Along with the description of the chest of Kypselos (see below, pp. 47-51), it is one of the most informative pieces of literary evidence for the type of narrative subjects which were favored in Archaic art.

Pausanias III, 18, 9-III, 19, 2: By Bathykles the Magnesian, who made the throne of the god of Amyklai, there are Graces, set up as votives upon the completion of the throne, and a statue of Artemis *Leukophryene*. Whose pupil this Bathykles was, and in the reign of what Lakedaimonian [Spartan] king he made the throne, these questions I pass over; but I saw the throne itself, and I will describe what sort of things there are upon it. Two Graces and two Seasons hold it up in front, and, in the same manner, in the back. On the left stand Echidna and Typhos, on the right Tritons. To go through the reliefs one by one in detail would only be a bore to my readers. But, to give a brief description (since many of them are not unfamiliar), Poseidon and Zeus are shown carrying Taÿgete, the daughter of Atlas, and her sister Alkyone. Also represented on it are Atlas, the single combat of Herakles with Kyknos, and the battle of the centaurs at the dwelling of Pholos. With regard to the creature called the "bull of Minos," I do not know why Bathykles represented it as being bound and led away alive by Theseus.[79] The dance of the Phaiakians is also represented on the throne and likewise Demodokos singing.[80] The exploit of Perseus against Medusa is also depicted. Passing over the battle of Herakles against Thourios, one of the giants, and the battle of Tyndareus against Eurytos, one comes to the rape of the daughter of Leukippos. He has also represented Dionysos and Herakles; Hermes is there carrying the former,

78. Several reconstructions of the throne, based on the extant fragments and Pausanias' description, have been proposed. A good example is that of E. Buschor, *Ath. Mitt.*, LII (1927), pp. 1 ff.

79. The most common tradition was that Theseus killed the Minotaur.

80. Cf. *Odyssey*, VIII, 471 ff.

still a child, to heaven; while Athena is leading Herakles to live from that time forth among the gods. Peleus is shown handing over Achilles to be brought up by Cheiron, who is said to have been his teacher. Kephalos is there too, who on account of his beauty was abducted by Hēmera, and also there are the gods who bring gifts to the marriage of Harmonia. The single combat of Achilles against Memnon is represented, and so is Herakles getting revenge upon Dionysios the Thracian and upon Nessos by the river Euenos. Hermes leads the goddesses to be judged by Paris, and Adrastos and Tydeus restrain Amphiaraos and Lykourgos the son of Pronax from fighting. Hera gazes at Io, the daughter of Inachos, who is already a cow, and Athena is shown fleeing Hephaistos who pursues her. After these there are depicted, from the labors of Herakles, the Hydra and how he led up the dog from Hades. Then there are Anaxias and Mnasinous, each of them seated on horseback, but there is just one horse carrying Megapenthes, the son of Menelaos, and Nikostratos. Bellerophon is killing the beast in Lycia, and Herakles drives the cattle of Geryones. At the upper edges of the throne are placed the sons of Tyndareus, one on each side, on horseback. There are sphinxes beneath the horses and wild beasts higher up,[81] a leopard on one side and a lioness on the side by Pollux. On the highest spot on the throne a group of dancers has been made, representing the Magnesians who worked on the throne along with Bathykles. Running beneath the throne and, on the inside, away from the Tritons, is the hunt for the Kalydonian boar and Herakles killing the children of Aktor; and also Kalaïs and Zetes, who are driving the harpies away from Phineas. Peirithoös and Theseus are there, having just seized Helen. Herakles is strangling the lion, and Apollo and Artemis are shooting Tityos. Also represented there is the combat of Herakles with the centaur Oreios and of Theseus with the bull of Minos. In addition there is represented the wrestling match of Herakles with Acheloös and the story which is told about Hera, that is, how she was bound by Hephaistos; also the agonistic festival which Akastos held in honor of his father and the story of Menelaos and the Egyptian Proteus, as told in the *Odyssey*. And finally there is Admetos yoking a boar and lion to his chariot and the Trojans bringing libations to Hector.

The part of the throne where the god would sit is not a single continuous plane, but rather it is furnished with several chairs, and by each chair there is left a wide space; the space left in the middle is the widest and it is there that the image stands. I know of no one who has ascertained the height of the image by actual measurement, but, to give a rough estimate, it must be about 30 cubits high. It is not the

81. Or "running upwards." The text is ambiguous. The top of the throne was perhaps composed of two or three steps.

work of Bathykles, but rather it is primitive and not made with much art, for although it has a face, and feet, and hands, it looks, for the most part, like a bronze column. It has a helmet on its head, and, in the hands, a spear and a bow.

Gitiadas of Sparta

Pausanias III, 17, 1-3:   Among the Lakedaimonians there is no acropolis rising to a conspicuous height, like the Kadmeia at Thebes or the Larisa at Argos. But there are hills in the city, and to the one which projects higher into the air than the others they give the name "acropolis." In this place there is built a sanctuary of Athena, called both "Protectress of the city" and "the Lady of the Brazen House." The construction of the sanctuary was begun, they say, by Tyndareus. When he died his children wanted to make a second attempt to carry out this building project, and it was intended that the spoils from Aphidna would provide them with the means for beginning the work. But they too left it unfinished, and it was many years later that the Spartans made both the temple and the image of Athena of bronze.[82] The builder was Gitiadas, a local man. This Gitiadas also composed Dorian lyric odes and other works, including a hymn to the goddess. There are reliefs wrought into the bronze showing many of the labors of Herakles, as well as many of the deeds which he performed of his own free will; and there are other reliefs showing exploits of the sons of Tyndareus, including the rape of the daughters of Leukippos. Also there is Hephaistos releasing his mother from fetters. . . . There too are the Nymphs giving gifts to Perseus as he is about to set out on his expedition against Medusa in Libya—a helmet and the shoes by which he was to be carried through the air. Also wrought there are figures illustrating the birth of Athena and also Amphitrite and Poseidon; these are the largest figures and, in my opinion, those which are most worth seeing.

Descriptions of Ancient Temples and Other Structures

The Temple of Hera at Olympia (built c. 600 B.C.)

Pausanias V, 16, 1:   It remains for me after this to describe the temple of Hera and as many objects [83] within the temple as are worthy of interest. It is said by the Eleans that it was the Skillountians, the people of one of the cities of Triphylia, who built the temple eight years after

---

82. For the representation of this statue on coins cf. Lacroix, *Reproductions,* pp. 217-218, pl. XVIII, nos. 1, 2.

83. Some of these objects have been described previously, pp. 15-16; for others, see pp. 47-55, 134.

Oxylos attained the kingship in Elis. The order of the temple is Doric, and columns stand all around it. In the opisthodomos one of the columns is of oak. The length of the temple is . . . .[84] Whoever the architect was, they do not remember.

The "Alkmaionid" Temple of Apollo at Delphi

Herodotus V, 62: The Alkmaionidai, an Athenian family in exile under the Peisistratidai, when their attempt, along with the other Athenian exiles, to achieve their return by force was of no avail, and they suffered greatly as they attempted to reestablish freedom in Athens (they had fortified Leipsydrion above Paionia), these Alkmaionidai, making use of every possible device against the Peisistratidai, contracted with the *Amphiktyones* [85] to build the temple in Delphi, the one which is there now, but did not exist then. Being wealthy men and of distinguished lineage, they finished off the temple in a manner which made it more beautiful than its original design, and among other things, although the plan called for the temple to be made of local limestone, they made the front of it of Parian marble.[86]

The Siphnian Treasury at Delphi

Herodotus III, 57: . . . The affairs of the Siphnians were at the peak of their prosperity at that time, and they were much richer than the other islanders. Their prosperity came from gold and silver mines which existed on the island, mines so rich that, with a tithe taken from the money derived from them, the Siphnians constructed a treasury at Delphi which was equal to the richest ones there.[87]

Great Achievements in Engineering at Samos

Herodotus III, 60: I have spoken at unusual length about the Samians, because three of the greatest works among all the Hellenes were built

84. The measurements of the temple, which followed, are lost in the text. In modern units, the dimensions of the stylobate are c. 61 × 162½ feet.

85. The representatives of various states who were the overseers of the sanctuary at Delphi.

86. This was the earliest temple in which there was a substantial use of marble. It was built c. 513-505 B.C.

87. Much of the sculptural decoration of this treasury is now in the Museum at Delphi. The friezes offer some of the finest examples of archaic relief sculpture. Cf. R. Lullies and M. Hirmer, *Greek Sculpture* (New York: 1957), plates 44-51. According to Herodotus, the era of prosperity in Siphnos came to an end shortly after the building of the treasury, when the island was plundered by an expedition of Samian mercenaries. The Samian raid is dated to the year 525/4 B.C. Cf. also Pausanias X, 11, 2.

by them. There is a mountain there 900 feet in altitude [88] and through the base of it runs a tunnel with mouths on either side of the mountain. The length of the tunnel is seven stades,[89] while the height and the width are each eight feet. Through the whole length of it there is another cutting 20 cubits in depth and three feet in width, through which water, carried along in pipes, is supplied to the city from a large spring. The architect of this tunnel was the Megarian Eupalinos, son of Naustrophos. This is one of the three things; the second is a mole built out into the sea around the harbor, twenty fathoms deep; the length of the mole is more than two stades. The third thing built by them is a temple, the largest of all the temples which I have seen; the first architect of it was Rhoikos, the son of Phileas, a local man.

THE MINOR ARTS

The Greek word toreutikē *meant the art of working the surface of an object with borer* (toros), *punch, hammer, drill, and so forth, that is, the art of "chasing." It applied equally to the working of the surface of a bronze statue, cauldron, or ring, to a stone gem, and to the working of ivory, wood, and other materials. Although there can be no sharp distinction between* toreutikē *and "sculpture," we include under the heading "minor arts" all examples of* toreutikē *used to decorate the surface of portable objects (that is, not temples) which had a function which was not purely sculptural (bowls, rings, and the like).*

The Bequests of the Lydian Kings to Delphi and Other Sanctuaries

Herodotus I, 14: When Gyges [90] became ruler, he sent offerings to Delphi which were by no means insignificant; in fact, most of the offerings which are made of silver at Delphi were sent by him; besides the silver he dedicated a vast number of gold offerings, among which the most worthy of mention are six gold kraters.[91] These stand in the Corinthian treasury and weigh thirty talents.[92] To be quite accurate, however, this is not really the treasury of the Corinthian people but rather of Kypselos, the son of Eëtion. This Gyges was the first of the barbarians whom we know to have set up offerings at Delphi after Midas, the son of Gordias, the king of Phrygia. For Midas set up the royal throne on

88. Literally 150 *orguiai*, or fathoms, which equals about 900 feet.
89. A stade equalled about 600 feet.
90. The first ruler in the Lydian dynasty called the Mermnadae. He usurped the throne of Lydia c. 685 B.C. and ruled until c. 657 B.C.
91. Krater—a mixing bowl used especially for mixing wine.
92. A talent was the equivalent of about 57 pounds.

which he used to sit when he gave judgments, an object well worth seeing. This throne stands right by the kraters of Gyges. The gold and silver which Gyges set up is called "Gygian" by the people of Delphi in honor of the donor.

Herodotus I, 25:   Alyattes[93] the Lydian died just after completing his war against the Milesians and after a reign of 57 years. Earlier, after recovering from his illness, he made offerings at Delphi (being the second man of his house to do so) of a great silver krater and a welded iron krater-stand, an object particularly worth seeing among all the votives in Delphi, the work of Glaukos of Chios, who alone of all men invented the welding of iron.

This stand which Glaukos made for Alyattes' krater remained in Delphi for many centuries and is described in greater detail by later writers:

Pausanias X, 16, 1:   Of the offerings which the Lydian kings sent to Delphi, the only one which still remains is the iron stand for the krater of Alyattes. This is the work of Glaukos of Chios, the man who invented the art of welding iron. Each plate of the stand is connected with another plate not by pins or rivets, but rather the welding alone connects them and is itself the binding matter for the iron. The shape of the stand is similar to that of a tower, wider at the bottom and tapering as it rises. Each side of the base is not solid throughout, but there are cross-bars of iron like the rungs of a ladder. The upright iron plates are curled outwards at the top, so as to form a seat for the krater.

Athenaeus, *Deipnosophistai* **V, 210 c:**   [The stand by Glaukos of Chios] is truly worth seeing on account of the small figures which have been wrought upon its surface as well as other animal and vegetable forms. . . .

Herodotus I, 50-52:   . . . Croesus[94] propitiated the god in Delphi with great sacrifices. For he sacrificed 3,000 sacrificial animals, and when he had heaped up into a great pyre couches gilt with gold and silver as well as golden offering bowls and purple robes and tunics, he burned them, hoping by such offerings to win the favor of the god. Moreover he commanded each and everyone of the Lydians to sacrifice whatever he could. After the sacrifice had taken place, he melted down a vast quantity of gold and cast ingots from it, making them six palms in length, three palms in width, and one palm in thickness; the number

93. King of Lydia from c. 610 to 560 B.C.
94. Ruled 560-546 B.C. The last and best known of the Lydian kings.

of them was 117. Four of them were of pure gold, weighing two and a half talents each, while the others were of white gold [95] and weighed two talents each. He also made an image of a lion in pure gold, having a weight of ten talents. The lion, when the temple in Delphi was burned, fell from the ingots (for it had been set up on top of these); it is now situated in the treasury of the Corinthians and weighs only six and a half talents, for three and a half of its talents melted away.

When he completed these offerings, Croesus sent them to Delphi, and other things along with them. There were two kraters of great size, one of gold, the other of silver, of which the golden one stood on the right as you entered the temple, and the silver one on the left. These two were moved as a result of the burning of the temple; the golden one is now in the treasury of the Klazomenians and weighs eight and a half talents plus twelve *minae,* while the silver one is in a corner of the pronaos of the temple and holds 600 *amphorai.*[96] It is filled by the Delphians at the time of the Theophania. The Delphians also say that it is the work of Theodoros of Samos and I believe it, for it impresses me as a work of more than average quality. He also sent four silver storage jars, which now stand in the treasury of the Corinthians, and two lustral vases, one golden, the other silver. On the gold one "of the Lakedaimonians" is inscribed, and the Lakedaimonians claim that it is their votive, although they are inaccurate in saying so. For this too is an offering of Croesus, and one of the Delphians wrote the inscription, wishing to please the Lakedaimonians. I know his name but I will not record it. The boy, through whose hand water runs, is a votive of the Lakedaimonians, but this is certainly not true of either of the lustral vases. Along with these Croesus sent other offerings of less import, including round silver bowls and also a gold statue of a woman three cubits high, which the Delphians say is the baking woman of Croesus. In addition he dedicated the necklaces and the belts of his own wife. These were the things which he sent to Delphi; and to Amphiaraos, of whose excellence and misfortune he was aware, he dedicated a shield completely of gold and also a solid gold spear, the shaft along with the head being completely of gold. Both of these were still in existence in my time, stored in the temple of Ismenian Apollo in Thebes.

Herodotus I, 92: There are many other offerings in Greece by Croesus besides those already mentioned. For example in Thebes in Boeotia there is a gold tripod, which he dedicated to Ismenian Apollo, while at Ephesos the golden bulls and the majority of the columns are his offerings; and in the temple of [Athena] *Pronaia* at Delphi there is a great

95. White gold: that is, alloyed.
96. More than 5,000 gallons.

golden shield. These offerings were still in existence in my time, while others have been destroyed. In Branchidai in the territory of the Milesians there were offerings by Croesus, which, I am told, were of an equal weight and of a similar quality to those in Delphi.

A Spartan Gift to Croesus

When Croesus was preparing for his war against Persia, he sought to form an alliance with the strongest of the Greek states and finally decided that Sparta was the most promising potential ally. Herodotus here describes some side aspects of the negotiations.

Herodotus I, 69-70: [The Spartans on an earlier occasion] had sent envoys to Sardis to buy gold, wishing to use it for a statue (the one of Apollo which is now set up in Thornax in Lakonia), and Croesus gave the gold as a gift to the men who had come to buy it.

For this reason the Lakedaimonians accepted the alliance, and also because he had chosen them to be his allies out of all the other Greeks. Accordingly they remained ready to answer his summons for aid, and they also made a bronze krater which was decorated with animals along the outside of the rim and was large enough to hold 300 *amphorai*,[97] their intention being to make a gift of it to Croesus in return for his gifts. But this krater never did get to Sardis, and there are two versions of the reasons for this. The Lakedaimonians say that when it reached Samos, in the process of being transported to Sardis, the Samians heard about it, and, putting to sea in their warships, seized it. The Samians say, however, that the Spartans who were bringing it arrived too late, and when they perceived that both Sardis and Croesus had fallen into enemy hands, they sold the krater in Samos; furthermore they say that the buyers, who were private citizens, set it up in the sanctuary of Hera. Of course, it is quite natural that those who sold it would say, when they returned to Sparta, that the Samians had stolen it.

The Art of Weaving

The art of weaving was highly developed at the earliest stages of Greek history and is frequently mentioned in Homer. Akesas and Helikon from the city of Salamis on Cyprus appear to be the first artists known by name who won fame as weavers. While no date is preserved for them, the tradition that they made the first robe for Athena Polias (presumably the venerable statue of Athena Polias on the Acropolis in

97. C. 2,700 gallons.

Athens, which was clothed in a new robe every four years as part of the Panathenaic festival) suggests a date at least as early as c. 560 B.C. when the Greater Panathenaia was established.

Athenaeus II, 48 B: The art of weaving fine fabrics reached its peak at the time when the Cypriotes Akesas and Helikon were the outstanding practitioners of this art. They achieved fame as weavers. Helikon, moreover, was the son of Akesas. . . . At Delphi, at any rate, there is an inscription on one of the works which reads:

> Helikon the Salaminian, son of Akesas, fashioned
> this, into whose hands
> The lady Pallas breathed divine grace.

Zenobius, *Proverb* I, 56: The works of Akesas and Helikon: these belong in the class of those works which are worthy of wonder. For these men were the first who wrought the peplos for Athena *Polias*. Akesas [98] was born in Patara, and Helikon was a Karystian.[99]

Plutarch, *Life of Alexander*, 32: [Alexander] also wore a shoulder mantle which was fancier than the rest of his armor. This was the work of the venerable [100] Helikon and was a mark of honor from the city of Rhodes, whence it had come as a gift.

The Chest of Kypselos at Olympia

Kypselos was tyrant of Corinth from c. 655 to c. 625 B.C. As already noted, the chest which he dedicated at Olympia is one of the primary literary sources for information about the themes of Archaic art.[101]

Pausanias V, 17, 5: There is also a chest made of cedar-wood and on it are figures, some made of ivory, some of gold, and some carved out of the cedar-wood itself. It was in this chest that the mother of Kypselos, the tyrant of Corinth, hid him when the Bacchiadai [102] were eager to find him just after his birth. In gratitude for the saving of Kypselos,

---

98. The text at this point gives the name as "Aceseus."

99. Patara was in Lycia on the southern coast of Asia Minor; Karystos is in Euboia. Possibly the artists later migrated to Cyprus.

100. The Greek *palaios* implies that Helikon was already considered ancient at the time of Alexander's campaigns, 333-323 B.C.

101. Several attempts have been made to reconstruct the appearance of the chest; cf. notably H. Stuart Jones, *J.H.S.*, XIV (1894), pl. 1. Many of the scenes which Pausanias describes have reasonably close parallels in Greek vase painting. For a general parallel to what the style of the figures on the chest must have been like, cf. Corinthian vases of the second half of the seventh century B.C.; for example, the "Chigi vase" in the Villa Giulia in Rome. Cf. Arias, Hirmer, *Greek Vase Painting* (New York: 1961), pls. 16, 17, and IV.

102. Bacchiadai: the ruling clan of Corinth which was overthrown by Kypselos.

his descendants, who were called "Kypselids," set up the chest as an offering at Olympia. The Corinthians of that time called chests *kypselai*, and it is from this that the name "Kypselos" was given to the child. Near most of the figures on the chest there are inscriptions, written in the archaic characters. Some of the letters run straight along, but others are arranged in the scheme which the Greeks called *Boustrophedon*. It is like this: at the end of a line of words the second line turns back again like a racecourse which has two stretches. In addition to this, the inscriptions on the chest are written in twisting characters which are difficult to make out. Beginning our inspection of the chest from the lower section, we find that the content of the first space is as follows. Oinomaos is shown pursuing Pelops who holds Hippodameia. Each of them has two horses, but those of Pelops are endowed with wings. Next is shown the house of Amphiaraos and some old woman who carries the infant Amphilochos. Before the house stand Eriphyle holding the necklace, and by her are her daughters Eurydice and Demonassa, as well as the child Alkmena, who is naked. Asios, in his epic, makes out Alkmena to be the daughter of Amphiaraos and Eriphyle. Baton, who is the charioteer for Amphiaraos, holds the reins in one hand and a spear in the other. Amphiaraos has already placed one foot up on the chariot, but he holds an unsheathed sword and, having turned around toward Eriphyle, is so beside himself with anger, that he just barely restrains himself from striking her.[103] After the house of Amphiaraos come the games in honor of Pelias and also the spectators who watch the contestants. Herakles is depicted there seated on a throne and behind him there is a woman. For this woman, whoever she may be, the inscription is lacking, but she is playing Phrygian pipes and not Greek ones. . . .

There follows an enumeration of the particular events in the games and the contestants involved.

Tripods are also set up here, obviously as prizes for the victors, and the daughters of Pelias are also shown. The name is inscribed for only one of them, Alkestis. Iolaos, who of his own free will shared in the labors of Herakles, is shown on his chariot after he has won a victory. After this the games in honor of Pelias come to an end, and the Hydra is shown, the creature in the river Amymone, being shot at with a bow by Herakles as Athena stands by. Inasmuch as Herakles is not unfamiliar both because of his exploits and also because of the scheme

103. A scene nearly identical to the one described is depicted on the "Amphiaraos krater," a Corinthian vessel of the mid-sixth century B.C. Cf. E. Pfuhl, *Masterpieces of Greek Drawing and Painting* (New York: 1955), Fig. 14.

by which he is represented, the name is not inscribed by him. Also there is Phineus the Thracian and the sons of Boreas, who chase the Harpies away from him.

(Sec. XVIII, 1):   In my perusal of the second area on the chest, I had better begin from the left. A figure of a woman is represented there holding a white child, which is asleep, on her right arm, and on her other arm she holds a black child similar to the one who is sleeping; both children have their feet twisted. The inscriptions make it clear (and one could figure it out without the inscriptions), that the figures are Death and Sleep, with Night as nurse of both. There is also a beautiful woman who chastises an ugly one by choking her with one hand, while with the other she beats her with a staff.[104] There are also two other women pounding mortars with pestles, whose occupation would seem to be the art of medicine, since there is otherwise no inscription to identify them. . . .

A series of scenes follows illustrating the themes of deception and violence in love and adventure: Idas leading home Marpessa, whom Apollo had abducted; Zeus seducing Alkmena; Menelaos threatening to kill Helen after the sack of Troy; Jason, Medea, and Aphrodite; Apollo and the Muses, a scene perhaps connected with the Idas and Marpessa story; Herakles attempting to trick Atlas into giving him the apples of the Hesperides; Ares leading Aphrodite, possibly a reference to the tale of illicit love told in the Odyssey *VIII, 266-369; Peleus wooing Thetis; and the sisters of Medusa pursuing Perseus.*

(Sec. XVIII, 6):   Military scenes are placed on the third section of the chest. The majority of the figures are shown as foot-soldiers, but some cavalrymen are shown on two-horse chariots. As far as the soldiers are concerned, one may infer that they are going into battle, and that as they go into battle they will recognize and greet one another. . . .

Pausanias then discusses the meaning of this scene and decides that it is a reference to the struggle which the ancestors of Kypselos had in gaining admission to Corinth as settlers.

(Sec. XIX, 1):   On the fourth section of the chest as you go around from the left is Boreas, who has abducted Oreithyia; he has serpent

---

104. This was possibly one of the earliest examples of personification and allegory in Greek art. The question of personification in Greek art is complicated, however, by the fact that subjects which would now be viewed as abstractions (for example, "Justice," "Strife") or natural phenomena (for example, "the north wind," "night," or "sleep") were sometimes viewed as actual divinities by the Greeks. Hence their forms were as "real" as those of Zeus, Apollo, and Athena.

tails instead of feet; and there is also the struggle of Herakles against Geryones. The latter is represented as three men joined together. Theseus holds a lyre and by him is Ariadne, who holds a wreath. There also is the fight between Achilles and Memnon, whose mothers stand by them; Melanion is also represented and by him is Atalanta holding a fawn. After that is the single combat of Hector against Ajax resulting from the former's challenge, and between them stands Strife in the form of an extremely ugly woman. . . .

The next scenes showed Aithra, the daughter of King Pittheus of Troizen and the mother of Theseus, at the time when she was consigned as a slave to Helen and the Dioscuri; and Agamemnon slaying the Trojan warrior Koön as described in the Iliad *XI, 248-263.*

Then there is Hermes who leads the goddesses to Alexander the son of Priam in order that their beauty may be judged, and the inscription by them says:

> This is Hermes who indicates to Alexander that
> he must judge between
> The beauty of Hera, Athena, and Aphrodite.

I do not know the reason why Artemis has wings on her shoulders; she also holds a leopard in her right hand and a lion in her left.[105] Also represented is Kassandra whom Ajax drags away from the image of Athena, and the inscription says:

> Ajax the Lokrian is dragging Kassandra away
> from Athena.

Of the children of Oedipus Eteokles is shown advancing against Polyneikes, who has fallen on one knee. Behind Polyneikes stands a woman with teeth which are no less savage than those of a beast. The nails on her fingers are curved like claws. The inscription by her says that she is Doom, suggesting that Polyneikes was carried off by fate, and that Eteokles' end came to him with some justice. Dionysos is shown reclining in a cave; he is bearded, holds a golden cup, and is dressed in a tunic which reaches to his feet. There are vines around him and also apple trees and pomegranate trees.

(Sec. XIX, 7): The uppermost area—for they are five in number—offers no inscription, and one is left to guess at the meaning of the reliefs. To proceed then, there is a cave, and in it a woman is sleeping

---

105. Artemis is represented here as the *"potnia thērōn," "*mistress of animals,*"* a format also known in Archaic vase painting. Cf. Arias and Tirmer, *op. cit.,* pls. 11 and 46.

with a man upon a couch. I guessed that they were Odysseus and Circe, basing my guess on the number of servant women who are placed before the cave and on the things which they are doing. For there are four women, and they are engaged in the tasks which Homer mentions in his epic.[106] There is also a centaur whose legs are not all like those of a horse, for the two front legs are those of a man.[107] Next come two-horse chariots, and there are women shown standing on these. The horses have golden wings, and there is a man who is giving armor to one of the women. All these things suggest that the scene deals with the death of Patroklos. The women on the chariots must be Nereids, and it must be Thetis who takes the armor from Hephaistos, for, besides the other evidence, the man who is giving the armor is not very sturdy in the feet, and a servant follows behind him carrying fire-tongs. It is said of the centaur, that he is Cheiron, now set free from men and deemed worthy to dwell among the gods, who has come to provide whatever solace he can to Achilles in his grief. Two maidens riding a wagon drawn by mules, one holding the reins, the other wearing a veil on her head, are thought to be Nausikaa the daughter of Alkinoös and her handmaiden, driving to the washing pools. There is also a man shooting arrows at centaurs, some of whom he has killed; this archer is clearly Herakles, and the scene is one of the deeds of Herakles.

As to who the person was who made the chest, I have been able to form no idea at all; the inscriptions on it, although some other person might conceivably have composed them, are most probably, by my conjecture, to be ascribed to Eumelos of Corinth. . . .

106. *Odyssey* X, 348 ff.
107. This scheme appears on some of the earliest mythological vase paintings. Cf. Beazley, *The Development of Attic Black Figure* (Berkeley and London: 1951), pp. 5-7 and Fig. 2.

3

The Early Classical
and
High Classical Periods

The repulse and eventual defeat of the invading Persian army in 480/479 B.C. gave rise to a wave of intellectual and artistic liberation in the Greek world. By facing and overcoming a ponderous Oriental empire the Greeks became more acutely conscious of the distinct and unique qualities of their own culture. The confidence and yet restraint with which Aeschylus in the Oresteia trilogy rejected ancient moral attitudes and set out to redesign the Greek's image of himself and the world is paralleled in art by the final renunciation of the ancient workshop formulas which Greece and the Orient had shared as a common heritage.

The art of the Classical period was both more realistic and at the same time more formal than Archaic art. The forms of Greek sculpture and painting began, on the surface, to simulate more closely the artist's optical experience of the natural world, and yet simultaneously the theoretical, formal principles by which forms were constructed—principles such as symmetria and rhythmos—became infinitely more subtle and demanding. This duality in the nature of the Classical style made it a fit vehicle to express both the idealism and the awareness of the tragic which characterize Greek thought in the fifth century B.C.

SCULPTURE

The Early Classical Period

Kritios and Nesiotes

Although the literary sources give little information about them, the two sculptors Kritios and Nesiotes were among the most influential artists of the Early Classical period. Their most famous work, the "Tyrant Slayers,"[1] is dated to 477 B.C. by the Marmor Parium. This group stood in the Agora at Athens.

Pausanias I, 8, 5: Not far off are figures of Harmodios and Aristogeiton who slew Hipparchos. The reason for this deed and the way it was done

1. This famous group is known through copies in various media. Cf. Richter, *Sculpture and Sculptors*,[2] Figs. 565-577; S. Brunnsaker, *The Tyrant Slayers of Kritios and Nesiotes* (Lund, 1955). Another work described by Pausanias (I, 23, 9) was a statue of an Athenian named Epicharinos, who won a victory in the foot-races of armed warriors. Pausanias mentions only Kritios, but the inscribed base of the work, found on the Acropolis, bears the signatures of both Kritios and Nesiotes. Cf. Raubitschek, *Dedications*, pp. 124-125, 513-517.

have been told by others.[2] Of these statues one group is the work of Kritios, while Antenor made the older group.[3]

Lucian, *Philopseudes*, 18: As you are entering, pass by the statues on the right, among which stand the Tyrannicides, the figures by Kritios and Nesiotes.

Pythagoras of Rhegion

Pythagoras was apparently one of the Samians who migrated in 496 B.C. to Zankle (modern Messina) and came under the sway of the tyrant Anaxilas of Rhegion (cf. Herodotus VI, 23-25). This change of residence gave rise to the almost certainly erroneous tradition that there were two sculptors named Pythagoras, one from Samos and one from Rhegion. Pythagoras made a statue at Olympia of a boxer named Euthymos (from Lokroi Epizephyroi in South Italy), which is described by Pausanias (VI, 6, 6). Although he does not call him "Pythagoras of Rhegion" in this passage, Pausanias clearly considered the statue to be the work of the same Pythagoras whose work he describes and praises elsewhere. The base of the statue, however, has been found at Olympia and on it Pythagoras signs himself "the Samian." [4]

Most of Pythagoras' works seem to have represented athletes (especially those from the Greek cities in Sicily) who had been victorious in the various athletic festivals. His career as a sculptor is thus very much like that of Pindar as a poet.

On his role as a theorist of proportions and his place in ancient art criticism, see Introduction, p. xvii.

Pliny, *N.H.* XXXIV, 59: Pythagoras from Rhegion in Italy surpassed him [Myron] with his Pankratiast which was set up at Delphi . . . and his Leontiskos.[5] He also made a statue of the runner Astylos, which is on display at Olympia, and also in that place a Libyan [and] a boy holding a whip,[6] and a nude figure bearing apples; likewise at Syracuse there is a figure of a lame man, which makes people who look at it actually feel the pain of its sore; also an Apollo transfixing the serpent [7]

2. Herodotus V, 55 ff.; Thucydides I, 20; VI, 54, 56-58.
3. See p. 33.
4. Loewy, *Inschriften*, no. 23.
5. As the text stands Pliny says at this point, "in the same event he also surpassed Leontiskos." Leontiskos was actually an athlete whose statue was made by Pythagoras, not an artist (see Pausanias' description which follows). Either the text is faulty or Pliny has misinterpreted his sources.
6. Reading *et puerum tenentem flagellum* as suggested by H. Stuart Jones. The statues referred to are probably those of Mnaseas and Kratisthenes described by Pausanias, *vide infra*.
7. Serpent: Pytho, the dragon which Apollo slew at Delphi.

with his arrows, and a man playing the *kithara*,[8] a work which is called "the just," because, when Alexander captured Thebes, a sum of gold which was hidden in a fold of its garment by a fugitive remained undisturbed. Pythagoras was the first to represent sinews and veins, and he was more exact in his representation of the hair.

There was another Pythagoras, a Samian, who was initially a painter. His statues of seven nude figures and an old man which stand by the temple of Today's Fortune [in Rome] are much praised. It is recorded that he resembled the above-mentioned Pythagoras in appearance to the point of being indistinguishable.

Diogenes Laertius VIII, 46: Some say there was another Pythagoras, a sculptor, of Rhegion, who seems to have been the first to aim at *rhythmos* and *symmetria*,[9] and that there was still another sculptor [of that name], a Samian.

Some of the statues referred to by Pliny in the first passage quoted above were also seen and described by Pausanias.

Pausanias VI, 13, 1 (the statue of the runner Astylos at Olympia): The statue of Astylos of Kroton is the work of Pythagoras. He won victories in three successive Olympiads in the one stade dash and in the double-length race. But because on the occasion of the latter two victories, in order to win the favor of Hieron the son of Deinomenes, he proclaimed himself a Syracusan, the people of Kroton condemned his house to be a prison and pulled down his statue which stood by the temple of Hera *Lakinia*.

Pausanias VI, 4, 3 (the wrestler Leontiskos): . . . there is a statue of Leontiskos, a wrestler in the men's category,[10] who was a Sicilian by birth and came from Messene on the strait. It is said that he was crowned by the Amphiktyones and twice by the people of Elis, and that his style of wrestling was like that of Sostratos of Sikyon in the *pankration*.[11] For it is said that Leontiskos did not know how to throw his opponents in wrestling but that he won by bending their fingers. The statue is by Pythagoras of Rhegion—if ever there was an artist gifted in the art of modelling, it was he. They say that he was a pupil of Klearchos,[12] who was also of Rhegion and was a pupil of Eucheiros.

8. The *kithara* was an elaborate form of the lyre. In connection with this statue see also Athenaeus I, 19 B.
9. *Rhythmos*—compositional patterns, especially of figures in movement; *symmetria*—proportion, the commensurability of all the parts of a statue.
10. As opposed to the boys' category.
11. See Chapter 2, note 29, p. 22.
12. On Klearchos see pp. 15-16.

Eucheiros is said to have been a Corinthian, and to have learned at the school of the Spartans Syadras and Chartas.

Pausanias VI, 13, 7 and VI, 18, 1 (a statue at Olympia of Mnaseas and Kratisthenes from Cyrene in Libya, presumably the same Libyans mentioned by Pliny):   By the side of Bykelos stands a statue of a man in armor, Mnaseas, surnamed the Libyan, from Cyrene.

There is also a chariot in bronze of Kratisthenes of Cyrene, and mounted on the chariot are a figure of Victory and Kratisthenes himself. Obviously his victory occurred in the chariot races. It is said that Kratisthenes was the son of Mnaseas the runner, surnamed "the Libyan" by the Greeks. His votive offerings at Olympia are the work of Pythagoras of Rhegion.

Besides statues of victorious athletes Pythagoras also did mythological groups. It has been suggested that the "lame man" mentioned by Pliny in the first passage refers to a statue of Philoktetes and that the following epigram from the Greek Anthology *refers to the statue by Pythagoras:*

Anthologia Graeca IV, 180, 294 (Planud. IV, 112):

> (On a statue of Philoktetes.)
> My enemy above all the Danaans is the sculptor
>   who made me, another Odysseus,
> Who reminds me of my trouble and baneful sickness,
> Not sufficient were the rocks, the tattered garment,
>   the gore, the wound, the sorrow,
> But he has also worked even the pain into bronze.

It has also been suggested that the "seven nude figures" referred to by Pliny were part of a group representing the "Seven against Thebes," and that the figures of Eteokles and Polyneikes mentioned by Tatian were part of that group.[13]

Tatianus, Epis. adv. Graecos 54 (p. 118 ed. Worth):   Is it not a bitter thing that you honor among yourselves the murder of brothers, you who look upon the representations of Polyneikes and Eteokles, and do not, by burying them along with their maker, Pythagoras, destroy the memorial of their evil.

Still other mythological subjects represented by Pythagoras were a bronze of Europa and the Bull and a bronze representing Perseus.

13. Originally suggested by L. Urlichs, *Chrestomathia Pliniana* (Berlin, 1857), p. 321.

Varro, de Lingua Latina V, 31: The word "Europe" comes from Europa the daughter of Agenor, whom as Mallius writes, the bull carried off from Phoenicia; Pythagoras made a remarkable image in bronze of this scene in Tarentum.

Dio Chrysostom, Or. XXXVII, 10 (comparing later statues to those of Daedalus): All these [statues] remain in their position and place unless someone moves them; the bronze of which they are constituted is incapable of movement, even though possessed of wings, as in the case of the Perseus of Pythagoras.

Kalamis

Kalamis was a prolific sculptor, apparently an Athenian, whose work was given an important place in the late Hellenistic comparative canon of sculptors (cf. Chapter 6, pp. 220-221).

A number of scholars believe that there were two artists named Kalamis, one a sculptor active in the second quarter of the fifth century B.C. and the other a silversmith and sculptor who was active in the fourth century B.C. and who may have been the grandson of the Elder Kalamis.[14] *(On Kalamis the silversmith, see below pp. 233-234; for passages which may reasonably be said to refer to the younger Kalamis, see p. 140 and footnote 42).*

We give here a selection of passages which can be referred to the fifth century Kalamis:

Pausanias I, 3, 4 (the Apollo "the Averter of Evil" in Athens): In front of the temple [of Apollo *Patroös*] there is a statue of Apollo . . . which they call "the Averter of Evil," made by Kalamis. They say that this name became associated with the god, because, by means of an oracle from Delphi he stayed the plague which afflicted them during the Peloponnesian War.[15]

Strabo VII, 319 (a colossal Apollo in Apollonia on the Black Sea): Apollonia, a colony of the Milesians . . . has on a certain island a sanctuary of Apollo, from which Marcus Lucullus took away the colossal statue of Apollo, a work of Kalamis, and set it up on the Capitol.[16]

14. Cf. F. Studniczka, "Kalamis," *Abhandl. d. Sächs. Ges. d. Wiss., Phil.-Hist. Kl.,* 25, 4 (1907); also Raubitschek, *Dedications,* pp. 505-508.

15. This is a natural assumption on Pausanias' part but probably incorrect if the statue was made by Kalamis. It has often been suggested that the figure known as the "Omphalos Apollo," a Roman copy of an Early Classical original, is a copy of the Apollo *Alexikakos* ("Averter of Evil") of Kalamis. Cf. Richter, *Sculpture and Sculptors,*2 p. 206; Figs. 36, 37.

16. Cf. also Appian, *Illyrica,* 30 and Pliny, *N.H.* XXXIV, 39, who says that the statue was 30 cubits high. The work is apparently pictured on the coins of Apollonia; cf. Lacroix, *Reproductions,* pp. 248-249 and plate XX, 6-9.

Pausanias II, 10, 3 (an image of Asklepios at Sikyon):   As you enter you see the god, who is beardless, a work executed in gold and ivory by Kalamis. He holds a scepter in one hand and the cone of the cultivated pine tree in the other.

Pausanias V, 26, 6 (a statue of Nike [Victory] at Olympia):   Beside the Athena there is a statue of Nike. The Mantineans set it up, but they do not make clear in the inscription, what war it commemorates. Kalamis is said to have made it without wings, in imitation of the wooden statue in Athens called "the wingless." [17]

Pausanias IX, 22, 1 (a statue of Hermes in Tanagra):   There are also sanctuaries of Hermes the "Ram-bearer" and of Hermes whom they call the "Vanguard." With regard to the former name, they relate that Hermes warded off a plague from them by carrying a ram around the city wall; to commemorate this event Kalamis made an image of Hermes carrying a ram on his shoulders.[18]

Lucian, in his Imagines, *envisualizes a woman of perfect beauty, whom he calls "Panthea." He derives the features which he would attribute to her from famous statues, among them the "Sosandra" ("Saviour of Men") of Kalamis. This figure, as Lucian tells us (Imag. 4), stood on the Acropolis of Athens and may be identical with the figure of Aphrodite by Kalamis which Pausanias (I, 23, 2) saw on the Acropolis.*[19]

Lucian, *Imagines* 6:   The Sosandra and Kalamis shall adorn her with modesty, and the holy and inscrutable smile will also be like hers, and the simplicity and orderliness of her dress shall also come from the Sosandra, except that her head shall be left uncovered.

Lucian, *Dialogi Meretricii*, III, 2 (one courtesan criticizes a young man's admiration of another courtesan):   Diphilos praised lavishly her rhythmic movements and the way she led the dance, and how well her step

17. The reference is to the old image of Athena Nike *Apteros* (the "wingless") whose sanctuary was on a bastion flanking the entrance to the Athenian Acropolis.
18. Represented on the coins of Tanagra; cf. Lacroix, *Reproductions*, pp. 246-248, plate XX, 4.
19. This Aphrodite was dedicated by a man named Kallias who may be the rich and distinguished Athenian citizen who married Elpinike, the sister of the Athenian political leader Kimon. Kimon had been imprisoned because of a debt incurred by his (then deceased) father Miltiades, but Kallias paid the debt and freed him. It may be that the name "Sosandra" was connected in some way with Kimon's "salvation" (cf. Herodotus VI, 136; Plutarch, *Life of Cimon*, IV). A base presumed to be that of the Aphrodite dedicated by Kallias has been found on the Acropolis; cf. Raubitschek, *Dedications*, no. 136.

followed the *kithara,* how fair her ankle was, and ten thousand other things, as if he were praising the Sosandra of Kalamis, and not Thaïs.

Kalamis also made a number of votive victory monuments (commemorating both military and athletic victories), which, as we have seen, constituted one of the basic types of commission which an ancient artist could receive.

Pausanias V, 25, 5 (an Agrigentine votive at Olympia): On the cape in Sicily which is turned toward Libya and the south, the cape called Pachynos, is the city of Motye. The people who dwell in it are Libyans and Phoenicians. It was against these foreigners in Motye that the people of Akragas [20] waged war, and, when they took booty and spoils from them, set up bronze statues of boys, who hold out their right hands and are hence depicted as if praying to the god. These figures are placed on the wall of the *Altis.* I supposed that they were the works of Kalamis, and the tradition about them supports my suppositions.

Pausanias VI, 12, 1 (another votive at Olympia): Nearby is a bronze chariot and a man mounted on it; race-horses stand by the chariot, one on each side, and there are children seated on the horses. These are memorials to the Olympic victories of Hieron the son of Deinomenes, who ruled as tyrant over the Syracusans after his brother Gelon. But Hieron did not send these offerings; rather it was Deinomenes, the son of Hieron, who gave them to the god. The chariot was the work of Onatas of Aegina, while the horses on either side of it and the children upon them are the work of Kalamis.[21]

Myron of Eleutherai

See also Chapter 6, pp. 220-221.

Pliny, *N.H.* XXXIV, 57-58: Myron, who was born at Eleutherai, and was a pupil of Ageladas, was most renowned for his statue of a heifer, a work which is praised in well-known verses—for many people gain their reputations through someone else's inventiveness rather than their own. He also made a dog, a Discus-thrower, a Perseus and the sea

20. Akragas—Agrigento.
21. Although we have classed Onatas among the Late Archaic sculptors, his career lasted well into the Early Classical period. Kalamis was clearly a younger contemporary of Onatas, perhaps even a pupil.
Pliny, *N.H.* XXXIV, 71, preserves a somewhat similar anecdote about a group for which Kalamis made a chariot with horses but Praxiteles made the charioteer (see p. 130). It is possible that this passage refers to the younger Kalamis or to an elder Praxiteles. It is also possible that Pliny's information is muddled, and he is really referring to the group by Onatas and Kalamis.

monsters,[22] a Satyr marvelling at the flutes, and an Athena,[23] contestants in the *pentathlon* at Delphi, pankratiasts, and a Herakles which is now in the round temple of Pompey the Great [24] in the Circus Maximus. He also made a monument to a cicada and a locust, as Erinna indicates in her poem.[25] He also made an Apollo which was carried off by the Triumvir Antony but restored again by the divine Augustus after being warned in a dream. Myron [26] seems to have been the first to extend the representation of reality; [27] he used more compositional patterns in his art than Polykleitos [28] and had a more complex system of symmetry; [29] he too, however, though very attentive as far as the bodies were concerned, failed to express a sense of inner animation; moreover he did not render the hair and the pubes any more perfectly than the rude art of an earlier period had.

Of the various works of Myron mentioned by Pliny, the "Discus-thrower" (Diskobolos), *which has been reconstructed with considerable accuracy from a series of Roman copies, is the best known today.*[30] *It provides an illuminating example of the* rhythmos *which Pliny praises in the art of Myron.*

Lucian, *Philopseudes* **18:** Surely, I said, you do not speak of the discus-thrower, who is bent over into the throwing position, is turned toward the hand that holds the discus, and has the opposite knee gently flexed, like one who will straighten up again after the throw? Not that

22. Latin *pristes;* another reading is *pristas,* "sawyers." If sea monster is correct, the reference may be to the story of Perseus and Andromeda. Possibly the *pristes* or *pristas* constituted a separate work, not connected with the Perseus and Medusa of Myron seen by Pausanias (I, 23, 7) on the Athenian Acropolis.

23. This work has been reconstructed from the evidence of Greek coins and vase paintings and Roman sculptural copies. Cf. Richter, *Sculpture and Sculptors,*2 Figs. 584-593.

24. This temple was dedicated to Herakles and was built by Pompey the Great.

25. Pliny derived this bit of misinformation from a poem in the *Palatine Anthology* (VII, 190) which actually refers to a girl named Myro.

26. On this passage, see Introduction, pp. xi-xii.

27. Latin *multiplicasse veritatem; veritas* translates the Greek *alētheia,* which referred to a physical reality of which the nature was confirmed by objective measurement rather than simply appearance.

28. Latin *numerosior in arte quam Polyclitus.* Latin *numerus* translates the Greek *rhythmos,* "shape, pattern"; *ars* may translate *technē,* and refer to the theoretical precepts which Myron applied to his art and by which he explained it.

29. Latin *diligentior in symmetria; diligens* translates the Greek *akribeia* which refers to precision or exactness in the handling of minute details. The meaning of Pliny's phrase may be not that Myron's system of *symmetria* was superior to that of Polykleitos but that it involved more proportional measurements and fewer common denominators.

30. Cf. Richter, *Sculpture and Sculptors,*2 Figs. 578-582.

one, he said, for the *Diskobolos* of which you speak is one of the works of Myron.

Quintilian II, 13, 8-10: It is often expedient to make variations in some established, traditional order and it is occasionally fitting to do so, as, for example, when we see the dress, face, and pose varied in statues and paintings. For indeed there is very little grace in a body which stands upright; the face, for example, looks straight ahead, the arms are allowed to hang down, the feet are joined, and the work as a whole is rigid from head to toe. But the familiar relaxed curvature and, as I might even call it, movement, provides a kind of liveliness and emotion. Therefore, the hands are not arranged in one manner alone, and there are a thousand varieties of expression in the face. Some figures have a sort of running or charging format, while others sit or recline. Some are nude, some are dressed, while others offer a mixture of both. What work is there which is as distorted and elaborate as that *Diskobolos* of Myron? But if anyone should criticize this work because it was not sufficiently upright, would he not reveal a lack of understanding of the art, in which the most praiseworthy quality is this very novelty and difficulty?

In antiquity, however, the most famous work of Myron was the cow (or heifer), about which the verses, mentioned by Pliny, were written. The fame of this work is attested by the fact that there are, in addition to other references, thirty-six epigrams about it preserved in the Greek Anthology. *A selection of them is given here. Most of them, as will be seen, laud the statue's realism.*

Anth. Graec. **I, 165, 42 (*Palat.* 719), by Euenos:**

> Either a hide completely of bronze covers this cow
> On the outside, or the bronze has a soul within it.

Anth. Graec. **I, 249 18 (*Palat.* 734), by Dioskorides:**

> O bull, in vain do you nudge this heifer. For it is lifeless;
> Myron, the cow-sculptor has deceived you.

Anth. Graec. **II, 64, 2 (*Palat.* 731), by Demetrios:**

> It was Myron who thus set me up,—a young cow,
> And the shepherds throw stones at me, as if I
> were left behind.

Anth. Graec. **III, 198, 14 (*Palat.* 737), by Julianus of Egypt:**

> It is a bronze heifer which you strike. Greatly has art
> tricked you,
> O shepherd—Myron did not put the soul within it.

Anth. Graec. III, 198, 15 (Palat. 793), by Julianus of Egypt:

> Seeing the heifer of Myron you would quickly cry out:
> Nature is lifeless but art is alive.

Anth. Graec. III, 198, 21 (Palat. 738), by Julianus of Egypt:

> In this cow Nature and Lady Art waged a battle.
> And Myron bestowed the prize on both equally,
> For to those who behold it, Art has stolen the
>   power of Nature,
> But to those who touch it, Nature is Nature.

Myron's fame as a sculptor of animals is also reflected in the following passages:

Propertius, II, 31, 7-8:

> And around the altar stood the herd of Myron,
> Four cows, made by art, statues full of life.

Petronius, Satyricon, 88:   Myron, who could almost capture the spirits of men and animals in bronze, found no heir.

As the two preceding passages indicate, Myron's sculpture was exceptionally popular with the Romans, and a number of his works were carried off to Rome and given prominent places there.

Strabo XIV, 637 b (in the temple of Hera on Samos):   Three colossal statues by Myron were set on a single base; these were carried off by Antony, but Augustus Caesar set two of them up again on the same base, the Athena and the Herakles. The Zeus, however, he transferred to the Capitoline and made a shrine for it there.

Cicero, Verrine II, iv, 3, 5-7 (concerning a shrine belonging to Heius Mamertinus, which was plundered by Verres):   Indeed, to get back to the shrine, there was a statue there, of which I speak, a Cupid made of marble, and in the opposite part there was a Herakles, an outstanding work, made of bronze. This was said to be a work of Myron. . . . [sec. 7] All these statues which I have mentioned, Verres carried off from the shrine of Heius.

Cicero, Verrine II, iv, 43, 93:   Did you not carry off from the very holy shrine of Aesculapius in Agrigentum a monument of the same Publius Scipio, a beautiful statue of Apollo, on the upper leg of which the name of Myron was inscribed in small silver letters?

Pausanias IX, 30, 1 (on Mt. Helikon):   Sulla set up the standing image of Dionysos, which, among the works of Myron, is the most worthy of note after the Erechtheus in Athens; the statue which he [Sulla] set up was not from his own resources; he took it from the Minyai of Orchomenos. This is an example of the saying among the Greeks: "to worship the divine with other people's incense."

Myron also did a number of victorious athletes, which were seen by Pausanias. Since little information, other than the names of the athletes, is given, we omit the text of these references.[31] One statue, however, that of an athlete named Ladas, was the subject of an interesting elegiac poem (here translated in prose) in the Greek Anthology.

Anth. Graec. IV, 185, 318 (Planud. IV, 54):   As you once were, O Ladas, full of life, when you left behind wind-swift Thymos, straining your sinews as you ran on the tip of your toes; so did Myron cast you in bronze, and stamp everywhere on your body your anticipation of the crown of Pisa.

He is full of hope; and on the edge of his lips the breath from his hollow flanks is visible; soon the bronze will leap for the crown nor will the base be able to hold it back. Oh, art is swifter than a breath of wind.

Telephanes of Phokis

Nothing is known about the sculptor Telephanes other than what Pliny tells us; but, if his information is accurate, Telephanes may have been one of the outstanding sculptors of the Early Classical period.

Pliny, N.H. XXXIV, 68:   Artists who have written composite volumes on this subject [sculpture and/or *toreutikē*] extol with the highest praises one Telephanes of Phokis, who is otherwise unknown, because . . . [lacuna in text] he lived in Phokis, and his works remained in obscurity there; nevertheless, by the testimony of these writers, he should be placed on an equal level with Polykleitos, Myron, and Pythagoras. They praise his Larisa, and his Spintharos who was a victor in the *pentathlon,* and his Apollo. Others speculate that the cause of his lack of reputation is not this [that he lived in a remote area], but rather it is that he offered his services to the workshops of Kings Xerxes and Darius.

31. Cf. Pausanias VI, 2, 2 (Lykinos of Sparta, winner in the horse races); Paus. VI, 8, 4 (Timanthes of Kleonai in the *pankration*); Paus. VI, 8, 5 (Philippos of Pellana in the boys' boxing); Paus. VI, 13, 2 (Chionis the Lakedaimonian).

The High Classical Period, c. 450-400 B.C.

In the second half of the fifth century B.C., Athens began to wield the same great influence in the arts which she was beginning to wield in literature, philosophy, and politics. Under the political hegemony (c. 461-429 B.C.) of Pericles a grand rebuilding program was undertaken to replace the monuments which had been destroyed by the Persians. The overseer of Pericles' building program was the sculptor Pheidias (on the Periclean building program see also under architecture, pp. 114-121).

Pheidias

Pheidias' personal contribution, other than being general overseer, to the Periclean building program, was to make the great gold and ivory cult statue of Athena for the Parthenon. In doing so, he ran into opposition from Pericles' political enemies.

Plutarch, Life of Pericles, 13 (excerpts): The man who directed all the works and was the overseer for him [Pericles] was Pheidias, although individual works were executed by other great architects and artists. . . . Pheidias himself worked on the golden image of the goddess, and his name is inscribed as the artist on the stele.[32] Almost everything was under his supervision, and, as we have said, he was in charge, owing to his friendship with Pericles, of all the other artists. This brought envy against the one and, against the other, slander to the effect that Pheidias was in the habit of procuring for Pericles free-born women who visited the building site.

Plutarch, Life of Pericles, 31: Pheidias the sculptor was commissioned to make the cult statue, as we have already said. Being a friend of Pericles and having considerable influence with him, he on that account had a number of jealous enemies; these enemies decided to test the populace by bringing a charge against Pheidias, in order to find out what the popular judgment would be against Pericles. Having bribed a certain Menon, one of Pheidias' co-workers, they had him sit down in the agora as a suppliant and beg for immunity in return for giving information and making a charge against Pheidias. The man was received as a witness by the people, and an inquiry was held in the assembly, but acts of theft were not proven. For right from the very beginning and on the advice of Pericles Pheidias had so worked and put in place the gold for the image that it was quite possible to remove it and test its weight. And this is what Pericles challenged his accusers

32. Just what stele is not clear. The reference may be to the base of the statue.

to do. But it was the reputation of his works that aroused jealousy against Pheidias, and particularly that, in making a relief of the battle of the Amazons on the shield [of the Athena *Parthenos*], he included a figure of himself as a bald old man who lifts up a stone with both hands and a very handsome portrait of Pericles fighting against an Amazon. The position of Pericles' arm, however, which holds up a spear in front of his eyes, is ingeniously contrived for the purpose, it would appear, of concealing the likeness which is only visible on either side.[33] Pheidias ultimately was led away to prison and died of a disease, or, as some say, by poison, which had been prepared by the enemies of Pericles in order to bring a false accusation against him. As for the informer, Menon, . . . the populace gave him immunity and ordered the generals to guarantee the man's safety.

A different version of the trial and death of Pheidias is told by scholiasts writing on lines 605-609 of the Peace *of Aristophanes, which read:*

First Pheidias began it all by acting ill
And Pericles dreaded that he might be involved;
He feared your tempers and the way you grind your teeth;
So before the worst could come, he set ablaze a town,
By throwing in the little spark, the Megarian decrees.[34]

Scholia on Aristophanes' *Peace*, 605 (First Scholiast): Philochoros[35] writing of the archonship of Theodoros[36] says as follows:[37] The gold image of Athena was set up in the great temple and had a weight of forty-four talents; Pericles was in charge, and Pheidias made it. And Pheidias, after he had made it, was tried for having embezzled some of the ivory which was used for the scales [of the snake represented with Athena]. Having gone into exile in Elis, he is said to have undertaken to make the image of Zeus at Olympia, and, after making it, to have been put

33. Some of the free Roman copies of the shield do contain figures which fit this description. It is perhaps doubtful, however, that the figures were really portraits of Pericles and Pheidias. The story may be a popular tradition of the Roman period, when portraits, of course, were commonplace. The tradition about the portraits is also recorded by Dio Chrysostom, *Or.* XII, 6; Pseudo-Aristotle, *De Mundo,* 399 B; Valerius Maximus VIII, 14, 6; and Apuleius, *De Mundo,* 32.
34. In 432 B.C. Pericles was responsible for a decree which forbade the Megarians access to any port allied to Athens. The decree had the effect of crippling Megara economically and was one of the contributing causes of the Peloponnesian War.
35. Philochoros: an Athenian historian of the third century B.C. who specialized in Athenian history and politics. His work survives only in small fragments.
36. The name is corrupted in the text. Theodoros is known to have been archon in 438 B.C.
37. Just how much, if any, of what follows, is a direct quotation from Philochoros is difficult to say. For a discussion of the question, cf. Jacoby, *Fragmente der griechischen Historiker,* III b (suppl.), Vol. II (Leiden, 1954), pp. 391-401 (commentary on Philochoros, frag. 121).

to death by the Eleans in the archonship of Pythodoros,[38] who came seven years later. (Second Scholiast): Some say that when Pheidias the sculptor was convicted of having defrauded the city and was banished, Pericles, in fear because he had overseen the preparations of the statue and had known about the theft, proposed the Megarian decrees and brought on the war, in order that, with the Athenians being preoccupied with the war, he would not have to submit his accounts to scrutiny. . . . But the suspicion against Pericles seems groundless, since the affair about Pheidias occurred seven years prior to the beginning of the war. Pheidias, as Philochoros says, worked on the statue of Athena during the archonship of Pythodoros [39] and stole the gold from the snakes of the chryselephantine statue of Athena, an act for which he was condemned and punished by exile. He happened to be in Elis where he had taken on the commission to do the statue of Zeus at Olympia for the Eleans, and having been thus condemned by them,[40] he was killed while in exile.

Pliny, *N.H.* XXXIV, 54:   Pheidias, besides his Olympian Zeus, which no one can rival, also made an Athena of gold and ivory in Athens, the one which is in the *Parthenon* and is represented as standing; and, in bronze, besides the Amazon mentioned above [see Chapter 6, p. 225] he made another Athena of such outstanding beauty that it has received the surname "the beautiful." He also made a "key-bearer" [41] and another Athena, which Aemilius Paulus dedicated in Rome in the temple of Today's Fortune, and also two statues in Greek dress which Catulus dedicated in the same temple, and another colossal nude figure; Pheidias is rightly judged to have opened up the art of *toreutikē* and to have demonstrated it.[42]

38. The text says "Skyphodoros," but no archon by that name is known. Pythodoros was archon in 432 B.C.

39. The text says Pythodoros (432 B.C.), but the correct reading is perhaps Theodoros, whose archonship (438 B.C.) seems to coincide with the time when Pheidias finished the Athena *Parthenos* and went to Olympia.

40. The "them" here is ambiguous but most likely refers to the Athenians, not the Eleans. The first scholiast's story to the effect that Pheidias swindled the Eleans as well as the Athenians seems unlikely. It probably reflects either the scholiast's misunderstanding of Philochoros or Philochoros' misunderstanding of the facts. The truth may be that Pheidias died in Elis while in exile, or that he subsequently returned from Elis to Athens to stand trial and died there.

41. "Key-bearer"—Greek *kleidouchos,* possibly a priest or priestess (the key symbolized the control of a sanctuary) or a deity of whom the keys were an attribute, conceivably the Athena *Promachos* (see below).

42. *Toreutikē,* as already noted, is the Greek term for the art of "chasing." It would seem, however, that Pliny uses the term in the broader sense of "sculpture" or at least "chryselephantine and metal sculpture." Since all Greek sculpture received a fine surface finish which necessitated the use of at least certain aspects of the technique of chasing, it may be that, in referring to the part, Pliny is thinking of the whole. For bibliography on this question and also for a dissenting opinion, cf. G. M. A. Richter, *A.J.A.,* 45, 1941, pp. 375-383, and M. J. Milne, *ibid.,* pp. 390-398.

THE WORKS OF PHEIDIAS

In the preceding passages mention has already been made of the most famous works of Pheidias—the gold and ivory cult statue of Athena Parthenos *at Athens and the Zeus at Olympia. The question as to whether Pheidias executed the Zeus before or after the Athena was debated for many years, with cogent reasons being offered for both points of view. In the recent excavations of the workshop of Pheidias at Olympia, however, a number of molds on which some of the gold sheets of the statue were hammered were discovered and also a cup with Pheidias' signature as well as some other pottery. The style of these objects seems to prove once and for all that the Zeus was made after the Athena.*[43]

Both the Athena and the Zeus are mentioned many times in ancient literature. Some of the more informative passages follow.

THE ATHENA PARTHENOS [44]

Pausanias I, 24, 5-7 (in his description of the Athenian Acropolis): In the temple which they call the *Parthenon* . . . the cult image itself is made of ivory and gold. In the middle of her helmet there is placed an image of a sphinx, and on each side of the helmet griffins are represented . . . griffins are beasts which look like lions but have the wings and the beak of an eagle. . . . The statue of Athena stands upright and wears a tunic which reaches to the feet and on her breast the head of Medusa,[45] made of ivory, is represented. In one hand she holds a figure of Victory about four cubits high and in the other she holds a spear; at her feet is placed a shield, and near the shield is a serpent. This serpent would be Erichthonios. On the base the birth of Pandora is represented in relief. The poems of Hesiod and others tell how Pandora was the first woman. Before this Pandora the race of women had not yet come into being.

Pliny, *N.H.* XXXVI, 18: That Pheidias is extremely famous among all peoples who appreciate the reputation of his Zeus at Olympia, nobody doubts, but in order that those who have not seen his works may know that he is justly praised, I will offer some small points of evidence to prove how great his inventiveness was. To do this, I shall neither use as

---

43. On the finds see E. Kunze, *Gnomon*, 1955, pp. 222 ff. and 1956, pp. 318 ff.

44. The general format of the Athena *Parthenos* is preserved in a number of smaller Roman copies. Cf. Richter, *Sculpture and Sculptors*,[2] Figs. 594-605. Some of the expenses for the statue are recorded in inscriptions, which indicate that it was dedicated in 438 B.C. (see p. 117).

45. That is, the "aegis," which is characteristic of most representations of Athena.

proof the beauty of the Zeus at Olympia, nor the size of the Athena which he made at Athens (since she is 26 cubits high and is made of ivory and gold), but rather I shall use the battle of the Amazons which is carved in a circular pattern on the convex side of her shield; like-wise on the concave side of it he represented the struggle of the gods and giants, and on her sandals that of the Lapiths and Centaurs, so fully did every part offer the opportunity for the application of his art. On the base is carved the scene which they call "the Birth of Pandora," with twenty gods present at the birth.[46] The Victory is especially marvellous, but experts admire the serpent and also the bronze sphinx which is placed below the point of her spear.[47]

Thucydides II, 13, 5 (part of Pericles' enumeration of the Athenian financial resources at the beginning of the Peloponnesian War):   And he added still further the money from the other sanctuaries, no small sum, which they could use, and, if they should be completely cut off from all other resources, they could use the gold plates which were placed on the goddess herself. For the statue, he pointed out, had forty talents of pure gold, and it was all removable. This, he said, they could use for their own salvation, but afterwards they must not put back less than they took away.[48]

THE ZEUS AT OLYMPIA

The Zeus was perhaps the most highly venerated statue in the ancient world. (See also the references in Chapter 6, pp. 221-223.)

Pausanias V, 10, 2:   The temple and the image were offerings to Zeus from the spoils which the Eleans seized when they conquered Pisa and as many of the surrounding peoples as sided with the Pisans in the war.[49] Pheidias is reputed to have been the sculptor of the image, and as evidence of this, there is an inscription beneath the feet of Zeus which reads:

Pheidias, the son of Charmides, the Athenian, made me.

Pausanias V, 11, 1-11:   The god is seated on a throne made of gold and ivory. A garland, which is made to look like olive shoots, is placed on his head. In his right hand he holds a figure of Victory, also made of

46. Reading *dii adsunt nascenti* (Urlichs).
47. Presumably a reference to the sphinx on the helmet.
48. The gold was actually removed (and apparently never replaced) in c. 297 B.C. by the Athenian tyrant Lachares, cf. Pausanias I, 25, 6; Athenaeus XI, 405 F.
49. The particulars about this war are not known. The Eleans conquered Pisa in 570 B.C., but this seems much too early for the war which led to the building of the temple. Perhaps the Elean campaigns mentioned by Herodotus IV, 148, are referred to here.

ivory and gold, who holds a fillet and has a garland on her head. In the god's left hand there is a scepter, which is inlaid with many kinds of metal; the bird which is seated on the top of the scepter is the eagle. The shoes of the god are of gold and so also is his robe. On the robe there are animate figures and also lily flowers represented. The throne is variegated with gold and stones, and still further with ebony and ivory. Upon it, moreover, there are painted figures and sculptured images. There are four Victories, represented in the pose of dancers, on each leg of the throne, and two others at the foot of each leg. On each of the front feet are placed the children of the Thebans who are seized by sphinxes, and under the sphinxes Apollo and Artemis are shooting down the children of Niobe with arrows. Between the legs of the throne there are four bars, each one extending from one foot to the next. On the bar which directly faces the entrance there are seven sculptured images; the eighth of them has disappeared, but they do not know how. These must be representations of ancient contests, for the contests for boys [50] had not yet been instituted in the time of Pheidias. They say that the figure of a youth binding a fillet on his head resembles Pantarkes in appearance, the Elean youth who was the object of Pheidias' love. Pantarkes won a victory in the boys' wrestling contest in the 86th Olympiad [436 B.C.]. On the other bars there is a company of warriors which, along with Herakles, fights against the Amazons. The number of figures, taking both sides together, is twenty-nine, including Theseus, who is lined up among the allies of Herakles. There are not only legs supporting the throne, but also columns which stand between the legs and are equal [in size and number] to them. It is not possible to go underneath the throne in the same way as we enter the interior of the throne at Amyklai. At Olympia there are fences constructed like walls which serve as barriers. Of these fences the section which is opposite the door is painted with a glaze of blue enamel; the rest of them have paintings by Panainos. Among them is Atlas holding up heaven and earth; Herakles stands by ready to take the burden from Atlas. Further along are Theseus and Peirithoös and also Hellas and Salamis, who has in her hand the ornament which goes on the ships' prows; from the labors of Herakles there is the battle with the Nemean lion, which is followed by the outrage against Kassandra committed

---

50. Pausanias does not say to what contests he is referring. He says himself that the boys' contests in running and wrestling were instituted in the 37th Olympiad (632 B.C.; cf. Paus. V, 8, 9). For this reason some editors have felt that Pausanias makes an error here or that the text is corrupt. Changes in the rules and in the types of contests offered, however, were frequently made in the Olympic games. It is quite possible that boys were excluded from certain games in Pheidias' day which were open to them in the time of Pausanias (for example, the *pankration* which was not open to boys until the 145th Olympiad [200 B.C.]).

by Ajax, Hippodameia the daughter of Oinomaos with her mother, and Prometheus, who is still bound in chains, although Herakles has climbed up to him. For this story is told about Herakles, namely, that he killed the eagle which was causing Prometheus agony in the Caucasus and that he freed Prometheus from his bonds. Finally there is a picture of Penthesileia giving up the ghost with Achilles there holding her up. There are also two Hesperides who carry the apples which are said to have been turned over to their care. This Panainos was the brother of Pheidias, and the *Battle of Marathon* in the Stoa *Poikilē* in Athens was also painted by him.[51] On the highest part of the throne, above the head of the image, Pheidias has made Graces on one side and Seasons on the other, three of each. In the epics these are said to be the daughters of Zeus. Homer, for example, in the *Iliad* [*Iliad*, V, 749 ff] says that they were entrusted with the sky just like the guards of a king's court. The stool beneath the feet of Zeus, which in the Attic dialect is called a *thranion*, has golden lions and also, in relief, the battle of Theseus against the Amazons, the first heroic deed of the Athenians against people of a different race. On the base which supports the throne and all the other ornamentation which surrounds Zeus, there are works of gold: Helios mounted on his chariot, Zeus and Hera, [Hephaistos],[52] and, next to him, Charis. After her comes Hermes, and, after Hermes, Hestia. After Hestia is Eros receiving Aphrodite as she rises from the sea; Persuasion is crowning Aphrodite. Also represented are Apollo, with Artemis, and Athena and Herakles; finally, toward the end of the base are Amphitrite and Poseidon, and also Selene, who appears to me to be riding a horse. It is said by some that the goddess is borne by a mule, not a horse, and there is a certain simple-minded story which they tell about the mule. The measurements of the Zeus at Olympia, both its height and breadth, have been written down and are known to me, but I will not bestow praise upon those who did the measuring, because the measurements which have been recorded by them are far less impressive than the effect which the statue makes on those who see it. In fact they say that the god himself bore witness to Pheidias' artistic skill. For when the image had just been completed, Pheidias prayed to the god to send him a sign if the work was pleasing to him, and at that very moment, they say, a lightning bolt struck the floor on the spot where in my day there was a bronze water-jar which served as a cover for it.

The section of the floor in front of the image is fitted out, not

51. On Panainos see pp. 107-108.
52. "Hephaistos" was added to the text by H. Brunn. Some antecedent is needed for the phrase "next to him"; Charis, "Grace," was, according to Homer (*Iliad*, XVIII, 382) the wife of Hephaistos.

with white, but with black tiles. A raised rim of Parian marble runs around the border of the black stone, and serves to hold in the olive oil which is poured out. For olive oil is beneficial to the image at Olympia, and it is olive oil which prevents any injury from occurring to the ivory due to the marshiness of the *Altis*. On the Acropolis in Athens it is water, and not olive oil, which benefits the ivory on the image which is called the *Parthenos*. For the Acropolis is extremely dry owing to its excessive height, and the image, being made of ivory, yearns for water and the moisture which comes from water. When I asked at Epidauros the reason why neither water nor olive oil is poured on the image of Asklepios,[53] those in charge of the sanctuary told me that both the image of the god and his throne were built over a well.

Strabo VIII, 353-354:   The greatest [of the offerings in the temple of Zeus at Olympia] was the image of Zeus, which Pheidias, the son of Charmides, made of ivory, and which is of such great size that, though the temple is indeed one of the largest, the artist seems to have failed to take into account the question of proportion; for although he represented the god as seated, he almost touches the peak of the roof, and thus gives the impression that, if he were to stand up straight, he would take the roof off the temple. Some authors have written down the measurements of the statue, and Kallimachos mentioned it in one of his iambic poems. Panainos the painter, Pheidias' own brother and his co-worker, was a great help to him in the decoration of the statue, especially the drapery, with colors. There are a good number of quite marvellous paintings on display around the sanctuary which are the work of that artist. And they recount this tradition about Pheidias: when Panainos asked him what model he intended to employ in making the image of Zeus, he replied that it was the model provided by Homer in the following lines:

> Thus spoke the son of Kronos and nodded his dark brow and the ambrosial locks flowed down from the lord's immortal head, and he made great Olympos quake [*Iliad*, I, 527-530].

Dio Chrysostom, *Or.* **XII, 50-52** (In this his *Olympian Oration* Dio puts into the mouth of Pheidias a long disquisition on the capabilities and limitations of the plastic arts; prior to that disquisition, Dio and his audience express to an imaginary Pheidias their impressions of his Zeus):   O best and noblest of artists, that it is a sweet and engaging sight, an inescapable delight for the vision, which you have made for all the Greeks and barbarians, all those who have come here on many different occasions—this nobody will deny. For it would even overwhelm those beings in creation which have an irrational nature—the animals—

53. The work of Thrasymedes of Paros; see pp. 152, 182.

if they could once see this work. It would overwhelm creatures like the bulls, for example, which are always being led to this altar, so that they would willingly submit to those who prepare them for sacrifice, if they could do it as a kind of favor to the god. It would also affect the nature of eagles and horses and lions, so that they, quelling their savage and wild side, would feel great peace of spirit as they were charmed by the sight [of the statue]. And among men, whoever might be burdened with pain in his soul, having borne many misfortunes and pains in his life and never being able to attain sweet sleep, even that man, I believe, standing before this image, would forget all the terrible and harsh things which one must suffer in human life. Such is the vision which you have conceived and rendered into art, a vision which is really: "An assuager of sorrow, gentle, an obscurer of the memory of all evils" [*Odyssey,* IV, 221]. Such is the light and such is the grace which comes from your art. For not even Hephaistos himself would find fault with the work, if he judged it by the pleasure and delight it gives to mortal eyes.

THE ATHENA PROMACHOS

Pausanias I, 28, 2 (on the Acropolis in Athens): [Among the monuments on the Acropolis] is a bronze image of Athena, [made from] a tithe [from the spoils] taken from the Persians who landed at Marathon, a work of Pheidias—but they say that the battle of Lapiths and Centaurs on her shield, as well as the other scenes which are wrought upon it, were engraved by Mys, and that these and the rest of the works of Mys were drawn for him by Parrhasios the son of Euenor. The point of the spear of this Athena and the crest of helmet are visible to approaching sailors from Cape Sounion.

Scholiast on Demosthenes, *Contra Andration*, 13: . . . for there are three images of Athena on the Acropolis in different places, one which has existed from the beginning, made of olive wood, which they call Athena *Polias,* since the city is hers; a second, exclusively of bronze, which they made when they were victorious at Marathon and is called the Athena *Promachos;* and a third which they made from gold and ivory . . . [the Athena *Parthenos*].

THE ATHENA LEMNIA

Pausanias I, 28, 2: . . . the most worth seeing of the works of Pheidias, the image of Athena which is called "the Lemnian," after those who dedicated it.

Lucian, *Imagines*, 4-6 (a dialogue dealing again with the ideal characteristics to be embodied in Panthea, cf. p. 60): LYKINOS: Of the works of Pheidias which one do you praise most highly? POLYSTRATOS: Which if not the *Lemnia,* on which he thought it fit to inscribe his name. . . . The *Lemnia* and Pheidias shall furnish the outline of her [Panthea's] whole face, the softness of the sides of her face, and the well-proportioned nose.

OTHER WORKS OF PHEIDIAS

The Athena Areia at Plataea

Pausanias IX, 4, 1:   The Plataeans have a sanctuary of Athena surnamed *Areia* ["the warlike"]; it was built from the spoils which the Athenians apportioned out to them from Marathon. The image is a *xoanon* overlaid with gold, except for the face, the hands and the feet which are of Pentelic marble.[54] In size it is only a little smaller than the bronze [the Athena *Promachos*] on the Acropolis, which the Athenians also set up as first fruits from [the spoils of] the battle of Marathon, and here too it was Pheidias who made the image for the Plataeans.

An Athena at Pellene in Achaea

Pausanias VII, 27, 2:   Along the roadside as you come to the city is a temple of Athena, built of local stone, but the image is of ivory and gold. They say that it was made by Pheidias before he made the images on the Acropolis in Athens and in Plataea. The people of Pellene say that there is also an underground shrine of Athena and that this shrine is directly under the base of the image; further that the air from the shrine is damp and for that reason beneficial to ivory.

An Athena in Elis

Pausanias VI, 26, 3:   On the acropolis in Elis there is a sanctuary of Athena, with an image of ivory and gold. They say that it is by Pheidias. A cock is represented on the helmet, because cocks are a sort of bird which is very ready to fight. This bird could also be thought of as being sacred to Athena *Ergane* ["the worker"].

The Aphrodite Ourania in Elis

Pausanias VI, 25, 1 (in the town of Elis):   Behind the stoa built from the spoils taken from Corcyra is a temple of Aphrodite; the precinct is in the open air not very far from the temple. In the temple is the image of the goddess whom they call *Ourania* ["Celestial"]; it is made of ivory and gold and is the work of Pheidias; it stands with one foot upon a tortoise.

54. Wooden statues of which the extremities were done in stone were called "acrolithic."

Plutarch, *Coniugalia Praecepta*, 32:   Pheidias represented the Aphrodite of the Eleans as stepping on a tortoise, a symbol of good housekeeping and silence, for women.

The Athenian Tribal Heroes in Delphi

Pausanias X, 10, 1:   On the base . . . there is an inscription which says that the statues were set up from a tithe of the spoils from the battle of Marathon. They represent Athena, Apollo, and a man who was one of the generals, Miltiades. Of those who are called heroes there are Erechtheus, Kekrops, Pandion, Leos, Antiochos (the son of Herakles and Meda, the daughter of Phylas), and also Aegeus and Akamas, one of the children of Theseus. These heroes gave their names to the Athenian tribes in accordance with a response from the Delphic oracle. As for Kodros, the son of Melanthos, and Theseus and Neleus, however, these heroes are no longer among the Eponymous heroes. Pheidias made the statues which I have catalogued, and it is quite true that these are a tithe from the battle.

The preceding passages show clearly that almost all of Pheidias' artistic effort was applied to making images of the gods, most of them cult images. Pausanias makes one reference, however, which does seem to refer to a portrait statue of a human being:

Pausanias VI, 4, 5 (At Olympia):   As for the boy binding his hair with a fillet, let him too be brought into my account of Pheidias because of Pheidias' skill as a sculptor; we have no idea, however, as to whose image it was that Pheidias made.

Alkamenes [55]

Alkamenes was a pupil of Pheidias and second in reputation only to his master. He may have inherited the job of supervising the Periclean building program after the death of Pheidias. His best known work was the "Aphrodite in the Gardens" in Athens.[56]

Pliny, *N.H.* XXXVI, 15-16:   "I must not omit pointing out that this art [sculpture in marble] is much older than painting or sculpture in bronze, both of which began with Pheidias in the 83rd Olympiad [448 B.C.]. . . . There is a tradition that Pheidias himself did sculpture

55. For a good summary of all the works plausibly connected with Alkamenes see C. Picard, *Manuel d'Archéologie Greque, La Sculpture,* II (Paris, 1939), pp. 551-586; hereafter cited as Picard, *Manuel.*
56. See also Pausanias I, 19, 2.

in marble, and that the extremely beautiful Venus which is in the buildings of Octavia in Rome, is his. It is certain at least that he was the teacher of Alkamenes the Athenian, a sculptor of the first rank, by whom there are a number of works in the temples in Athens, and also a particularly famous statue of Venus outside the walls which is called the "Aphrodite in the Gardens." It is said that Pheidias himself put the finishing touches on this work.

Lucian, *Imagines*, 6 (further features of the Panthea):   The cheeks and the front part of the face he will take from the "Aphrodite in the Gardens" of Alkamenes, and as for the hands, the shapeliness of the wrists, and the subtle taper of the fingers, these too he will take from the statue "in the Gardens."

Like Pheidias, most of Alkamenes' works were images of the gods.

Pausanias II, 30, 2:   Alkamenes, it seems to me, was the first to represent Hekate by three images joined together,[57] a figure which the Athenians call Hekate *Epipyrgidian* ["on the tower"]. It stands by the temple of Nike *Apteros*.

Pausanias I, 20, 3 (an image of Dionysos in Athens):   The most ancient sanctuary of Dionysos is right by the theater. There are two temples within the precinct and also two statues of Dionysos, the *Eleuthereus* ["the Liberator"] and the one which Alkamenes made of ivory and gold.[58]

Cicero, *De Natura Deorum*, I, 83:   At Athens we praised that statue of Hephaistos which Alkamenes made, a figure standing upright and draped, in which there is visible a slight lameness which, however, is not ugly.[59]

Pausanias IX, 11, 6 (in Thebes):   Thrasyboulos, the son of Lykos, and those Athenians who, along with him, overthrew the tyranny of "the Thirty" (for it was from Thebes that they set out when they made their descent upon Athens),[60] set up colossal statues of Athena and Herakles in Pentelic marble, works by Alkamenes, in the sanctuary of Herakles.

---

57. Hekate was, among other things, a goddess of the crossroads; hence she had to look in many directions at once and a three-headed image was appropriate.

58. For the representation of this figure on Athenian coins, cf. Lacroix, *Reproductions*, pl. XXXVI, 3.

59. The same description is given by Valerius Maximus VIII, 11, ext. 3. The statue in question was perhaps the cult image of the *Hephaisteion* in the Agora in Athens.

60. The date of this event was 403 B.C.

Other figures of deities by Alkamenes, seen by Pausanias, were an Ares in Athens (Paus. I, 20, 3); an image of Hera in a temple situated between Athens and Phaleron (Paus. I, 1, 5); and an Asklepios in Mantineia (Paus. VIII, 9, 1).

Alkamenes, like Pheidias, seems to have made at least one portrait statue of an athlete.

Pliny, N.H. XXXIV, 72:   Alkamenes, the disciple of Pheidias, made marble statues and also a bronze statue of a winner in the *pentathlon*, known as the *enkrinomenos*.[61]

Agorakritos of Paros

Among the disciples of Pheidias, Agorakritos seems to have been most closely associated with the master. In antiquity, in fact, there is some confusion about whether certain works should be attributed to Pheidias or Agorakritos. This is true, for example, of the most famous statue ascribed to Agorakritos, the Nemesis of Rhamnous.[62] In such cases it is probably best to look for the truth in the lectio dificilior; that is to say, if a well-known work is ascribed to a very famous artist and to a more obscure one, the latter is probably the correct attribution, since tradition does not usually honor the less famous rather than the more famous unless there is some good reason for it.

Pliny, N.H. XXXVI, 17:   Another disciple of his [Pheidias'] was Agorakritos of Paros, who was pleasing to him because of his youth and beauty; as a result, it is said that Pheidias allowed Agorakritos' name to be put on a number of his [Pheidias'] own works. In any case, the two disciples [Alkamenes and Agorakritos] competed with one another in the making of an Aphrodite, and Alkamenes was the victor, not because of the quality of his work, but through the votes of the citizenry who favored one of their own people against a foreigner; [63] whereupon Agorakritos, according to tradition, sold his statue with the proviso that it should not remain in Athens and that it should be called "Nemesis." [64] It was set up in Rhamnous, a deme of Attica, and is a work which Marcus Varro [65] preferred to all other statues. There

61. *Enkrinomenos*—either "he who is approved" or "he who had been admitted to the games."
62. Fragments of the head and the base of the Nemesis have been found at Rhamnous. (The former is in the British Museum; the latter in Athens.) Cf. Richter, *Sculpture and Sculptors,*[2] Figs. 633 and 635.
63. Agorakritos, being from the island of Paros, was considered a foreigner.
64. Nemesis was the goddess of retribution for unjust acts.
65. Marcus Terentius Varro (116-27 b.c.). See appendix.

is also a work of Agorakritos in the same town in the shrine of the Great Mother.[66]

Pausanias I, 33, 2-8: About sixty stades from Marathon as you go along the seacoast toward Oropos is Rhamnous. The houses where the people live are on the sea, and inland a little, away from the sea, is the sanctuary of Nemesis, who is the most inexorable of the gods toward men of sinful violence. It would seem that the wrath of this goddess also fell upon those of the barbarians who landed at Marathon. For thinking that no obstacle stood in the way of their taking Athens, they were bringing with them some Parian marble to use for a trophy, just as if the whole thing were over and done with. It was this stone that Pheidias made into a statue of Nemesis; on the head of the goddess is a crown on which are represented deer and some images of Victory which are not very big. In her left hand she holds the branch of an apple tree, and in her right hand she holds a *phialē*,[67] on which Ethiopians are represented. . . . [At this point Pausanias examines inconclusively the question of why the Ethiopians are represented on the bowl, and is led into a digression on the geography of Ethiopia.] This statue does not have wings nor is any other of the ancient statues of Nemesis represented with them, since not even the extremely holy *xoana* which belong to the people of Smyrna have wings. But later artists, maintaining that the goddess makes her epiphany most of all after a love affair,[68] represent Nemesis with wings just as they do Eros. I now go on to the images which are represented on the base; what I have indicated up to this point was for the sake of clarity. The Greeks say that Nemesis was the mother of Helen, but that Leda suckled her and brought her up. As to Helen's father, the Greeks as well as everyone else think that it was Zeus and not Tyndareus. Having heard these stories Pheidias represented Helen as being brought before Nemesis by Leda; likewise he represented the children of Tyndareus and a man named Hippeus who stands by with a horse. Also there are Agamemnon, Menelaos, and Pyrrhos the son of Achilles; it was he who first took Hermione, the daughter of Helen as his wife. Orestes was left out on account of the daring act against his mother, yet Hermione remained by him through

66. It is not completely clear whether "the same town" means Athens or Rhamnous. Arrian (*Peripl. Pont. Euxin*, 9) describes a statue of the "Mother of the Gods" in the *Metroön* in the Agora at Athens. The image held a cymbal in one hand and was flanked by lions. A number of terracotta statuettes reproducing this image have been found in the Agora excavations (cf. for example, *A.J.A.*, XLI (1937), p. 183, Fig. 9). Both Arrian and Pausanias (I, 3, 5), who also saw it, ascribe the statue to Pheidias, but Pliny's reference suggests that it may have been by Agorakritos.

67. *Phialē:* a round, shallow bowl, frequently used in sacrificial rites (= Latin *patera*).

68. "After a love affair"; it could also mean "in opposition to loving."

everything and even bore him a child. Next on the base is someone called Epochos and another youth. With regard to them, the only thing I heard was that they were brothers of Oinoë, from whom the name of the deme comes.

Pausanias IX, 34, 1 (in Boeotia):   Before you reach Koroneia as you come from Alalkomenai, there is a sanctuary of Athena *Itonia*. . . . In the temple there are bronze images of Athena *Itonia* and Zeus. They are the works of Agorakritos, the pupil and loved one of Pheidias.

Kolotes

Pliny, *N.H.* XXXV, 54:   . . . Panainos [the brother of Pheidias] who painted the inside of the shield of an Athena in Elis,[69] which Kolotes made, the disciple of Pheidias and his assistant in the making of the Zeus at Olympia.

Strabo VIII, 334:   It is a moderate-sized village (Kyllene, the port of Elis), which has an image of Asklepios by Kolotes, an ivory statue which is a marvel to look upon.

Pliny, *N.H.* XXXIV, 87:   Kolotes, who worked with Pheidias on the Zeus at Olympia, made statues of philosophers.

For Pausanias' description of a gold and ivory table at Olympia ascribed to an artist named Kolotes, cf. p. 214.

Kresilas of Kydonia (Crete)

Pliny, *N.H.* XXXIV, 74-75:   Kresilas made a man wounded and expiring, in which one can sense how little life remains; [70] he also made the "Olympian Pericles," a work worthy of the title; [71] it is a marvellous thing about this art that it can make famous men even more famous. . . . Kresilas [72] also made a *Doryphoros* ["spear-bearer"] and a wounded Amazon.[73]

---

69. Probably the Athena of Pheidias on the acropolis in Elis; see p. 75.
70. This figure is thought to be identical with the statue of the Athenian Dieitrephes which is described by Pausanias (I, 23, 3) as being "wounded with arrows." The evidence for this conclusion is a base found on the Acropolis in Athens which bears the name of Hermolykos, son of Dieitrephes, as the dedicator and the signature of Kresilas as sculptor. Cf. Raubitschek, *Dedications*, no. 132, pp. 141-144, 510-513.
71. For Roman copies (busts only), cf. Richter, *Sculpture and Sculptors,*2 Figs. 623-624.
72. The text reads "Ctesilas."
73. On this figure of an Amazon, see also Chapter 6, p. 225.

Other works by Kresilas were a Demeter in Hermione (cf. Loewy, Inschriften, *no. 45) and a Pallas (Athena)* Tritogeneia (Anth. Graec. IV, 142, 119; Anth. Pal. XIII, 13).

Styppax of Cyprus

Pliny, *N.H.* XXXIV, 81: Styppax the Cypriote is famed for one statue, the *splanchnoptes;* [74] the subject of this statue was a slave [75] of the Olympian Pericles roasting entrails and kindling a fire with the breath from his puffed-out cheeks.

Lykios the son of Myron

Athenaeus, XI, 486 D: [Lykios] was a Boeotian by birth from Eleutherai, and was the son of Myron the sculptor. . . .

Pliny, *N.H.* XXXIV, 79: Lykios was a disciple of Myron, who made a figure of a boy blowing on dying embers, a work worthy of his preceptor, and also figures of Argonauts. . . .[76] Lykios also made a figure of a boy burning incense.

Pausanias I, 23, 7: I remember having seen other works on the Acropolis of Athens, including a bronze by Lykios the son of Myron of a boy who holds a *perirranterion* [a vessel for sprinkling lustral water].

Pausanias V, 22, 2 (at Olympia): Alongside what is called the *Hippodamion* there is a semi-circular base of stone, and the image which stands on it represents Zeus along with Thetis and Hemera ["Day"] who are praying for their children. These stand in the middle of the base, while Achilles and Memnon, arranged as if they were ready for combat, are present, one at each end of the base. Other groups also oppose one another in man-to-man combat in the same manner, that is, barbarian against Greek: Odysseus against Helenos (for these two had the greatest reputation for wisdom in the respective armies), Alexander [that is, Paris] against Menelaos (because of their long-standing hatred), Aeneas against Diomedes, and Deiphobos against Ajax the son

---

74. *Splanchnoptes:* "the roaster of *splanchnia,*" which were the inner parts of a sacrificial animal such as the heart, kidneys, and the like.

75. Further anecdotes about this slave are given by Pliny in *N.H.* XXII, 44.

76. In the section omitted Pliny mentions several works by other artists, including one of the Pankratiast Autolykos which is ascribed to the fourth century sculptor Leochares. Since Autolykos was the victor in the *pankration* in 421 B.C. (cf. Xenophon, *Symposium,* 2), well before the time when Leochares was active, some scholars (for example, Overbeck and Stuart Jones) ascribe the Autolykos to Lykios.

of Telamon. These were the works of Lykios the son of Myron, and they were set up by the people of Apollonia on the Ionian sea. . . .[77]

For the text of three inscriptions found on the Athenian Acropolis; cf. Raubitschek, Dedications, nos. 135, 135a, 135b:

The knights [dedicated this] from the [spoils of] the enemy. The cavalry commanders were Lakedaimonios, Xenophon, and Pronapos. Lykios of Eleutherai, the son of Myron. made them.

The three Athenian cavalry commanders are known to have been active around the middle of the fifth century B.C. *(Cf. Raubitschek, op. cit., pp. 150-151.) The statue may have been set up sometime after the Athenian victory at Oinophyta (457* B.C.*) or after the suppression of the Euboean revolt (446/5* B.C.*).*

Of the three inscriptions, no. 135 is the original and the other two are copies executed in the Roman period. The inscriptions may be connected with a group which Pausanias saw near the entrance to the Acropolis and which he identified as the "sons of Xenophon," or, if not that, mere ornamental figures (Pausanias I, 22, 4). It has been suggested that the original group represented the Dioscuri; Pausanias, knowing that the sons of the writer Xenophon were sometimes called "the Dioscuri" (cf. Diogenes Laertius II, 52), may have misinterpreted the inscription. The statues which he saw were, in any case, probably Roman copies. (Cf. E. Bethe in Pauly-Wissowa Real-Encyclopaedie, V, 1029c, s.v. "Dioskuren"; Raubitschek, op. cit., pp. 518-519.)

Paionios of Mende (Thrace)

Paionios is one sculptor who may be even better known today than he was in antiquity. His "Flying Nike," now in the museum in Olympia, is one of the rare examples of an original Greek statue from the hand of a known master.[78] The statue was seen, when it stood in its original position in Olympia, by Pausanias.

Pausanias V, 26, 1:   The Dorian Messenians who at one time received Naupaktos from the Athenians set up at Olympia an image of Nike which was placed on a column. This image is the work of Paionios of Mende, and was made from the spoils taken from the enemy, when they

---

77. The dedicatory inscription which follows indicates that the Apollonians set up this group after a victory over the Abantes of Euboea.

78. Cf. Richter, *Sculpture and Sculptors*,2 Fig. 637; Lullies, Hirmer, *Greek Sculpture*, pl. 176.

waged war against the people of Akarnania and Oiniadai; at least so it seems to me. The Messenians themselves say that the offering resulted from their exploit on the island of Sphakteria along with the Athenians but that they did not inscribe the name of their enemy through fear of the Lakedaimonians, whereas they had no fear at all of the people of Oiniadai and Akarnania.[79]

The base of the statue which Pausanias mentioned has been found at Olympia (cf. Loewy, Inschriften, no. 49). It reads:

The Messenians and the Naupaktians set up [this statue] to Olympian Zeus as a tithe from the spoils taken from the enemy. Paionios of Mende made it, and he also won the commission to make the akroteria for the temple.

We should also note that Pausanias ascribes the pedimental sculptures of the temple of Zeus at Olympia (cf. pp. 113-114), which were made c. 460 B.C., to Paionios and Alkamenes. While it is not impossible that Paionios could have worked on the pediments, and then, forty years later, having undergone a radical change of style, made the Flying Nike, it does seem unlikely, and most modern scholars reject Pausanias' ascription. The akroteria of the temple, as the inscription on the base of the Flying Nike shows, were made by Paionios, and it may be that Pausanias confused them with the pedimental sculptures. The same may be said about Alkamenes, who may have been active as late as 403 B.C.

Strongylion

Pliny, *N.H.* XXXIV, 82:   Strongylion made an Amazon, which they call *euknemon* on account of the excellence of its legs; it was also on account of this that the statue was carried around in the retinue of the emperor Nero. The same sculptor also made a statue of a youth; which, by falling in love with it, Brutus of Philippi formed an illustrious connection between it and his own name.

The last mentioned work is also referred to in the epigrams of the Roman poet Martial.

79. The Messenian campaign against Oiniadai, which took place in 452 B.C., was not notably successful (cf. Pausanias IV, 25, 9 ff.). The Athenian victory over the Spartans at Sphakteria took place in 424 B.C. (cf. Thucydides IV, 8-41). Since Paionios' statue seems to date from c. 420, it may be that the Messenians were right and Pausanias was wrong about the occasion of the battle.

Martial XIV, 171:

> The glory of so small a statue is not obscure.
> Of this very boy Brutus was the lover.

(Cf. also Martial II, 77; IX 51.)

Strongylion also seems to have made a latter-day version of the Trojan horse in bronze on the Acropolis of Athens. The work is referred to in the Birds *of Aristophanes line 1128, and a scholiast on that line notes that the dedicator was one Chairedemos, son of Euangellos, from the Deme of Koile. The base of the statue, from which the scholiast probably derived his information, has been found in the sanctuary of Brauronian Artemis on the Acropolis of Athens, and it bears the signature of Strongylion as scuptor.*[80] *The horse was also seen by Pausanias, who does not mention the scuptor's name.*

Pausanias I, 23, 7-8:   There is also a sanctuary of Brauronian Artemis. . . . A horse is set up there called "the Wooden" but made of bronze. That the horse made by Epeios[81] was a siege machine for breaching the wall [of Troy] is known to everyone who does not ascribe absolute simple-mindedness to the Phrygians. But of course it is said of that horse that it held within it the best of the Greeks, and the design of this bronze one has been made accordingly. Both Menestheus and Teukros are peeking out of it and so too are the children of Theseus.

Pausanias IX, 30, 1 (on Mt. Helikon):   The first images of the Muses are the work of Kephisodotos, all of them; a little farther on there are three more, again by Kephisodotos, and then three others by Strongylion, an artist responsible for excellent [images of] cattle and horses.[82]

Pausanias I, 40, 2-3 (in Megara):   Not far from the fountain is an ancient sanctuary; portraits of Roman emperors, from our own time, stand in it and also located there is a bronze image of Artemis called the "Savior." They say that a detachment from the army of Mardonios, having overrun the Megarid, wished to pull back to Mardonios at Thebes, but by the will of Artemis night came on them as they were on the road and, losing their way, they turned into the hilly region of the country. In an attempt to find out if there was an enemy detachment nearby, they hurled some missiles, and the rock, which was

---

80. Cf. Raubitschek, *Dedications*, no. 176. The base is dated in the last quarter of the fifth century B.C.

81. Epeios was the legendary builder of the original Trojan horse; cf. *Odyssey*, VIII, 492.

82. Kephisodotos (see pp. 127-128) was mainly active in the early fourth century B.C. Strongylion's career probably belongs to the late fifth and early fourth centuries.

near them, groaned as it was hit; after that they shot their arrows with even greater zeal. Eventually they used up all their arrows, thinking that they were shooting at the enemy. At daybreak the Megarians attacked, and, it being a case of armed men fighting unarmed men who no longer even had missiles, they killed most of them. It was for this reason that they made an image of Artemis the Savior. . . . The image of Artemis herself was made by Strongylion.

Pausanias I, 44, 4:   The hilly region of the Megarid is on the border of Boeotia, and in it the city of Pagai has been built by the Megarians. . . . In Pagai there remains something well worth seeing—a bronze image of Artemis called the "Savior." It is equal in size to the one in Megara and no different from it in design.[83]

Kallimachos

Pliny, *N.H.* XXXIV, 92:   Of all [sculptors], however, Kallimachos is most remarkable for his surname: he was a perpetual deprecator of his own work, nor was there ever an end to his attention to minutiae; for this reason he was called the *katatexitechnos,* a memorable example of the need for establishing a limit to meticulousness. Also by him are the "Lakonian Dancers," a technically flawless work, but one in which meticulousness has taken away all charm.

Pausanias I, 26, 6 (in the *Erechtheion* on the Acropolis in Athens): . . . the most holy object, and one which by common agreement was held to be so many years before the people from the demes united [into a city] is the image of Athena, on what is now the Acropolis, but was then simply called the *polis* ["city"]. There is a tradition that this image fell from heaven, but I will not go into whether this is true or not. Kallimachos made a gold lamp for the goddess. When they have filled the lamp with oil, they wait [before refilling it] until the same day of the following year, and the oil which is in the lamp suffices for the intervening time, even though it is lit both day and night alike. The wick which is in it is of Karpasian flax, which is the only type of flax which is not consumed by fire. Above the lamp is a bronze palm tree [84] which reaches to the roof and draws up the smoke. Kallimachos who made the lamp, although inferior to the foremost practitioners of this art, was so much superior to all of them in inventiveness, that he became the first sculptor to drill through stones, and he took the name

83. The statue is represented on late coins of Megara and Pagai; cf. Lacroix, *Reproductions,* pl. XXVI, nos. 4, 5, and 6.
84. Perhaps some kind of Corinthian column, which Kallimachos is supposed to have invented; see p. 121.

katatexitechnos,[85] or possibly, when others used the name, he adopted it himself.

Minor Athenian Sculptors

NIKERATOS

Pliny, *N.H.* XXXIV, 80:   Nikeratos made an Asklepios and a Hygieia which are [now] in the temple of Concord in Rome.

Pliny, *N.H.* XXXIV, 88:   Likewise Nikeratos, having attempted everything which other sculptors had done, represented Alcibiades and his mother Demarate performing a sacrifice by the light of torches.[86]

Tatian, *Ep. adv. Graecos*, 53 (Tatian, a Christian apologist, is ridiculing the statues which his pagan contemporaries admire):   Why do you feel that Glaukippe gave birth to a holy child? Well suppose someone gave birth to a portentous child, as is shown in her statue by Nikeratos the bronze-worker, son of Euktemon and an Athenian by birth; even if she did carry an elephant in her womb, is that any reason why Glaukippe should enjoy public honors?

DEINOMENES

According to Pliny, N.H. XXXIV, 50, Deinomenes was active in the 95th Olympiad (400 B.C.). Pliny also notes that Deinomenes made statues of Protesilaos and a wrestler named Pythodemos (N.H. XXXIV, 76).

Pausanias I, 25, 1 (on the Acropolis in Athens):   Deinomenes made the [two] statues of women which stand nearby, Io the daughter of Inachos and Kallisto the daughter of Lykaon; the events in the stories about both of these women are exactly alike—that is, the love of Zeus, and anger of Hera, and the transformation which, in the case of Io, was into a cow; in the case of Kallisto, into a bear.

Tatian, *Ep. adv. Graecos*, 53:   Deinomenes, by means of his art, made a work which perpetuated the memory of Besantis, the queen of the Paionians, because she carried in her womb a child who was black.

85. *Katatexitechnos* would literally mean the "one who melts down his art." The manuscripts of Pausanias read *kakizotechnos*, "the spoiler of art," a title which would fit Pliny's discussion of Kallimachos (where it does not occur) better than Pausanias'. Vitruvius uses the name *katatechnos*, which could mean "the artificial one" but is probably an error; cf. p. 122 below.

86. Alcibiades died in 404 B.C.; the name of his mother is given as Deinomache by other writers.

SOCRATES

Pausanias I, 22, 8:   Right at the entrance to the Acropolis there is a
Hermes which they call *Propylaios*,[87] and statues of "the Graces" which,
they say, were made by Socrates the son of Sophroniskos, to whose reputation as the wisest of men the Delphic oracle was a witness.

Pausanias IX, 35, 3 ff.:   And in front of the entrance to the Acropolis
there are Graces, three in number, beside which they perform mystic
rites which must not be spoken of to the many. . . . (Sec. 6) Who the
man was who first represented the Graces naked in sculpture or painting, I was not able to find out, since, in the earlier periods, the sculptors
represented them as draped, and the painters made them the same
way. . . . (Sec. 7) Socrates the son of Sophroniskos made images of the
Graces for the Athenians in front of the entrance to the Acropolis. And
these too are all draped.

Pliny, *N.H.* XXXVI, 32:   Nor are the Graces in the *propylaia* of the
Athenians less esteemed, the ones which Socrates made; this is another
man, not the painter, though some think he is the same.[88]

*The tradition that the philosopher Socrates was also a sculptor
was apparently taken for granted in the Roman period,[89] although
some degree of uncertainty is indicated in the passage from Pliny and
in Pausanias' use of the phrase "they say." A number of modern Plato
scholars,[90] however, have doubted that there is any truth in the tradition
and perhaps with good reason. The earliest sources for the tradition are
the sensational chronicler Douris of Samos [91] (c. 340-260 B.C.) and the
Sceptic philosopher Timon of Phlios (c. 320-230 B.C.).[92] Undoubtedly
there was a group of the Graces carved by a sculptor named Socrates,
but the name was not uncommon, and the attribution to the sculptor
may be a later tradition. The story may have arisen from Socrates' playful reference to himself as a descendant of Daedalus (Plato, Euthyphro,
10 c).*

87. That is, "before the gate." This was possibly, although not necessarily, the
Hermes *Propylaios* of Alkamenes, of which Roman copies have been found; cf. Richter,
*Sculpture and Sculptors,*2 p. 238 and fig. 628.
88. On the painter Socrates, see below, p. 171.
89. Cf. Diogenes Laertius II, 18; Lucian, *Somnium,* 12; Valerius Maximus III,
4, ext. 1.
90. Cf. J. Burnet's edition of the *Euthyphro, Apology and Crito* (Oxford, 1924),
notes p. 51; A. E. Taylor, *Socrates, the Man and his Thought* (1933; reprint New York,
1956), pp. 40-42.
91. Quoted by Diogenes Laertius II, 9. Douris apparently said that Socrates was
a slave as well as a stone cutter—a good indication of his reliability.
92. Cf. H. Diels, *Poetarum Philosophorum Graecorum Fragmenta* (1901), fr. 25.

The sculptors of the High Classical period treated up to this point have been those whose artistic fortunes were bound up in some way with Athens, either because they were citizens or because their Patrons were Athenians (or Athenian allies).

The other great center for the production of sculpture in this period was Argos. The leader of the Argive school, Polykleitos, was a great theoretician, whose fame was rivalled only by that of Pheidias.

Polykleitos of Argos

See also Chapter 6, pp. 220 ff.

Pliny, N.H. XXXIV, 55: Polykleitos of Sikyon, a disciple of Ageladas [93] made a *Diadoumenos* [one who binds a fillet on his head], a soft-looking youth which is famous for having cost one hundred talents; and a *Doryphoros* [spear bearer],[94] a virile looking boy. He also made a statue which artists call the "Canon" and from which they derive the basic forms of their art, as if from some kind of law; thus he alone of men is deemed to have rendered art itself in a work of art.[95] He also made a man scraping himself with a strigil and a nude figure attacking with a javelin,[96] and two boys, also nude, playing with knucklebones, who are called the *astragalizontes* [dice players] and are now in the Emperor Titus' atrium —a work than which, some claim, there is none more perfect. He also made a Hermes which was once in Lysimacheia,[97] a Herakles, which is in Rome, a military commander [98] putting on his armor, and a statue of Artemon, who was called the *periphorētos*.[99] Polykleitos is deemed to have perfected this science and to have explained the art of *toreutikē* just as Pheidias had opened up its possibilities. It was strictly his invention to have his statues throw their weight on one leg; Varro says, how-

93. Plato and Pausanias, as well as Polykleitos' own signatures (cf. Loewy, *Inschriften,* no. 91), indicate that he was an Argive; Sikyon succeeded Argos as the leading artistic center of the Peloponnesos; Pliny may here be under the influence of Xenokrates (cf. Introduction) who was a member of that school. On Ageladas see above pp. 24-25.

94. The *Doryphoros* and the "Canon" are the same work.

95. *Artem ipsam fecisse artis opere indicatur.* Ars (Greek *technē*) in the first instance probably refers to artistic theory; compare Pliny's passage on Myron, p. 62, n. 28.

96. Reading *telo incessentem.*

97. Lysimacheia, a city on the Hellespont built by the Hellenistic monarch Lysimachos (c. 360-281 B.C.).

98. Some take the text to mean that the "military commander" is another name for the Herakles.

99. *Periphorētos* can mean either "the infamous" or "he who is carried around." If the second meaning is intended, the reference may be to an engineer named Artemon who worked under Pericles (Plutarch, *Pericles,* 27). Artemon was lame and had to be carried around in a litter.

ever, that they are "square" and almost all composed after the same pattern.[100]

Of the works of Polykleitos mentioned by Pliny, at least two, the Doryphoros *and the* Diadoumenos, *are known through good Roman copies.*[101]

Polykleitos' theories of proportion were embodied in a treatise known as the Canon, *of which, according to Galen, the* Doryphoros *was an illustration.*

Galen, de Placititis Hippocratis et Platonis, V, (ed. Müller, p. 425): Beauty, he [Chrysippos] believes, arises not in the commensurability of the constituent elements [of the body], but in the commensurability [102] of the parts, such as that of finger to finger, and of all the fingers to the palm and the wrist, and of these to the forearm, and of the forearm to the upper arm, and, in fact, of everything to everything else, just as it is written in the *Canon* of Polykleitos. For having taught us in that work all the proportions of the body, Polykleitos supported his treatise with a work; he made a statue according to the tenets of his treatise, and called the statue, like the work, the "Canon."

Galen, de Temperamentis, I, 9: Modellers and sculptors and painters, and in fact image-makers in general, paint or model beautiful figures by observing an ideal form in each case, that is, whatever form is most beautiful in man or in the horse or in the cow or in the lion, always looking for the mean within each genus. And a certain statue might perhaps also be commended, the one called the "Canon" of Polykleitos; it got such a name from having precise commensurability of all the parts to one another.

100. The phrase "this science" (*hanc scientiam*) seems to refer in the text to the art of metal sculpture as a whole; perhaps in Pliny's original source the reference was to Polykleitos' theories of *symmetria* and the like. Whether *hanc scientiam* is synonymous with or separate from *toreutikē* is not clear (on *toreutikē*, see p. 43). "Square-like" here translates the Latin *quadrata* (Greek *tetragōnos* in Pliny's source) which has been interpreted in several ways. Some have interpreted it in a metaphorical way as "four-square"; others view it as a reference to the carefully balanced and essentially torsionless composition of Polykleitos' figures and translate it with phrases like "squarely built" (Cf. Rhys Carpenter, *Greek Sculpture* [Chicago: 1960], p. 107). The Italian scholar Silvio Ferri interprets the terms *quadratus* and *tetragōnos* by analogy to their use in rhetoric, where they refer to the balancing of four cola in a sentence through either a paratactic or chiastic scheme. Elements in the statues of Polykleitos are similarly balanced. Cf. S. Ferri, "Nuovi Contributi esegetici al 'Canon' della Scultura Greca," *Rivista del R. Istituto d'Archeologia e Storia dell' Arte,* 7 (1940), pp. 117-152.

101. Cf. Richter, *Sculpture and Sculptors,*[2] Figs. 645-654.

102. Commensurability—Greek *symmetria* (cf. p. 57). When used in the plural *symmetria* is translated by "proportions."

Quintilian, *Inst. Or.* **V, 12, 21:**   And indeed the outstanding sculptors and painters, when they wish to represent bodily forms which are as beautiful as possible, have never fallen into this error—namely that they use some Bogoas or Megabyzus [103] as the model for their work— but rather they use the *Doryphoros,* a work suitable both for the military and for the wrestling-court. . . .

The role of Polykleitos as a "sculptor's sculptor" which is reflected in the Doryphoros, *however, represents only one side of his career, for he also executed at least one large-scale public commission—the colossal gold and ivory statue of Hera* [104] *at the Argive* Heraion.

Pausanias II, 17, 4:   The image of Hera is seated on a throne; it is very large, made of gold and ivory, and is the work of Polykleitos. On her head is a crown which has the Graces and the Seasons worked upon it; in one of her hands she holds a pomegranate and in the other a sceptre. As for the details about the pomegranate [105]—since it is a teaching which must not be talked about—I will pass over it. They say that it is a cuckoo which is perched on the sceptre and explain it by the story that Zeus, when he was in love with the virgin Hera, changed himself into this bird, and that she caught it to have as a pet. This story and others like it which are told about the gods I record without believing them; nevertheless I do record them. It is said that the image of Hebe which stands next to the Hera is the work of Naukydes; [106] it too is of ivory and gold. By it there is an ancient image of Hera on a column. This most ancient image is made of wild pear wood; it was set up in Tiryns by Peirasos the son of Argos, and when the Argives sacked Tiryns they carried it off to the Heraion.

Strabo VIII, 372:   . . . The *Heraion* near Mycenae was the common property of both [Argos and Mycenae]; in the temple there are statues by Polykleitos, which in artistic quality are the most beautiful of all works, but in value and grandeur they are inferior to those of Pheidias.[107]

103. The names are perhaps intended to suggest an oriental eunuch.
104. The statue is represented on Argive coins minted in the time of the Roman empire. Cf. Lacroix, *Reproductions,* pp. 254-258, pl. XXI, nos. 13, 14.
105. The pomegranate was sacred to Demeter and Persephone and was connected with the symbolism of death and resurrection in some of the Greek mystery cults.
106. See pp. 92-93.
107. The words "value" and "grandeur" are here translated with intentional ambiguity. The Greek words *polyteleia* and *megethos* may literally mean "cost" and "size," or they may have a metaphorical meaning, as for example, "richness" and "grandeur of conception."

In addition to the Hera and the Hermes mentioned by Pliny, Polykleitos made several other images of deities which are simply mentioned by Pausanias: a Zeus Meilichios in Argos (Paus. II, 20, 1) and a group of Apollo, Leto, and Artemis on Mt. Lykone between Argos and Tegea (Paus. II, 24, 5). There was also a statue of Aphrodite at Amyklai which Pausanias (III, 18, 7-8) says was "by Polykleitos" set up after the battle of Aigospotamoi (405 B.C.), but this may have been the work of the younger Polykleitos (see below pp. 153, 182).

Polykleitos also made many statues of victorious athletes. The Doryphoros and Diadoumenos, in fact, may have been originally in this category, although no specific name is connected with them. Pausanias also mentions a number of these athlete statues without describing them: Thersilochos of Corcyra and Aristion of Epidauros (VI, 13, 6),[108] Xenokles of Mainalos (VI, 9, 2), Antipater of Miletos (VI, 2, 6) and Kyniskos [109] of Mantinea (VI, 4, 11)—all at Olympia.

Another work of Polykleitos was a pair of statues called the Kanephoroi (basket bearers). The exact nature of the subject and the purpose of the statues is obscure, but they must have represented women or girls who took part in some religious procession.

Cicero, *in Verrem*, II, IV, 3, 5 (discussing the art collection of Heius in Sicily, which was plundered by Verres): In addition there were two bronze statues, not large, but of truly outstanding beauty, clothed in garments such as virgins wear, who, with their hands raised, were carrying certain sacred objects which are placed on their heads in the manner of the Athenian virgins. These are called the *Kanephoroi*. Who is the artist who made them? Who indeed? You admonish rightly; they were said to be by Polykleitos.

As the passages on the Doryphoros *indicate, Polykleitos was deeply concerned with questions of artistic theory and technique. Plutarch and Philo Mechanicus preserve what appear to be two direct quotations which are attributed to Polykleitos and are possibly from his writings.*

Plutarch, *Quaestiones Convivialae*, II, 3, 2: The artists first of all model their figures so as to be without surface detail and shapeless, and

---

108. Aristion's victory was in 452 B.C. This was probably one of the earliest works of Polykleitos.

109. The base of this statue with its accompanying inscription has been found at Olympia. Cf. Loewy, *Inschriften,* no. 50. The "Westmacott Athlete" (a Roman copy) in the British Museum has been plausibly connected with the Kyniskos; cf. Richter, *Sculpture and Sculptors,*2 p. 251, Fig. 658.

then later distinguish the individual forms. For this reason, Polykleitos the sculptor said "the work is hardest when the clay is on the nail." [110]

Philo Mechanicus, Syntaxis, IV, 1, p. 49, 20 (ed. Schöne [Berlin, 1893]; cf. also Diels, *Fragmente der Vorsokratiker*,[7] 40 B 2): . . . thus the statement made by the sculptor Polykleitos may be suitably repeated for the future. For "perfection," he says, "arises *para mikron* [111] through many numbers." Indeed it happens in the same manner in that art [sculpture] that, in finishing off works through many numbers [measurements], they make a slight deviation in each part and in the end these add up to a large error.

And finally we may add an anecdote from Aelian which, though of doubtful historical veracity, may perhaps be a true reflection of Polykleitos' attitude as an artist.

Aelian, Varia Historia, XIV, 8: Polykleitos made two statues at the same time, one which would be pleasing to the crowd and the other according to the principles of his art. In accordance with the opinion of each person who came into his workshop, he altered something and changed its form, submitting to the advice of each. Then he put both statues on display. The one was marvelled at by everyone, and the other was laughed at. Thereupon Polykleitos said, "But the one which you find fault with, you made yourselves; while the one which you marvel at, I made."

Naukydes of Argos

Naukydes, who, as has already been noted, did the statue of Hebe which stood next to Polykleitos' Hera at Argos, was the son of Patrokles

110. Cf. also Plutarch, *De Perfectibus in Virtute*, 17. "On the nail" was a proverbial phrase meaning something like "in the fine points." The reference originally was perhaps to the fact that the artist put the finishing touches on his clay model with his fingernails.

111. *Para mikron*—the meaning of this Greek phrase is debated. Philo's interpretation seems to be that it means "from a minute calculation," that is, a very slight difference in measurements can make the difference between a work which is successful and one that is not. (This meaning is accepted in Diels [and Kranz], *Fragmente der Vorsokratiker*,[7] 40 B 2.) Another interpretation is that the phrase means something like "except for a little" or "almost," implying that, when all the correct measurements are made, there is still something else needed (for example, alterations based on the artist's subjective preferences) before a work can achieve beauty. Cf. Rhys Carpenter, *The Esthetic Basis of Greek Art*, reprint (Bloomington: 1959), p. 124; also D. Schulz, "Zum Kanon Polyklets," *Hermes*, 83 (1955), pp. 215 ff. Others take the phrase to mean "from a small unit," that is, a module. Cf. H. Stuart Jones, *Ancient Writers on Greek Sculpture*, p. 129; still another meaning might be "gradually," "little by little." For a summary of the interpretations, cf. Schulz, *op. cit.*

(attested by an inscription, cf. Loewy, Inschriften, no. 86). It has been suggested that these two artists were relatives of Polykleitos, although in exactly what relationship they stood to him is difficult to determine. Patrokles had another son named Daidalos (cf. Loewy, no. 88). According to Pausanias (II, 22, 7) Naukydes was the brother of a sculptor named Polykleitos.[112] *This may have been the younger Polykleitos, whose existence is well attested (see pp. 153, 182). In that case, Naukydes, Daidalos, and Polykleitos the younger may all have been sons of Patrokles, who in turn may have been a brother or cousin of the elder Polykleitos. Pliny (N.H. XXXIV, 50) dates Naukydes and Patrokles in the 95th Olympiad (400 B.C.). Daidalos and Polykleitos the Younger were presumably somewhat younger than Naukydes and were active mainly in the first quarter of the fourth century B.C.*

Of Patrokles we know only that he made figures of athletes, warriors, hunters, and men engaged in sacrifice (Pliny, N.H. XXXIV, 91), and that he worked on a large Spartan votive at Delphi (cf. p. 94).

Pliny, N.H. XXXIV, 80: Naukydes is valued for his Hermes and his discus-thrower and his figure of a man sacrificing a ram.[113]

Pausanias VI, 9, 3 (at Olympia): The portraits which are the most splendid works of Naukydes in my opinion are this one of Cheimon in Olympia and the one which was carried off from Argos to the temple of Peace in Rome.

Other works of Naukydes were his portrait of the athlete Eukles of Rhodes (cf. Pausanias VI, 6, 2) and of Baukis of Troizen (Paus. VI, 8, 4).

The Disciples of Polykleitos

Pliny, N.H. XXXIV, 50: . . . Polykleitos had as his disciples Argeios, Asopodoros, Alexis, Aristeides, Phrynon, Deinon, Athenodoros, and Dameas of Kleitor.

Some of these sculptors are otherwise completely unknown, but a number of them worked on a large votive monument set up by the Spartans at Delphi to commemorate their victory over the Athenians.

Pausanias X, 9, 7: Opposite are offerings of the Lakedaimonians from the spoils of their victory over the Athenians: the Dioscuri and Zeus,

112. One manuscript reads "Perikleitos," however, and Naukydes is called the son of Mothon, not Patrokles.
113. The last is sometimes associated with a group of Phrixos sacrificing a ram which was seen by Pausanias on the Athenian Acropolis (I, 24, 2).

Apollo and Artemis, and, by them, Poseidon and Lysander,[114] the son of Aristokritos, who is being crowned by Poseidon; also there are Agias, who was the soothsayer for Lysander on that occasion and Hermon, who piloted the flag-ship of Lysander. The statue of Hermon was made, as one might expect, by Theokosmas of Megara because he had been enrolled as a citizen by the Megarians. The Dioscuri were by Antiphanes of Argos, and the soothsayer was the work of Pison of Kalaureia, which belongs to Troizen. As for Athenodoros and Dameas, the latter made the Poseidon and the Artemis, and also the Lysander, while Athenodoros made the Apollo and the Zeus. These last artists were Arcadians from Kleitor. Behind the works just described, figures have been set up of those who gave aid to Lysander at Aigospotamoi, both Spartans and allies. These were Arakos the Lakedaimonian . . . [a list of ten names follows] . . . These were made by Tisander, but the following ones were made by Alypos of Sikyon [115] . . . [a list of seven names follows] . . . After these Axionikos, the Achaian, from Pellene . . . [nine names follow] . . . They say that these are the works of Patrokles and Kanachos.

Pausanias X, 9, 12 (following the above): Now as to the struggle between the Athenians and the Argives over the area called Thyrea [116]—this was prophesied by the Sibyl, who said that the battle would come out evenly. But the Argives, feeling that they had gotten the upper hand in the battle, sent a bronze horse—representing the "Wooden Horse" [of Troy], I suppose—to Delphi. This was the work of Antiphanes of Argos.[117]

Other Sculptors of the High Classical Period

THEOKOSMAS OF MEGARA

Theokosmas was one of the artists who worked on the Spartan victory offering at Delphi (see the previous passage) and hence has some association with the school of Polykleitos; but, as the following passage shows, he also had connections with Athens.

Pausanias I, 40, 4 (at Megara): After this, as you go into the sanctuary of Zeus called the *Olympieion* there is a temple which is well worth seeing. The image of Zeus, however, was not completed owing to the

114. Lysander: the Spartan admiral and director of military operations during the last years of the Peloponnesian war.
115. Alypos of Sikyon was a pupil of Naukydes; cf. Pausanias VI, 1, 3.
116. This battle at Thyrea (on the border between the Argolid and Lakonia) must be the one in 414 B.C. mentioned by Thucydides VI, 95.
117. Antiphanes was the pupil of a sculptor named Periklytos, who was in turn a pupil of Polykleitos. Cf. Pausanias V, 17, 3.

outbreak of the war of the Peloponnesians against the Athenians, in which every year the Athenians, in ravaging the country of the Megarians, destroyed public property and brought private land-owners to the brink of ruin. The face of the image of Zeus is of ivory and gold, while the remaining parts are of clay and gypsum. They say that it was made by Theokosmas, a local artist, and that Pheidias collaborated with him. Above the head of Zeus are the Seasons and the Fates. This makes it clear to all that Fate is obedient to him alone and that he is the god who apportions the seasons as he sees fit. Behind the temple are some half-worked pieces of wood. These Theokosmas intended to adorn with ivory and gold and thus finish the image.[118]

NIKODAMOS OF MAINALOS (IN ARCADIA)

Pausanias V, 26, 6 (at Olympia): . . . there stands an image of Athena with a helmet on her head and clad in an aegis. Nikodamos of Mainalos made it, and it is an offering of the Eleans.

Pausanias V, 25, 7 (at Olympia): On the same wall with the offerings of the people of Akragas [see p. 61 above] there are also two nude statues of Herakles as a boy. One represents him in the act of shooting with his bow at the Nemean lion. This statue of Herakles and likewise the lion [which is pitted] against Herakles were offered by Hippotion of Tarentum, and are the works of Nikodamos of Mainalos. The other image is the offering of Anaxippos of Mende, and was transferred to this place by the Eleans.

Pausanias also saw two statues at Olympia by Nikodamos of the athletes Antiochos of Lepreon (VI, 3, 9), Damoxenidas of Mainalos (VI, 6, 3), and Androsthenes of Mainalos (VI, 6, 1). The last of these was a victor in the Pankration in 420 B.C. *The base of the statue of Damoxenidas has been found at Olympia (Loewy,* Inschriften, *no. 98) and seems to date from the fourth century. Hence Nikodamos' career can be placed in the late fifth and early fourth centuries.*

PAINTING

Polygnotos of Thasos

See also Chapter 6, pp. 219, 221, 228.
Polygnotos' association with Kimon (c. 512-449 B.C.), who perhaps brought him from Thasos to Athens and helped him to acquire Athenian

118. The image is possibly represented on the Megarian coinage of the time of the Roman empire. Cf. Lacroix, *Reproductions*, p. 265, pl. XXII, 10.

citizenship, makes it clear that he was active in the Early Classical period. Pliny (N.H. XXXIV, 85) notes that Polygnotos was also a sculptor, although no specific statues by him are mentioned.

Pliny, N.H. XXXV, 58: Others were famous . . . before the 90th Olympiad [420 B.C.], such as Polygnotos of Thasos, who first painted women in transparent drapery, and represented their heads in multicolored headdresses; and he also made many innovations in painting, since it was he who introduced representing the mouth as open, showing the teeth, and varying the face from the rigidity which had existed previously. There is a picture by him in the Portico of Pompey (but which formerly was in front of the Curia) in which there is some doubt whether he has depicted the figure with the shield as moving upward or moving downward. He painted a chamber in Delphi, and he also painted the portico in Athens which they called the *Poikilē*, doing it for nothing, although Mikon painted a part of it for a fee. Actually the reputation of Polygnotos was greater, since the Amphiktyones, which is the common council of Greece, decreed free food and lodging for him.[119]

Plutarch, *Life of Cimon*, 4: They accused him [Kimon] of having intercourse in his youth with his own sister Elpinike, and they say that Elpinike was not particularly well-behaved in other respects, but that she lived in sin with Polygnotos the painter. And it was for this reason, they say, that, in painting the Trojan women in the stoa which was then called the *Peisianakteion* but later the *Poikilē*, he made the face of Laodike into a portrait of Elpinike. Polygnotos was not just one of the common workmen, and he did not paint the stoa for a profit, but rather he painted it free, thus showing his patriotic zeal for the city, as is related by the historians; the poet Melanthios expresses it in this manner:

> For at his own cost he decorated the temples of the gods
> And the Agora of Kekrops with the virtues of demi-gods.

Harpokration, *Lexicon*, s.v. "Polygnotos": . . . concerning Polygnotos the painter, a Thasian by birth, the son and pupil of Aglaophon, and how he achieved Athenian citizenship when he painted without a fee the *Stoa Poikilē*, or, according to others, the paintings in the treasury [120] and the *Anakeion* [121]—this history has been related by others including

---

119. Presumably the *Amphiktyones* of Delphi, where Polygnotos did some of his best-known work.

120. Perhaps a reference to the sanctuary of Theseus in Athens (*Theseōs hierōi* rather than *Thesaurōi*).

121. *Anakeion:* the sanctuary of the Dioscuri in Athens, *vide infra*.

Artemon in his book *About Painters* and Juba in his book *On Painting*.[122]

THE WORKS OF POLYGNOTOS

The Sack of Troy (Iliupersis) *and* Underworld (Nekyia) *in the* Lesche *of the Knidians in Delphi*

The Lesche *("clubhouse") dedicated by the people of Knidos was situated within the precinct of Apollo at Delphi. The famous paintings by Polygnotos were inside the building, either on its walls or on wooden plaques attached to the walls. Pausanias' description of them is extremely long and elaborate and is presented here in abridged form (with all omissions, except for minor discursive remarks, summarized in brackets).*

The language of the description—such phrases as "higher up," "above," and the like—makes it clear that Polygnotos placed his figures above and below one another as if they were disposed on a plane which could be seen receding toward the horizon. Polygnotos was probably the innovator of this type of spatial composition in Greek painting. His style of spatial and figural composition is probably reflected in the well-known "Niobid Krater" in the Louvre.[123]

Pausanias X, 25, 1: Above the Kassotis [124] is the building which has the paintings by Polygnotos; it is an offering of the Knidians and is called the *Lesche* by the Delphians because when they got together here in the old days they used to discuss weightier subjects, including everything connected with legends. . . . As you go into the building the whole portion of the painting to your right represents Ilium captured and the Greeks sailing away. On the ship of Menelaos they are getting everything ready for the departure. The ship is depicted and among the sailors there are grown men and, mixed up with them, children; in the middle of the ship is the helmsman Phrontis, holding two poles. Homer represented Nestor as talking about Phrontis, among other things, with Telemachos . . . [some remarks on the history of Phrontis intervene] . . . . This Phrontis, to continue, is in the painting of Polygnotos, and beneath him is a certain Ithaimenes carrying clothing, and Echoiax is seen going down the gangplank and holding a bronze

122. Nothing more is known of Artemon. Juba (c. 50 B.C.-23 A.D.), besides being a prolific and versatile writer, was king of Mauretania. He was one of the sources used by Pliny in compiling his chapters on the history of art.
123. Arias, Hirmer, *Greek Vase Painting*, pls. 173-175. Some conception of the original appearance of Polygnotos' paintings may be derived from Carl Robert's reconstruction of them; cf. C. Robert, "Die Nekyia des Polygnot," *Hallisches Winckelmannsprogram*, 1892; "Die Iliupersis des Polygnot," *Hallisches Winckelmannsprogram*, 1893.
124. A spring within the sanctuary at Delphi.

hydria [water jar]. Polites, Strophios, and Alphios are striking the tent of Menelaos which is not far from the ship. Amphialos is taking down another tent, while at his feet a boy is seated. There is no inscription by the boy; Phrontis above is represented with a beard. His name is the only one which Polygnotos learned from the *Odyssey;* [125] the names of the others, it seems to me, he invented himself.

Briseis stands there with Diomede above her and Iphis in front of both of them; they seem to be scrutinizing Helen's beauty. Helen herself is seated, and Eurybates is near her. I supposed that he was the herald of Odysseus, although he did not yet have a beard. The hand-maids Elektra and Panthalis are there; the latter stands next to Helen while Elektra is binding sandals on her mistress' feet. These names are also different from those which Homer gives, in the *Iliad,* [126] where he represents Helen, and her servants along with her, going to the wall. Seated above Helen is a man shrouded in a purple cloak and looking extremely downcast. One might surmise that it was Helenos, the son of Priam, even before reading the inscription. Near Helenos is Meges; he is wounded in the arm, just as Lescheos of Pyrrha, the son of Aeschylinos, represented him in the *Sack of Troy.* For he says that he was wounded by Admetos the son of Augeias in the battle which the Trojans fought in the night. Lykomedes the son of Kreon is depicted next to Meges with a wound in his wrist. Lescheos says that he was wounded in this way by Agenor. It is quite obvious that Polygnotos would not have painted their wounds in this way if he had not read the poem by Lescheos. He has added, however, another wound on Lykomedes' ankle and a third on his head. Euryalos the son of Mekisteos is also wounded on the head and on the wrist. These figures are placed higher up than Helen in the picture. After Helen comes the mother of Theseus with her hair shorn and Demophon, one of the sons of Theseus, who, I gather from his attitude, is trying to determine whether it will be possible for him to save Aithra . . . [details about his attempt to save Aithra, the mother of Theseus, who became Helen's slave, intervene] . . . .

The Trojan women seem to be captives already and are mourning their fate. Andromache is depicted and her child stands by her clutching her breast—this child, Lescheos says, met his end by being hurled from the tower. He further says that this was not a decree of the Greeks, but that Neoptolemos made a private decision to be the murderer. Also depicted is Medesikaste; she too is one of the illegitimate daughters of Priam. . . . Andromache and Medicaste are wearing

125. *Odyssey,* III, 278 ff.
126. *Iliad,* III, 144, where the maidens are Aithre and Klymene.

hoods,[127] while Polyxena has her hair braided as is customary with virgins. Poets sing about how she died at the tomb of Achilles, and I know of paintings which I have seen both in Athens and at Pergamon above the river Kaïkos which deal with the sufferings of Polyxena. To continue, Nestor is also represented with a cap on his head and a spear held in his hand. There is also a horse whose position suggests that he is about to roll in the dust. Right up to the spot where the horse is, there is a beach and on it pebbles are just visible; thereafter the representation of the sea breaks off.

(**X, 26, 1**): Up above this group of women at the point between Aithra and Nestor there are these other captive women—Klymene, Kreousa, Aristomache, and Xenodike . . . [a discussion of the literary sources for these figures—Stesichoros and Lescheos—intervenes]. . . . Represented on a couch above these are Deinome, Metioche, Peisis, and Kleodike. Of these, the name of Deinome alone occurs in the work called the *Little Iliad*. The names of the other women, I believe, were invented by Polygnotos. Epeios is represented as a nude figure who razes the wall of Troy to the ground. Above the wall rises the head, which is alone visible, of the Wooden Horse. There too is Polypoites the son of Peirithoös, who has his head bound with a fillet, and next to him Akamas the son of Theseus who has a helmet on his head; a crest has been wrought on the helmet. Also there is Odysseus . . . and Odysseus has put on his cuirass. Ajax the son of Oileus stands by an altar holding a shield, swearing an oath about his shameless act against Kassandra. Kassandra is seated on the ground and holds the image of Athena, since she pulled the image down from its base when Ajax was dragging her away from her place as a suppliant. Depicted there also are the children of Atreus who also wear helmets. Menelaos holds a shield on which a serpent has been wrought, a reference to the portent which appeared among the victims at Aulis. Below those who are making Ajax swear the oath, and parallel with the horse by Nestor, is Neoptolemos who has killed Elasos, whoever Elasos may be. He is represented with only a little life left in him. Astynoös, of whom Lescheos makes mention, has fallen on his knees and Neoptolemos strikes him with his sword. Polygnotos has represented Neoptolemos alone as still engaged in slaying Trojans, because it was his intention that the whole painting should be above the grave of Neoptolemos . . . also depicted is an altar and a small boy who clings to it out of fear. On the altar is a bronze cuirass . . . [a discussion of the cuirass follows].

127. Hoods—Greek *kalymmata*. The word can also mean veil. The garment is probably intended to be a sign of mourning.

Beyond the altar he has painted Laodike who is standing . . . [a discussion of the sources for the history of Laodike intervenes]. Next to Laodike there is a stand made of stone and on the stand is a bronze washing-basin. Medusa, holding on to the stand with both hands, is seated on the ground. She too should be counted among the daughters of Priam according to the Ode of the poet of Himera [Stesichoros]. Beside Medusa is an old woman with her hair shorn, or a man who is a eunuch, who holds a naked child on his knees. The child is represented as holding its hand in front of its eyes out of fear. (X, 27, 1) There are also corpses, including a naked man named Pelis who lies prostrate on his back; below this Pelis lie Eioneus and Admetos, still dressed in their cuirasses. . . . The others above these are, beneath the wash-basin, Leokritos the son of Poulydamas, killed by Odysseus, and, above Eioneus and Admetos, Koroibos the son of Mygdon . . . [a digression on Mygdon and Koroibos intervenes]. And higher up than Koroibos are Priam, Axion, and Agenor . . . [a discussion of the literary sources for the death of Priam and Hecuba intervenes] . . . . Sinon, the companion of Odysseus, and Anchialos are carrying off the body of Laomedon; and there is another corpse, the name of which is Eresos. No poet, as far as I know, has sung this story about Laomedon and Eresos. Also represented is the home of Antenor with a leopard skin hanging over the doorway, the sign of an agreement among the Greeks to keep their hands off the house of Antenor. Theano is also depicted along with her sons, Glaukos who is seated on a corselet which consists of two parts fitted together, and Eurymachos who is seated on a rock. By him stands Antenor and after that Krino, the daughter of Antenor. Krino carries an infant child. The look on the faces of all of them is that of people who have suffered a great disaster. Servants are loading a chest and other baggage on a donkey. Also seated on the donkey is a small boy. Below this section of the painting there is also the elegiac couplet of Simonides:

> Polygnotos, Thasian by birth, Aglaophon's son,
> Painted the sacking of Ilium's citadel.

The Underworld (Nekyia)

Pausanias (X, 28, 1): The other part of the painting, the part on the left-hand side, represents Odysseus, who has gone down to the region called Hades in order to ask the soul of Teiresias about how to achieve a safe homecoming. The details of the painting are as follows. There is water which is like a river, and is clearly intended to be Acheron. Reeds have grown up in it and there are forms of fish which are so faint that you might take them for shadows rather than fish. There is a ship on the river and a ferryman at the oars. Polygnotos followed, it seems

to me, the poem called the *Minyad*. For in the *Minyad* are the following lines about Theseus and Peirithoös:

> But at that spot they did not within the place of anchorage find
> the ship on which the dead embark, the one which the old ferryman,
> Charon, used to guide.

For this reason Polygnotos painted Charon as a man already well on in
years. Those who are on board the ship are not all clearly distinguish-
able to those who have arrived.[128] Tellis appears to have reached the
age of an ephebe,[129] and Kleoboia, who is still a virgin, holds a chest
on her knees of the type which they usually make for Demeter. With
regard to Tellis all I heard was that the poet Archilochos was his grandson, while they say that Kleoboia first brought the rites of Demeter from
Paros to Thasos.

On the bank of Acheron there is a group well worth seeing; it
it is placed below the boat of Charon and shows a man who has been
unjust to his father being choked by the father. . . . [Examples of how
earlier generations were dutiful to their parents intervene.] Near the
man in Polygnotos' painting who maltreated his father and for that
reason has a full measure of suffering in Hades, near him, I repeat, there
is a man who is receiving his punishment for having robbed sanctuaries.
The woman who is punishing him knows about drugs and such things
as are for the torture of men . . . [examples of piety among earlier
generations are given]. . . . Thus it appears all men at that time held
the divine in high honor, and for that reason Polygnotos painted the
scene about a man who robbed sanctuaries.

Higher up than the figures which I have thus far spoken of is
Eurynomos. The Delphian guides say that this Eurynomos is one of the
demons in Hades, and that he eats the flesh of corpses and leaves behind
only the bones. But Homer in the Odyssey and the poems called the
Minyad and the *Nostoi* [*Homecomings*]—for in these poems mention
is made of Hades and of the terrors which are in it—do not know of
this demon Eurynomos. Nevertheless I shall make clear what sort of
creature this Eurynomos is and in what sort of format he has been
depicted. The color of his skin is between blue and black like that of
flies which are always hovering around meat; he is showing his teeth
and is seated on a vulture's skin which is spread out beneath him.
After Eurynomos come Auge and Iphimedeia from Arcadia. Auge
turned up at the house of Teuthras in Mysia, and of all the women
with whom they say Herakles had an affair, she was the one who bore
a child most like its father. . . .

128. "To those who have arrived" is omitted by some editors.
129. Ephebe is the Greek term for a youth who had reached the age of 18 and
was undergoing military training.

(X, 29, 1):   Still higher up than the figures which I have already spoken of are Perimedes and Eurylochos the companions of Odysseus who are carrying sacrificial victims. These victims are black rams. After them there is a man who is seated; the inscription says that he is "Oknos" ["Sloth"]. He is represented as plaiting a rope, while a female donkey stands by him continually eating up the plaited portion of the rope. They say that this Oknos was a man who loved work, but that he had a spendthrift wife. And everything he earned by work was spent by his wife not much later. . . . [Other anecdotes about Oknos are given.] . . . Tityos is also depicted, no longer being punished, but completely consumed by continual torture, a faint and decomposed image.

Going on to the next group of figures in the painting, nearest to the man who twists the rope, is Ariadne. She is seated on some rocks and looks at her sister Phaidra, who in turn is swinging herself on a loop-swing, holding the rope in her hands on each side. This position, even though it is represented rather prettily, suggests the story of the death of Phaidra. . . . [Remarks on the story of Ariadne and Dionysos follow. This is followed by a brief description of other women, who, like Phaidra, had renowned marriages—Chloris, Thyia, Procris, Klymene, and Megara the wife of Herakles.]

Above the heads of the women just mentioned is the daughter of Salmoneus [Tyro] seated on some rocks and by her is Eriphyle, standing, who holds the ends of her fingers through her tunic by her neck; and you can imagine that in the folds of her tunic, in one or the other of her hands, she holds that well-known necklace. Above Eriphyle he has painted Elpenor and Odysseus who is crouching on his feet, and holds his sword above the pit; and the prophet Teiresias is coming forward toward the pit. After Teiresias is Antikleia, the mother of Odysseus, seated on the rocks. Elpenor, instead of garments, wears a plaited mat as is customary for sailors. Lower down than Odysseus are Theseus and Peirithoös seated on chairs; the former holds both Peirithoös' sword and his own, while Peirithoös stares at the swords. And you would guess that he was angry with the swords because they were useless and of no avail in their adventures. . . . [Details about the myth of Theseus and Peirithoös follow.]

(X, 30, 1):   Next Polygnotos has painted the daughters of Pandareos. . . . [A summary of Homer's story about these daughters, *Odyssey* XX, 66-78, follows.] Polygnotos has painted them as maidens garlanded with flowers and playing with dice, and their names are given as Kameiro and Klytie. . . . After the daughters of Pandareos is Antilochos, with one foot on a rock and leaning on a sceptre beneath his left armpit, and holding up a staff in his hands. Protesilaos, who is seated, is looking at Achilles. Such is the position of Protesilaos, and above Achilles stands Patroklos. These figures, except for Agamemnon, do not have beards. . . . [Scenes follow of Phokos showing to his friend Iaseus the ring which the latter had given him and of Maira, the daughter of Proteus seated on a rock.] . . . Next to Maira is Aktaion the son of Aristaios and Aktaion's mother. They hold in their hands a fawn and are seated on a deerskin. A hunting dog lies stretched out before them, suggesting both the life of Aktaion and the manner of his death.

Looking at a still lower part of the painting, we come, after Patroklos, to Orpheus, seated on a sort of hill; with his left hand he has hold of a *kithara,* and with the other hand he touches a willow. There are branches which he touches, and he is leaning against the tree. The grove seems to be that of Persephone, where black poplars and willows grew according to Homer. The manner in which Orpheus is represented is Greek and neither his clothing nor his headdress are Thracian. On the other side of the willow tree Promedon is seen leaning against it. There are those who think that the name Promedon was invented and introduced, just as if it were in a poem, by Polygnotos; it is said by others that the man was a Greek who was fond of listening to all kinds of music, but especially to the singing of Orpheus. In this area of the painting is Schedios who led the Phokians to Troy. With him is Pelias seated on a chair; his beard and his hair alike are grey, and he gazes at Orpheus. Schedios holds a dagger and has a garland of grass on his head. Seated near Pelias is Thamyris whose eyes have been blinded and is represented in the attitude of one who is completely humiliated; the hair on his head has grown long as has his beard. His lyre is thrown at his feet, with its horns broken and with strings which have snapped. Above him is Marsyas seated on the rocks and by him Olympos represented as a blooming boy who is learning how to play the flute. . . . [Remarks on Marsyas and the flutes follow.]

(**X, 31, 1**): If you look again at the upper part of the painting, there comes, after Aktaion, Ajax of Salamis, and also Palamedes and Thersites engaging in a game of dice, of which Palamedes was the inventor. The other Ajax looks at them as they play. The color of this Ajax might be likened to that of a man who has been in a shipwreck and whose skin is still caked with salt. Polygnotos has thus quite artfully brought together the enemies of Odysseus. . . . [The background of Odysseus' enemies is then mentioned.] Meleager, the son of Oineus, appears higher up in the painting than Ajax the son of Oileus, and seems to be looking at Ajax. . . . [The story of Meleager's death follows.]

In the lower part of the painting, after the Thracian Thamyris, Hector is seated, clasping his left knee with both hands, and represented in the attitude of one who grieves. After him comes Memnon, seated on a rock and right next to Memnon is Sarpedon. Sarpedon buries his face in both hands, while Memnon places one hand on Sarpedon's shoulder. They all have beards, and there are birds worked into the cloak of Memnon. . . . [These birds, it is explained, attend upon the tomb of Memnon.] By Memnon a naked Ethiopian boy is represented. . . . [A discussion of the route which Memnon took to Troy intervenes.]

Above Sarpedon and Memnon is Paris, who does not yet have a beard. He is clapping his hands just the way some rude country fellow would clap them. You will say that Paris appears to be calling Penthesileia to him by the sound of his hands. Penthesileia is also there looking at Paris; she seems by the toss of her head to look on him with disdain and to treat him as of no account. The representation of Penthesileia is that of a virgin; she carries a bow which is like Scythian bows and wears a leopard skin on her shoulders. . . . [Above these are represented two women carrying broken water pitchers who were never initiated into the mysteries and also Kallisto, daughter of Lykaon, the nymph Nomia, and Pero, the daughter of Neleus.]

After Kallisto and the women who are with her, there is the representation of a cliff, and Sisyphos, the son of Aiolos, is exerting himself to push the stone up the cliff. There are also in the painting a storage jar, an old man, and a boy and some women—a young woman below the stone and another who is beside the old man and of the same age as he. The others are carrying water, and you will no doubt guess that the old woman's water-jar is broken. And whatever water is left in the sherd, she is pouring back into the storage jar again. I surmised that these were people who attached no significance to the rites at Eleusis. For the earlier Greeks felt that the Eleusinian mysteries came before all others in holiness to the same degree that the gods were more worthy of honor than heroes.

Beneath this storage jar is Tantalos who has all the pains which Homer depicted with regard to him, and in addition to these there is also the fear caused by the stone which hangs over him. It is clear that Polygnotos has followed the version of Archilochos here. I do not know, however, whether Archilochos borrowed the story about the stone from others or whether he introduced it into the poem himself.

Such is the number and so great are the beauties which this painting of the Thasian possesses.

The Anakeion *(Sanctuary of the Dioscuri) in Athens*

Pausanias I, 18, 1: The sanctuary of the Dioscuri is an ancient one. . . . Here Polygnotos has painted an episode connected with them —the marriage of the daughters of Leukippos.

Paintings at Plataea

Pausanias IX, 4, 1: In Plataea there is a sanctuary of Athena called *Areia* . . . [the temple was built from the spoils of the battle of Marathon, and the image was made by Pheidias, see p. 75]. There are paintings in the temple, one by Polygnotos, showing Odysseus who has already trapped the suitors; the other, by Onasias, showing the earlier expedition of Adrastos and the Argives against Thebes.[130] These paintings are on the walls of the *pronaos*. . . .

Paintings in the Propylaia *of the Acropolis in Athens*

Pausanias I, 22, 6: The room on the left of the Propylaia contains some pictures.[131] Among those which time has not caused to grow faint, there are pictures of Diomedes and Odysseus, the latter in Lemnos taking away the bow of Philoktetes and the former stealing the image of Athena from Troy. Also there among the pictures is one of Orestes killing Aegisthus and Pylades killing the son of Nauplios who had come to aid Aegisthus. And there is Polyxena about to have her throat cut near the tomb of Achilles. Homer did well to pass over this savage act; he likewise did well, it seems to me, in composing a poem about the sack of Skyros by Achilles, thus differing from those who say that Achilles dwelt among the virgins in Skyros, which is the story which Polygnotos has painted. He also painted Odysseus by the river encountering the girls who were doing the washing along with Nausikaa—just as Homer has described it.[132]

Mikon of Athens

Mikon and Polygnotos seem to have been collaborators. They worked together on the paintings in the Stoa Poikilē, *the* Anakeion, *and the sanctuary of Theseus in Athens. Mikon also resembled Polygnotos in being a sculptor as well as a painter (cf. Pausanias VI, 6, 1; Pliny, N.H. XXXIV, 88).*

THE WORKS OF MIKON

The Amazonomachy *and the* Battle of Marathon *in the* Stoa Poikilē *in Athens (see also p. 108)*

130. This is the only known work by Onasias. The reading "Adrastos and" is based on a restoration of the text proposed by Dindorf.
131. Much of this room is still intact in the north wing of the *Propylaia* (built c. 438 B.C.). If the room was originally designed for the function which it fulfilled in Pausanias' day (and the windows and mouldings in it suggest that it may have been), it perhaps should be recognized as the world's earliest public art gallery.
132. Whether the paintings not specifically ascribed to Polygnotos are also by him is not clear.

Aristophanes, *Lysistrata*, 678-679 and scholiast: . . . just contemplate those Amazons which Mikon has painted, mounted on horseback and fighting against men!

Scholiast: The *Stoa Poikilē* in Athens is thus spoken of because of the paintings which are in it. Here Mikon made the battle of the Amazons. He was the son of Phanochos, an Athenian.

Aelian, *De Natura Animalium* VII, 38: A certain Athenian brought along a dog as an ally in the battle of Marathon, and each of them is represented in the painting in the *Poikilē;* the dog was not dishonored, but got his reward for having undergone the danger by being shown with Kynaigeiros and Epizelos and Kallimachos [the Athenian generals]. These men and also the dog were painted by Mikon. At least some say by him, but others say by Polygnotos.

The Return of the Argonauts *in the* Anakeion *in Athens*

Pausanias I, 18, 1 (see also under Polygnotos, pp. 96, 104-105): The sanctuary of the Dioscuri is an ancient one. There . . . Mikon has painted the men who sailed with Jason against the Kolchians. The intensity of his effort in this painting is particularly apparent in the figure of Akastos and the horses of Akastos.

Pausanias VIII, 11, 3 (concerning the daughters of Pelias, who, at the instigation of Medes, killed their father): No poet has recorded their names, at least within the scope of my reading, but Mikon the painter wrote the names Asteropeia and Antinoë on his portraits of them.[133]

Paintings in the Theseion *in Athens*

Pausanias I, 17, 2: By the gymnasium there is a sanctuary of Theseus. There are paintings here of the Athenians fighting the Amazons. . . . Also painted in the sanctuary of Theseus is the battle of the Lapiths and centaurs. Theseus is there and has already killed a centaur. Among the others the battle is still an equal match. The painting on the third wall is not very clear to those who have not heard what they tell about it, in part because of its age and in part because Mikon did not depict the whole story. . . . [A section follows narrating some of the exploits of Theseus in Crete, in Western Greece, and in the underworld, and also his death on Skyros. Which of these stories Mikon did or did not represent is not clear.]

133. These figures presumably belonged to the *Return of the Argonauts.* Another figure which perhaps belonged to this painting was that of the Argonaut Boutes, hidden behind a rock so that only his helmet and one eye were visible. This figure gave rise to the proverb, "Quicker than Boutes," because it was felt that Mikon could have executed the figure in a very short time. For the texts (Zenobios and other collections of proverbs) see Overbeck, *Schriftquellen,* no. 1085.

*The following anecdote is probably to be connected with one of
the mural paintings described above.*

Aelian, *De Natura Animalium*, IV, 50:   With regard to horses, they
say that they have no lower eyelids. They maintain, moreover, that it
was the fault of Apelles of Ephesos that, when painting a certain horse,
he did not take note of this peculiarity in the animal. Others say that
this fault should not be ascribed to Apelles but to Mikon, who was very
good at painting this animal, and erred only in the way just mentioned.

Panainos the Brother of Pheidias

*We have already seen that Panainos collaborated with Pheidias
on the ornamentation of the statue of Zeus at Olympia (cf. above, p.
72).*

Pausanias V, 11, 6:   This Panainos was the brother of Pheidias, and the
Battle of Marathon in the *Stoa Poikilē* in Athens was also painted by
him.

Pliny, *N.H.* XXXV, 54-58 (in a discussion on the chronology of Greek
painting):   . . . there is a tradition that Pheidias himself was originally
a painter and that the shield [of the Athena *Parthenos*] in Athens was
painted by him; moreover there can be no doubt that his brother
Panainos, who painted the inside of the shield of Athena in Elis which
was made by Kolotes [see above, p. 80], . . . was active in the 83rd
Olympiad [448 B.C.]. . . . (Sec. 57) Indeed Panainos, the brother of
Pheidias, even painted the battle of the Athenians against the Persians
at Marathon. Now at this time the use of color had increased to such
an extent and the art had become so highly perfected, that he is reputed to have painted portraits of the leaders in this battle—among the
Athenians Miltiades, Kallimachos, and Kynaigeiros, and among the barbarians Datis and Artaphernes.[134] (Sec. 58) Not only that but during
the time when he flourished competitions in painting were instituted
at Corinth and Delphi, and in the first of these he [Panainos] competed
with Timagoras of Chalkis, by whom he was defeated, which is clear
from an old poem by Timagoras himself. . . .

Pliny, *N.H.* XXXVI, 177:   There is a temple of Athena in Elis in which
Panainos the brother of Pheidias introduced the technique of the work-

---

134. Whether Panainos and Mikon painted separate pictures of the battle of
Marathon in the *Stoa Poikilē*, or whether they collaborated on a single picture is not
known.

ing of plaster with milk and saffron; as a result even today if saliva, applied to one's thumb, is rubbed into it, it gives off the odor and taste of saffron.

The Paintings in the Stoa Poikilē in Athens

As the preceding passages in this section have indicated, Polygnotos, Mikon, and Panainos all contributed to the paintings of the Stoa Poikilē *in the Agora in Athens. The fullest description of the paintings is that of Pausanias.*

Pausanias I, 15, 1:   . . . the stoa, which is called *Poikilē* from its paintings. . . . This stoa contains first a scene with the Athenians drawn up against the Lakedaimonians at Oinoë in the territory of Argos. The painting does not show the high-point of the struggle, nor has the action gotten to the point where there is already a display of valorous deeds, but rather the battle is just beginning and they are still in the process of coming to grips.[135] On the middle wall the Athenians and Theseus are shown fighting the Amazons [painted by Mikon]. Among these women alone, it would seem, defeats did not rob them of their recklessness in the face of danger, since Themiskyras was seized by Herakles and later their army, which they sent to Athens, was destroyed, but in spite of all that they came to Troy to fight against the Athenians and all the other Greeks as well. After the Amazons come the Greeks who have taken Troy and also the kings who have gathered together on account of the outrageous act of Ajax against Kassandra [painted by Polygnotos]. The painting includes Ajax himself and also Kassandra and other captive women. The final part of the painting represents those who fought at Marathon [painted by Mikon and Panainos]. The Boeotians who inhabit Plataea and the Attic force are coming to grips with the barbarians. In this section the struggle is an equal match. In the center of the battle, however, the barbarians are fleeing and are pushing one another into the marsh, and at the borders of the painting there are Phoenician ships and Greeks slaying those of the barbarians who are climbing into them. Here too is a portrait of the hero Marathon, after whom the plain is named; Theseus is represented as rising out of the earth, and Athena and Herakles are also here. For Herakles was first decreed to be a god by the Marathonians, as they themselves say. Of the combatants the most conspicuous in the painting are Kallimachos, who was chosen by the Athenians to be the supreme commander, and, of the other generals, Miltiades, and also the hero who is named Echettos.

---

135. Neither the painter nor the occasion of the battle is known.

Dionysios of Kolophon

Reference has already been made to a painter named Dionysios mentioned in an epigram of Simonides as having painted a certain set of doors along with Kimon of Kleonai (see p. 36). This epigram (which is a rare example of a contemporary reference) dates Dionysios in the first half of the fifth century B.C. *Aelian also suggests that he was a contemporary of Polygnotos.*

Aelian, *Varia Historia*, IV, 3: Polygnotos of Thasos and Dionysios of Kolophon were painters. Polygnotos painted large pictures. . . . Those of Dionysios, except for the size, imitated the art of Polygnotos in its precision, its representation of emotion and character, its use of patterns of composition, the thinness of the drapery, and so on.[136]

Plutarch, *Life of Timoleon*, 36: The poetry of Antimachos and the paintings of Dionysios, both from Kolophon, although they have vigor and tension,[137] seem forced and labored.

Pliny, *N.H.* XXXV, 113: . . . Dionysios on the contrary painted nothing other than human beings, and on account of this he was given the name *anthropographos* ["painter of men"].

In the above passage it is not certain that the Dionysios referred to is Dionysios of Kolophon. The name anthropographos, *however, suggests that he may be the same as the Dionysios mentioned by Aristotle (cf. Chapter 6, p. 230) who "painted men as they were."*

Agatharchos

Agatharchos, the son of Eudemos, was a Samian by birth. His great achievement was the invention of rules for the rendering of spatial perspective in painting. Perspective painting in Greece was called skēnographia, *which literally means "scene-painting," and, as the following passage shows, the technique was first employed in painting stage settings for the Athenian dramas.*

Vitruvius VII, praef. 11: For first of all Agatharchos, when Aeschylus was presenting a tragedy, made the setting [*scaena*] for it, and left be-

---

136. Aelian's information in this passage is of the sort which might have come from the history of Xenokrates (see Introduction, pp. xi-xii, xviii). On the "thinness of the drapery" compare Pliny's *tralucida veste pinxit* (*N.H.* XXXV, 58), see p. 96.

137. "Tension" here translates the Greek *tonos*, which possibly refers to the contrast of light and shade in a painting. Cf. Pliny, *N.H.* XXXV, 29.

hind a commentary about it. Instructed by him, Demokritos and Anaxagoras wrote on the same subject, demonstrating how it followed that, if a definite center is constituted for the line of vision and also the extension of the radii [therefrom], one follows these lines in accordance with a natural law, so that ill-defined images from a thing which is not clearly defined may produce the appearance of buildings in the pictures of a stage setting and, although all the things are figures on a flat vertical plane, some appear to be in the background and some in the foreground.

The other literary testimonies about Agatharchos are anecdotal:

Plutarch, *Life of Pericles,* **13:** And indeed they say that when Agatharchos the painter boasted that he could paint figures quickly and easily, Zeuxis [138] overheard him and said, "It takes me a long time." For facility and speed in making a thing do not give it lasting gravity or the sharpness of beauty.

Plutarch, *Life of Alcibiades,* **16** (discussing the faults of Alcibiades): He made the Athenians forgive all the other things and bear them with restraint, always giving the mildest of names to his misdeeds, such as "youthful pranks" and "good fellowship." A typical example was when he locked up the painter Agatharchos, and then, when he had painted his [Alcibiades'] house, let him go again with a reward.

Pauson

Pauson had a reputation for painting lowly or perhaps immoral subjects; see Aristotle's evaluation of him, Chapter 6, p. 230. His date is uncertain, but if he is the same as the indigent and depraved Pauson at whom Aristophanes pokes fun,[139] he belongs to this second half of the fifth century B.C. *One amusing anecdote about him is preserved:*

Lucian, *Demosthenis Encomium,* **24:** They relate about the painter Pauson that he was hired to paint a horse rolling on its back. But he painted it running, and with a great cloud of dust around it. While he was still painting it, the man who hired him interfered and blamed him for not executing the painting according to instructions. Consequently Pauson ordered his assistant to exhibit the painting upside down, and the horse was thus seen to be lying on its back and rolling around.

138. On Zeuxis see pp. 154-158.
139. Aristophanes, *Acharnians,* 854; *Thesmophoriazusai,* 948; *Ploutos,* 602.

The Relatives of Polygnotos: Aristophon and Aglaophon

We are told by Plato (Gorgias 448 B and scholiast) *that a painter named Aristophon, the son of Aglaophon, was Polygnotos' brother. A few works by this painter are mentioned by Pliny.*

Pliny, N.H. XXXV, 138: Aristophon [is praised for] his Ankaios wounded by the boar along with Astypale as his companion in the suffering and also a detailed picture in which Priam, Helen, "Credulity," Odysseus, Deiphobos and "Deceit" are represented.[140]

Another painter named Aglaophon was active in the later fifth century (he was a contemporary of Alcibiades) and was probably a grandson of Aglaophon the father of Polygnotos and Aristophon (since the custom of repeating names in every other generation was common among the Greeks). He may have been the son of Aristophon or even of Polygnotos. Pliny (N.H. XXXV, 60) dates him in the 90th Olympiad (420 B.C.).

Athenaeus, XII, 534 D (concerning Alcibiades): When he arrived in Athens from Olympia, he set up two paintings by Aglaophon. One of these showed [figures representing] "the Olympic games" and "the Pythian games" placing a wreath on his [Alcibiades'] head; in the other "Nemea" was shown seated and on her lap was Alcibiades, whose face was more beautiful than those of the women.[141]

Apollodoros of Athens

Apollodoros, although little is known about him, was one of the most important Greek painters. It was he who first developed the technique of what the Greeks called skiagraphia, *"shading," that is, the simulation of normal optical experience of figures in light and space by the modulation of light and shade in a painting.*

Pliny, N.H. XXXV, 60: . . . now all these [referring to Aglaophon and other painters active in the 90th Olympiad] are illustrious; however,

140. The names "Ankaios" and "Astypale" are reconstructed from a faulty text. Ankaios was involved in the Kalydonian boar hunt. For "Deceit" ("Dolus") some would read "Dolon."

141. The same picture is mentioned by Plutarch, *Life of Alcibiades,* 16, and may be identical with the portrait of Alcibiades seen by Pausanias in the picture gallery of the *Propylaia* in Athens; cf. Pausanias I, 22, 6.

our exposition must not linger over these while it is hastening to get to the luminaries of the art, among whom Apollodoros the Athenian first shone brightly in the 93rd Olympiad [408 B.C.]. He first established the method for representing appearances [142] and first conferred glory upon the paintbrush by a law.[143] By him are a *Priest Praying* and *Ajax Burned by a Lightning Bolt,* a work which may be seen today at Pergamon. Nor is there a painting [144] on display by any artist before Apollodoros which holds the eyes.

Plutarch, *De Glor. Athen.*, 2: Apollodoros the painter who first invented the fading out and the building up of shadow, was an Athenian, of whose works it is written:

> A person will criticize them better than he
> will imitate them.[145]

Scholiast on *Iliad*, X, 265: . . . painters and sculptors represent Odysseus wearing a cap. Apollodoros the *skiagraphos* first painted a cap on Odysseus. . . .

Scholiast on Aristophanes, *Ploutos*, 385: There is a painting, moreover, of the Herakleidai and Alkmene and the daughter of Herakles, who, in fear of Eurystheus, are supplicating the Athenians—a painting which is not by Pamphilos, as some say, but by Apollodoros.

ARCHITECTURE

The Temple of Zeus at Olympia *(Built c. 470-457 B.C.)*

The temple was made, as already noted (see p. 70) from the spoils taken by the Eleans from a war with Pisa. The foundations and many of the architectural members of the temple may still be seen at Olympia. Most of the famous pedimental sculptures and metopes are in the Museum in Olympia.[146]

142. "Established the method for representing appearances"—*hic primus species exprimere instituit.*
143. "By a law"—*iure.* The reference is perhaps to the "laws" or "rules" of Apollodoros' technique of shading, although others would simply translate *iure* as "by right."
144. "Painting"—*tabula,* which means an easel painting, probably done on wood. The meaning of the passage may be that all the great paintings prior to Apollodoros' were wall-paintings, and that he was the first to win a reputation through easel paintings.
145. This saying is elsewhere ascribed to Zeuxis. See p. 155.
146. In addition to the usual handbooks, cf. G. Rodenwaldt, W. Hege, *Olympia,* 1936.

Pausanias V, 10, 3-10: The style of the temple is Doric, and it has a peristyle around the outside. It is made of local stone. Its height up to the pediment is 68 feet, its width 95 feet, and its length 230 feet.[147] Its architect was Libon, a local man. The roof tiles are not of terra cotta, but of Pentelic marble carved in the form of tiles. They say that this was the invention of a man from Naxos named Byzes, by whom they say there are statues in Naxos on which the following inscription is written:

> To the offspring of Leto Euergos the Naxian dedicated me, the son of Byzes, who first wrought tiles of stone.

This Byzes was a contemporary of Alyattes and of Astyages the son of Cyaxaris who ruled over the Medes [c. 610-560 B.C.]. At Olympia a gilt cauldron is placed at each corner of the roof, and in the middle, at the point of the pediment, stands a Victory, which is also gilt.[148] Beneath the image of Victory a gold shield has been put in place, with Medusa the Gorgon worked in relief upon it. . . . [Pausanias then gives the inscription on the shield which states that it was a Spartan votive commemorating their victory over the Athenians at Tanagra in 457 B.C.] On the frieze which runs around above the columns of the temple at Olympia on the outside there are twenty-one gilt shields, dedications by the Roman general Mummius after he had won his war against the Achaeans, taken Corinth, and made the Dorian Corinthians abandon their houses. Turning to the pediments, the one in front [east] represents the struggle of Pelops and Oinomaos in chariot-racing, just about to get under way, with both sides still involved in the preparation for the actual race. An image of Zeus is placed in the center of the pediment, and to the right of Zeus is Oinomaos with a helmet on his head, and by him is his wife Sterope, one of the daughters of Atlas. Myrtilos, who drove the chariot for Oinomaos, sits in front of the horses, which are four in number. After him there are two men. There are no names for them, but they too must be under Oinomaos' orders to attend to the horses. On the very end Kladeos is reclining. In other ways as well he is the most honored of rivers by the Eleans after the Alphaios. To the left of Zeus are Pelops and Hippodameia, the charioteer of Pelops, the horses, and two men, who again seem to be grooms for the horses, in this case serving Pelops. The pediment once again grows narrow, and in the angle on this end Alphaios is represented. The name for the man who is Pelops' charioteer in the Troizenian version of the story is "Sphairos," but the guide in Olympia alleges that it was "Killas." The figures in the front pediment are by Paionios, who was born in Mende, in Thrace;

---

147. In modern English feet the measurements are approximately 91 by 210½ feet.

148. This victory was the work of Paionios of Mende; see p. 82.

those in the rear pediment are by Alkamenes, a man who was a contemporary with Pheidias and was second in skill only to him as a maker of images.[149] The sculptures by him in this pediment represent the battle of the Lapiths against the centaurs at the wedding of Peirithoös. In the center of the pediment is Peirithoös.[150] Next to him, on one side, is Eurytion who has seized the woman who is Peirithoös' wife and Kaineus defending Peirithoös, and on the other side is Theseus defending himself against the centaurs with an axe. One centaur has seized a maiden, and another has seized a handsome youth. Alkamenes represented these figures, it seems to me, because he had learned from the poems of Homer that Peirithoös was a descendant of Zeus and because he knew that Theseus was a great grandson of Pelops.

Also represented at Olympia are most of the labors of Herakles.[151] Above the doors of the temple is the hunt after the boar from Arcadia, and also Herakles' exploits against Dionysios of Thrace and against Geryones in Erytheia; he is also shown as he is about to receive the burden from Atlas and also cleansing the earth of dung for the Eleans. Above the doors of the *opisthodomos* he is shown taking the Amazon's girdle and also represented there are his exploits against the stag, against the bull of Knossos, the birds at Stymphalos, the Hydra, and the lion in the territory of Argos. As you enter through the bronze doors, there is, in front of the column on the right, [a statue of] Iphitos being crowned by a woman, "Ekecheiria" ["Truce"], as the elegiac inscription on it says. Columns also stand inside the temple, and there are colonnades placed on a higher level with an approach through them to the image.[152] A winding ascent up to the roof has also been constructed.

The Periclean Building Program

Plutarch, *Life of Pericles*, 12-13: What afforded the most pleasure and adornment to Athens, and the greatest astonishment to other men, and is the sole witness on behalf of Greece, that she does not lie in speaking of her power and her ancient wealth—this was his [Pericles'] building of public monuments; and it was this which his enemies disparaged and slandered by shouting in the assembly that the populace had lost its good reputation and was ill-spoken of as a result of hav-

---

149. The reasons for doubting Pausanias' ascription of the pediments to Paionios and Alkamenes have already been discussed (cf. p. 83). Pausanias may have confused his information about the *akroteria* with that about the pediments.
150. Modern scholars usually take this figure to represent Apollo.
151. The reference is to the metopes of the temple. These number twelve in all and were part of the frieze at the front and rear of the *cella;* six metopes belong to each frieze.
152. The chryselephantine Zeus of Pheidias.

ing appropriated for itself the common treasury of the Greeks from Delos. And that which was the most reasonable of excuses for them to him against his accusers, namely, that, in fear of the barbarians, they had taken the common funds away to a safe place to guard them, even this Pericles refused to allege. "Greece, it seems, [the opposition charged] is dealt a terrible, wanton insult and is openly tyrannized over, when she sees us using the money which was contributed under necessity for the war effort, gilding our city and embellishing it, like some pretentious woman bedecked with precious stones, with images and thousand-talent temples." Pericles, in reply, informed the people that they did not owe an accounting of the money to the allies as long as they protected them and kept off the barbarians; for the allies supplied "not a single horse, nor ship, nor soldier but only money, which belongs, not to those who give it but to those who receive it, providing that they furnish the services for which they receive it." And it was necessary, now that the city was sufficiently supplied with the necessities for war, to devote the surplus of the treasury to the construction of these monuments, from which, in the future, would come everlasting fame, and which, while in construction, would supply a ready source of welfare by requiring every sort of workmanship and producing a wide variety of needs; these in turn would call into service every art, make every hand busy, and in this way provide paid employment for almost the whole city, thus ornamenting and sustaining it at the same time. Just as military expeditions furnish those who are of the requisite age and strength with support from public funds, and wishing that the disordered mass of common workmen gain a portion of the profits and not spend their time in lazy idleness, he brought forth and proposed to the people great building projects and far-reaching artistic programs requiring an extended application of labor, so that, no less than those who were in the fleet or guarded the borders, or took part in military expeditions, the population at home would have a claim to derive benefit from and have a share in the public funds. For this undertaking the materials used were stone, bronze, ivory, ebony, and cypress-wood, and the artists who labored on them and wrought works of art were builders,[153] modellers, bronze-workers, stone-cutters, dyers, workers in gold and ivory, painters, embroiderers, and engravers; and those concerned with the organization and transport of the materials were, on the sea, the merchants, sailors, and ships' pilots, and, on land, the wagon-makers, those who bred draught animals, wagon drivers, rope makers, linen-weavers, road workers, and miners. Thus each art, just as each general has his own army under him, had its own private throng of laborers organized like an army, acting as an instrument and body of

153. "Builders"—*tektones* or what would now be called "construction workers."

public service; so, to sum the whole thing up, briefly, the opportunities for service reached every age and type, and they distributed the wealth accordingly.

(Sec. 13):   As the works rose, shining with grandeur and possessing an inimitable grace of form, and the workmen strove to surpass one another in the beauty of their workmanship, the rapidity with which they were executed was especially marvellous. For the projects, each of which they thought would require several successive generations to reach completion, were all being completed together in the prime of one man's administration. . . . [The anecdote about Agatharchos' rapidity in painting, given on p. 110, appears at this point.] For that reason the works of Pericles are even more admired—though built in a short time they have lasted for a long time. For, in its beauty, each work was, even at that time, ancient, and yet, in its perfection, each looks even at the present time as if it were fresh and newly built. Thus there is a certain bloom of newness in each work and an appearance of being untouched by the wear of time. It is as if some ever-flowering life and unaging spirit had been infused into the creation of these works.

Pheidias directed all the projects and was the overseer of everything for him [Pericles], although there were also great architects and artists employed on the works. The *hekatompedon* [154] *Parthenon* was executed by Kallikrates and Iktinos; Koroibos began the building of the *Telestērion* [155] in Eleusis, for it was he who set the columns in place on the floor and connected them with the epistyle. Upon his death, Metagenes of Xypete set in place the frieze and the upper columns. Xenokles of Cholargos roofed the opening over the *Anaktoron*.[156] The long wall,[157] which Socrates says he himself heard Pericles propose, was undertaken by Kallikrates. Kratinos makes fun of this work because it was completed so slowly:

> With words Pericles raised the wall long ago,
> But with deeds he doesn't budge it.

The *Odeion,* in its interior arrangement, consisted of many seats and columns, and in the style of its roof it was made so as to slope and descend from a single peak, an arrangement which, they say, was a reproduction of the tent of the [Persian] king; [158] Pericles had charge

154. *Hekatompedon*—100 feet in length. The term had also been applied to earlier temples on the Acropolis, presumably those on the site of the *Parthenon*.
155. *Telestērion*—the building in which the secret rites of the Eleusinian mysteries took place.
156. *Anaktoron*—the innermost shrine, within the *Telestērion*, at Eleusis.
157. The "long wall" (actually two parallel walls) ran between Athens and Peiraeus.
158. This tent was seized by the Greeks after the battle of Plataea. Cf. Herodotus, IX, 82.

of this too. And on account of this Kratinos, in his play *The Thracian Women,* once again made fun of him:

> This Zeus with the pointed head comes forth,
> Pericles, with the *Odeion* on his head,
> Since the time for ostracism has passed.

Again eager for honor Pericles had a resolution passed establishing a musical contest in the Panathenaic festival and he himself, having been selected as a judge, arranged how the competitors should play the flute and sing and play the *kithara.* And it was in the *Odeion* that they used to view the musical contests, both at that time and at other times.

The *Propylaia* of the Acropolis were built over a five-year period with Mnesikles as the architect. A remarkable occurrence took place during the building which indicated that the goddess was not standing aloof but that she was involved in the work and was helping to bring it to completion. The most able and eager man among the workmen slipped and fell from the height and lay there in very poor condition, given up for dead by the doctors. When Pericles was very despondent about this, the goddess appearing to him in a dream, prescribed a course of therapy, by which, when Pericles applied it, he quickly and easily cured the man. As a result of this he set up a bronze image of Athena *Hygeia* on the Acropolis, near the altar which they say was once there.

Vitruvius differs from Plutarch in maintaining that Iktinos was the architect of the Telestērion *at Eleusis.*

Vitruvius VII, praef. 16: At Eleusis Iktinos roofed over the sanctuary of Demeter and Kore, a room of immense size, in the Doric order with exterior columns so as to have an increased space for use in sacrifices.

A sizable number of inscriptions has been found which record the allocations of funds and expenses for the Periclean building program. Many of the inscriptions are worn or fragmentary; hence their readings are in some cases controversial, and they remain very much the province of the specialist. Notable among them are: (a) the accounts for Pheidias' Athena Parthenos *(I.G. I,^{2} 354-362); (b) the financial decrees proposed by Kallias in 434* B.C. *(I.G. I,^{2} 91, 92) which deal with the allocation of funds for various projects; (c) the inventory of the treasuries of the Parthenon from c. 434-406* B.C. *(I.G. I,^{2} 276-292, which refer to the westerly room in the* cella, *the room actually called the* Parthenon, *and I.G. I,^{2} 256-275, which refer to the main room in the* cella); (d) *the building accounts of the* Parthenon *(I.G. I,^{2} 339-353) dating from 447* B.C. *to 432* B.C. *(and thus dating the building period of the temple);*

(e) the building accounts of the Propylaia *(I.G. I,² 363-367) dating from 437-432* B.C.*; (f) the decrees authorizing the building (448* B.C.*) of and noting the inauguration (420* B.C.*) of the temple of Athena Nike Apteros (I.G. I,² 24, 25 and I.G. I,² 88-89); and, (g) the most extensive of all, the building accounts of the* Erechtheion, *the last of the great buildings in the program, dating c. 421-406* B.C. *(I.G. I,² 372-374).*[159]

Most of the inscriptions make interesting reading only to the initiated epigrapher, but since they are among the few "contemporary references" to the art of the Classical period, a few characteristic examples are given here.

I.G. I,² 24 (specifications for the sanctuary and temple of Athena Nike on the Acropolis in Athens; the improved text given by M. Tod, *Greek Historical Inscriptions,* 2nd ed. [Oxford: 1946], no. 40, has been used as the basis for this translation): It was decreed by the Council of the People . . . Glaukos made the proposal: that, for Athena Nike, a priestess, who shall hold the office for life, shall be appointed from among all the Athenians and that the sanctuary should be furnished with doors according to the specifications which Kallikrates draws up; that the controllers of state revenue shall arrange the contracts in the prytany of the tribe of Leontis; that the priestess shall get 50 drachmas [annually], and also the legs and the hides from the public sacrifices; that a temple should be built according to the specifications which Kallikrates draws up, and also a stone altar.

Hestiaios proposed: that three men be chosen from the Council; and that these, having drawn up the specifications with Kallikrates, shall inform the Council as to how the contracts have been made. . . .

I.G. I,² 352, lines 27-43, from the building accounts of the *Parthenon* (434-433 B.C.; text partly restored):

EXPENSES

. . . [numbers missing] 200 . . .
. . . 2 drachmas, 1 obol . . . . . . purchases
. . .

WAGES

. . .

20,000 [plus ?] drcahmas, 2 obols	. . . . to those who quarried the stones in Pentele and loaded them on the wheeled vehicles
16,392 drachmas	to the sculptors for the pedimental sculptures
1,800	to those hired by the month

159. For the interpretation of the information contained in these inscriptions, the reader is referred to the articles of W. B. Dinsmoor, *A.J.A.* XVII (1913), pp. 53-80, 242-265, 371-398.

[...] drachmas ....left over from this year
70 ....gold Lampsakene staters
27 ⅙ ....gold Kyzikene staters

I.G. I,² 372-374, lines 1 ff, excerpts from a report of 409/8 B.C. on the condition of the *Erechtheion*: [160]

The commissioners for the temple in which the ancient image is kept —Brysonides of Kephisia, Chariades of Argyle, Dionides of Kephisia, the architect Philokles of Acharnai, the secretary Etearchos of Kydathenaion— recorded the works on the temple as they found them, according to the decree of the populace proposed by Epigenes, both fully finished and partially worked, in the archonship of Diokles, in the first Prytany of the tribe of Kekropis, in the session of the Council in which Nikophanes of Marathon was the first secretary:
    The following parts of the temple were found partially worked.
    In the corner toward the *Kekropion:*

4	Plinths, not set in place, four feet long, two feet wide, one and one-half feet thick
	...
(lines 29 ff)	One column capital for the open space in the interior [three] feet long, one and one-half feet wide, one and one-half feet thick
5	Epistyle blocks not in place, eight feet long, two feet wide, and two feet thick
	...
(lines 40 ff)	All the rest of the work all around the perimeter begins with the Eleusinian stone [161] to which the figures [are to be attached], three blocks have been put in place by this commission
	...
(line 83)	On the porch toward the *Kekropion* it is necessary to do the relief carving on three ceiling blocks over the maidens,[162] thirteen feet long, five feet wide, five feet thick. The rosettes on the epistyle need to be carved
	...

I.G. I,² 373 (Expenses for the *Erechtheion,* 409/8 B.C.):

(line 5)	.. For setting in place blocks six feet long, two feet high, and one foot in thickness, to

160. For the complete text of the *Erechtheion* inscriptions with translation and commentary see G. P. Stevens, L. D. Caskey, H. N. Fowler, and J. M. Paton, *The Erechtheum* (Cambridge, Mass.: 1927), pp. 277-422.
161. The Ionic frieze of the *Erechtheion* was made of dark Eleusinian limestone.
162. The "maidens" are the caryatids of the south porch of the *Erechtheion.* Cf. Lawrence, *Greek Architecture,* pls. 68, 71.

Simon living in Argyle, for five blocks: 37 drachmas, 3 obols. For putting in place one block, two feet high, one foot thick, two feet long, to Simon living in Argyle: 2 drachmas, 3 obols . . .

. . .

(line 245)

To the workmen the fees agreed upon and day labor. For laying tile above the ceiling on the roof to Kteson of Lakiadai: 24 drachmas. For putting in place the rafters and the cross pieces each day, to Gerys: six days, 6 drachmas

. . .

(line 251)

For setting in place the intercolumnar partitions facing the *Pandroseion,* to Komon living in Melite: 40 drachmas. For turning the bosses for the coffer-lids, to Mikon, living in Kollytos: 3 drachmas, 1 obol. To the sawyer for sawing a beam into coffer-lids, to Rhadios, living in Kollytos: 5 drachmas

. . .

I.G. I,² 374 (408/7-407/6 B.C.), further expenses on the *Erechtheion:*

(line 74)

For erecting scaffolding for the painters in encaustic, in the interior, below the ceiling, to Manis living in Kollytos: 1 drachma, 3 obols

. . .

(line 95)

To the painters in encaustic, for painting the cymatium on the inner face of the epistyle, at five obols per foot, the contractor being Dionysiodoros living in Melite, the surety being Herakleides of Oa: 30 drachmas. The sum total to the painters in encaustic: 30 drachmas. To the gilders, for gilding the bronze rosettes, we give the sum owed from the previous prytany. . . .

(line 109)

To the architect Archilochos of Argyle: 37 drachmas

The next section records expenses paid to certain sculptors for the marble reliefs which were attached to the dark limestone frieze of the Erechtheion.

(lines 161 ff)

. . .the man holding the spear 60 drachmas. Phyromachos of Kephisia for the young man with the breastplate: 60 drachmas. Praxias living in Melite, for the horse and the man who is visible behind it and who strikes

its flank: 120 drachmas. Antiphanes from
Kerameis, the chariot, the young man, and
the horse being harnessed: 240 drachmas.
Mynnion living in Argyle, the horse and
the man striking it and the stele which he
added later: 127 drachmas. Sosklos living in
Alopeke, the man holding the bridle: 60
drachmas. Hiasos of Kollytos, the woman
and the small girl pressed against her: 80
drachmas. Total sum for the making of the
images: 3,315 drachmas.

Iktinos and the Temple of Apollo at Bassai

Pausanias VIII, 41, 7-9: On it [Mt. Kotilios in Arcadia] is the place
called Bassai and the temple of Apollo *Epikourios;* both it and the roof
are of stone. Of all the temples in the Peloponnesos, this one might be
looked upon, after the one in Tegea,[163] as the most admirable for the
beauty of its stone and on account of its harmony. This name was given
to Apollo for having given aid during a plague, just as he received
the name "Averter of Evil" from the Athenians for having turned the
plague away from them too. It was during the war between the Peloponnesians and Athenians [164] that he also stayed the plague for the Phigalians, and not at any other time. The points of evidence for this are that
both the surnames for Apollo have about the same meaning and that
Iktinos who was the architect of the temple in Phigalia, was a contemporary of Pericles and built the temple called the *Parthenon* for the
Athenians.

The Origin of the Corinthian Order

Vitruvius begins the fourth book of the De Architectura *by discussing the origins of the orders of Greek architecture. His sections on
the Doric and Ionic orders are fanciful, mythological interpretations,
but his treatment of the Corinthian order, which follows, may have a
kernel of truth in it.*

Vitruvius IV, 1, 8-10: The third order, however, which is called the
"Corinthian," is an imitation of the slenderness of a maiden, because
maidens, on account of the tenderness of their age, are represented as

---

163. On the Tegea temple, built by Skopas, see pp. 141-142.
164. The plague occurred in 430-429 B.C. Cf. Thucydides, II, 47 ff. Dinsmoor,
however, dates the colonnade of the temple to around 450 B.C.; on the other hand,
some of the interior details and the sculpture should perhaps be dated toward the
end of the century. Cf. W. B. Dinsmoor, *The Architecture of Ancient Greece,*[3] (London and New York: 1950), pp. 154-159.

slighter in build and allow more beautiful effects in ornamentation. Now the invention of that capital is recorded to have happened as follows. A maiden who was a citizen of Corinth and already old enough for marriage was attacked by a disease and died. After her funeral, her nurse collected the goblets in which the maiden had taken delight while she was alive, and, having put them together in a basket, she took them to the grave monument and put them on top of it. In order that they should remain in place for a long time, she covered them with a tile. Now it happened that this basket was placed over the root of an acanthus. As time went on the acanthus root, pressed down in the middle by the weight, sent forth, when it was about springtime, leaves and stalks; its stalks growing up along the sides of the basket and being pressed out from the angles because of the weight of the tile, were forced to form volute-like curves at their extremities. At this point Kallimachos, who, because of his elegance and subtlety in the art of working marble, was given the name *Katatechnos*[165] by the Athenians, happened to be going by and noticed the basket with this gentle growth of leaves around it. Delighted with the order and the novelty of this form, he made columns using this as his model and established a canon of proportions[166] for it. From that he distributed the proportions of the Corinthian orders throughout the details of the work.

THE MINOR ARTS

Myron, Pheidias, and Mentor

In the Roman period certain famous works of silver plate and the like were claimed to be by Myron, Pheidias, and other famous Greek sculptors. The most colorful references to such works occur in the Epigrams *of Martial.*

Martial, IV, 39:

> You have collected all types of silverware.
> Only you have ancient works by Myron;
> Only you have the handiwork of Praxiteles and Skopas;
> Only you have works chased by the graver of Pheidias;
> Only you possess the labors of Mentor;
> Nor are there lacking to you real works of Grattius,
> Nor works which are lined with Callaician gold,
> Nor relief sculpture from ancient tables.
> I marvel, however, that in all this chased silver,
> You, Charinus, have nothing which is chaste.

165. On Kallimachos and his title, see p. 86, note 85.
166. "Established a canon of proportions"—*symmetriasque constituit.*

Martial, VI, 92:

> Since a serpent is engraved on your cup,
> Ammianus, a work of art by Myron,
> You drink Vatican wine; that is, you drink venom.[167]

Pheidias' reputation as an engraver and jeweler is also supported by an observation by the Emperor Julian the Apostate.

Julian, *Epistola* 67 (377 A, B): The wise Pheidias was known not only for his statues in Olympia and in Athens, but also for having condensed a work of great art in a small gem, as they say he did with his grasshopper and a bee, and if you please, with a fly. And each of these, though its nature was of bronze, came to life through his art.

Mentor, who is mentioned in the first of the epigrams of Martial given above, was perhaps the most famous silversmith of the ancient world.[168] His exact date is not known, but he was probably active in the fifth century B.C.; *it is at least certain that he was active before 356* B.C., *when, according to Pliny (see Chapter 6, p. 233) some of his works were destroyed in the fire that consumed the* Artemision *at Ephesos.*

Cicero, *Verrine*, II, IV, 18, 38: Diodorus of Malta . . . has lived in Lilybaeum now for many years, . . . in connection with him Verres was told that he [Diodorus] had an excellent collection of engraved art objects, among them some cups, of the kind called *Thērikleia*,[169] works made by Mentor with the utmost skill of hand. When this man [Verres] heard about them, he was so inflamed with cupidity not only to inspect them but indeed to carry them off, that he summoned Diodorus to him and demanded them.

Pliny, *N.H.* XXXIII, 147: The orator Lucius Crassus has two cups [*skyphoi*] chased by the hand of the artist Mentor and costing 100,000 sesterces;[170] it is admitted, however, that, out of a sense of shame, he never dared to use them.

Lucian, *Lexiphanes*, 7, also uses the adjective *mentourgēs* in connection with some cups, about which a scholiast[171] observes: *Mentourgēs* is de-

---

167. The wine of the Vatican region of Rome was apparently of a very low order. An ironic contrast between the expensive cup and the cheap wine is intended.

168. For other references to Mentor by Martial and other Roman poets, see the references in Overbeck, *Schriftquellen*, nos. 2173-2181.

169. *Thērikleia*—a certain type of cup, named after the Corinthian potter Therikles, who invented it.

170. The reading of the number is not certain.

171. Cf. Overbeck, *Schriftquellen*, no. 2172.

rived from a certain glass worker named Mentor who made use of cups with this form: they were equipped with a large handle which ran down to the base, for which reason he [Lucian] calls them "easy to grasp."

On Mys, another famous toreutēs *(engraver, chaser, and the like) of the fifth century* B.C., *see p. 74 (the Athena* Promachos *of Pheidias) and p. 233.*

4

The
Fourth
Century

During the period from the end of the Peloponnesian War (404 B.C.) to the death of Alexander the Great (323 B.C.), Greek art did not move into any radically new paths, but a definite change of emphasis away from ambitious political and religious idealism toward a more private, personal type of art becomes apparent. Especially characteristic of the period is a new concern for the personal emotions of the individual both as a subject for art (see under Parrhasios, pp. 160-161) and as a guide for the artist (see Apelles' concept of charis, p. 164).

This chapter essentially includes artists and works which can be associated with the period up to and including the time of Alexander. However, works produced by artists who were contemporaries of Alexander but who survived him are also included in this chapter.

SCULPTURE

Kephisodotos of Athens

Pliny (N.H. *XXXIV, 50*) dates Kephisodotos in the 102nd Olympiad (372 B.C.).

Pliny, N.H. XXXIV, 87: There were two sculptors named Kephisodotos. By the first there is a Hermes nursing the infant Dionysos; he also made a man declaiming in public with his hand upraised—whom it represents is not certain; the subsequent Kephisodotos did some philosophers.[1]

Pausanias IX, 16, 2 (at Thebes): . . . there is a sanctuary of Tyche [Fortune]. She [the statue of Tyche] carries the child Ploutos [Wealth]. The Thebans say that the hands and the face of the image were done by Xenophon and the rest by Kallistonikos, a local man. It was a clever design on the part of these artists—that is, putting Ploutos in the hands of Tyche as if she were his mother or nurse; but no less clever was the design of Kephisodotos. For he made the image for the Athenians of Eirene [Peace] holding Ploutos.[2]

Pliny, N.H. XXXIV, 74: Kephisodotos made the marvellous Athena in the port of Athens [Peiraeus] and an altar for the temple of Zeus the

1. The Elder Kephisodotos was the father of Praxiteles; the later one was Praxiteles' son.
2. According to Pausanias I, 8, 2, this figure stood on the Areopagos in Athens. Roman copies of it are preserved in Munich and New York. Cf. Richter, *Sculpture and Sculptors*,[2] Figs. 659, 660; for the representations of it on the coins of several cities, cf. Lacroix, *Reproductions*, pl. XXVI, no. 8-10. The cult of Eirene was officially introduced into Athens in 375 B.C. (cf. Cornelios Nepos, *Timotheus*, 2, 2) which provides an approximate date for the statue.

Savior in the same harbor, a work with which few may be compared.[3]

Pausanias VIII, 30, 10:   Quite near the stoa [of Aristander in Megalopolis] in the direction from which the sun rises is a sanctuary of Zeus surnamed the Savior. It is ornamented with columns placed all around it. Next to Zeus, who is seated on a throne stands, on the right, "Megalopolis" and, on the left, is an image of Artemis the Savior. These are of Pentelic marble and the Athenians Kephisodotos and Xenophon made them.

For the statue of the Muses on Mt. Helikon by Kephisodotos see p. 84.

Praxiteles

Pliny (N.H. XXXIV, 50) dates Praxiteles in the 104th Olympiad (364 B.C.).

Pliny, N.H. XXXVI, 20:   I have mentioned the date of Praxiteles in my discussion of the sculptors who worked in bronze; yet it was in his fame as a worker of marble that he surpassed even himself. There are works by him in Athens in the *Kerameikos.* But superior to all the works, not only of Praxiteles, but indeed in the whole world, is the Aphrodite which many people have sailed to Knidos in order to see. He made two statues and offered them for sale at the same time; one of them was represented with the body draped, for which reason the people of Kos, whose choice it was (since he had put the same price on both) preferred it, judging that this was the sober and proper thing to do. The people of Knidos bought the rejected one, the fame of which became immensely greater. Later King Nikomedes[4] wished to buy it from the Knidians, promising that he would cancel the city's whole debt, which was enormous. They preferred, however, to bear everything, and not without reason. For with that statue Praxiteles made Knidos famous. Its [that statue's] shrine is completely open, so that it is possible to observe the image of the goddess from every side; she herself, it is believed, favored its being made that way. Nor is one's admiration of the statue less from any side. They say that a certain man was once overcome with love for the statue and, after he had hidden himself [in the shrine] during the nighttime, embraced the statue and that there is a stain on it as an indication of his lust. There are other statues in Knidos by illustrious artists, a Dionysos by Bryaxis and another Dionysos

3. Perhaps the same as the statues of Zeus and Athena in Peiraeus mentioned by Pausanias I, 3, 3.
4. Nikomedes III of Bithynia who ruled from 90 to 74 B.C.

and an Athena by Skopas; and there is no greater testimonial to the quality of Praxiteles' Aphrodite than the fact that, among all these works, it alone receives mention. By him [Praxiteles] also there is an Eros [Cupid], which Cicero used in his charges against Verres, and for the sake of which people used to visit Thespiai; it is now placed in the lecture rooms of Octavia.[5] There is another Eros by him, this one nude, in Parium,[6] the colony on the Propontis, which is equal to the Aphrodite at Knidos both for its fame and for the injury which it suffered; for Alketas the Rhodian fell in love with it and also left upon it the same sort of trace of his love. At Rome, the works of Praxiteles are a Flora, a Triptolemos, and a Demeter in the gardens of Servilius, a "Success" and "Good Fortune"[7] on the Capitoline, and also Maenads, which they called Thyiads, and Caryatids, Sileni, which are among the monuments belonging to Asinius Pollio,[8] and an Apollo and a Poseidon.

Pliny, *N.H.* XXXIV, 69-70: Praxiteles, who was more successful in marble [sculpture] and hence was more famous [in that medium] also made, however, very beautiful works in bronze: the Rape of Persephone, a *Katagousa*,[9] and a Dionysos with a figure of "Drunkenness" and the famous Satyr to which the Greeks attach the surname *periboëtos* ["the much talked of" or "the notorious"]; also the statues [10] which were once in front of the temple of "Felicitas" along with an Aphrodite and which were consumed in the fire which destroyed that temple during the principate of Claudius; the latter work was equal to her sister statue in marble which is famed all over the world [that is, the Aphrodite of Knidos]; also a woman bestowing a garland, a woman putting on an armlet, "Autumn,"[11] . . .[12] He also made a young Apollo who, close at

5. These were part of a large complex of buildings dedicated by Augustus to his sister Octavia. They consisted of a series of porticoes surrounding temples of Jupiter *Stator* and Juno *Regina*, a library and *curia* (hall for political assemblies), and the *scholae* mentioned here, which were rooms for philosophical disputation, lectures, and artistic exhibitions.

6. Represented on the coins of Parion of the Roman Imperial period, cf. Lacroix, *Reproductions*, pl. XXVIII, 1-4.

7. "Success"—Latin *Bonus Eventus*, probably Greek *Agathos Daimōn;* "Good Fortune"—Latin *Bona Fortuna*, Greek *Agathē Tychē*.

8. Gaius Asinius Pollio, 76 B.C.-5 A.D., a wealthy Roman politician, writer, literary critic, and patron of the arts.

9. Meaning either "a woman spinning thread" or possibly a reference to a figure who is "bringing home" Persephone from the underworld. The Greek admits both meanings, but the first alternative seems more likely.

10. The statues are apparently the "Thespiades," probably a group representing the Muses referred to by Pliny, *N.H.* XXXVI, 39, and by Cicero, *Verrine* II, IV, 2, 4.

11. Only one manuscript reads *Oporan*, "Autumn." The earliest edition of Pliny printed *oenophoram*, "wine bearer." Urlichs suggested *Canephoram*, "basketbearer."

12. At this point Pliny ascribes to Praxiteles the Tyrannicides group which was carried off by Xerxes. His information is clearly erroneous; see p. 33.

hand, is lying in wait with an arrow for a lizard which is creeping up, for which reason they call him the *Sauroktonos*.[13] Also well-regarded are two of his statues which express diverse emotions, his "Matron Weeping" and his "Courtesan Smiling." This last they believe to have been Phryne [Praxiteles' mistress], and they detect in it the love of the artist and the reward revealed in the face of the courtesan. There is also a statue which reveals his kindly nature. For he placed a charioteer made by himself in a quadriga made by Kalamis, lest the latter, who was better at representing horses, should be thought to have failed in representing men.

Of the many works of Praxiteles mentioned by Pliny in the preceding passages, the Aphrodite of Knidos was quite clearly the most famous. A number of copies of it exist,[14] but the effect of the original is perhaps more truly reflected in the following passages.

Lucian, *Imagines*, 6 (once again selecting features for the "Panthea"): LYKIOS: And now he will make it possible for you to see the statue coming into being as he fits it together, taking only the head from the Knidian [Aphrodite]. For he will not want to use the rest of the body since it is nude. But the area around the hair and the forehead and also the neat line of the eyebrows he shall let her have just as Praxiteles made them; likewise the dewy quality of the eyes with their joyous radiance and welcoming look, this too he shall preserve just as Praxiteles conceived it . . . and as to how old she should be, let the measure of this follow exactly that of the goddess in Knidos. Yes, this too shall be measured according to Praxiteles' standard.

Lucian, *Amores*, 13-14: When we had taken sufficient delight in the garden plants, we passed on into the temple. The goddess is set there in the middle of it—an exceedingly beautiful work of Parian marble— with a look of proud contempt and a slight smile which just reveals her teeth. The full extent of her beauty is unhidden by any clinging raiment for her nudity is complete except insofar as she holds one hand in front of her to hide her modesty. So strongly has the artist's art prevailed, that the recalcitrant and solid nature of the stone has become adapted to each limb. . . . The temple has two entrances, [the second being] for those who wish to see the goddess directly from the back, in order that nothing about the goddess should fail to be mar-

---

13. *Sauroktonos*—"Lizard Slayer." Roman copies in bronze and marble and also on coins exist. Cf. Richter, *Sculpture and Sculptors*,[2] Figs. 673-676.

14. Cf. Richter, *Sculpture and Sculptors*,[2] Figs. 668-672; see also the standard monograph on Praxiteles: G. E. Rizzo, *Prassitele* (Milan-Rome, 1932), pls. LXX-LXXXV.

velled at. . . . (Sec. 14) To see the goddess in her entire splendor, we went around to the back. As the doors were opened by the woman who was entrusted with the keys unforeseen amazement at the goddess' beauty seized us. . . .

The Aphrodite of Knidos is also the subject of a number of poems in the Greek Anthology. *The following is a typical example.*

Anth. Graec. I, 104, 9 (Planud. IV, 160) by a poet named Plato:

> Paphian Cythera came through the sea to Knidos
>   Wishing to see her own image.
> Having gazed from every angle in that conspicuous space
>   She cried: "Where did Praxiteles see me naked?"
> Praxiteles did not see what was unlawful, but the iron
>   Carved the Paphian just as Ares would have wanted her.

Athenaeus XIII, 590: [Phryne, Praxiteles' mistress] in the festival of the Eleusinians and in the festival of Poseidon took off her robes in view of all the Greeks, unbound her hair and went into the sea. It was with her as a model that Apelles [15] painted his Aphrodite *Anadyomenē* [rising from the sea]. And Praxiteles the sculptor, falling in love with her, made his Knidian Aphrodite with her as the model.

Phryne, Praxiteles' notorious mistress, so fascinated him that he set up a gold statue of her at Delphi.

Athenaeus XIII, 591 B: The local people had a gold statue made of this Phryne and set it up in Delphi on a column of Pentelic marble. Of this statue Krates the Cynic said, when he saw it, that it was an offering of the incontinence of the Greeks. The portrait stood between those of Archidamas the king of the Lakedaimonians and Philip, the son of Amyntas, and bore the inscription: "Phryne the Thespian, daughter of Epikles." . . .

Phryne is also reputed to have forced Praxiteles into a definitive judgment on his own work.

Pausanias I, 20, 1 (in Athens): There is a road leading from the *Prytaneion* which is called [the street of the] "Tripods." They give the place that name because there are temples just big enough for this purpose [that is, of holding tripods], and in them stand tripods, made of bronze; they also contain works of art which are especially worth

15. On Appeles see p. 166.

noting. For there is a Satyr there of which Praxiteles is said to have been very proud. And when Phryne once asked him for whichever of his works was the most beautiful, they say that he agreed, as a lover would, to give it to her but that he could not bring himself to confess which work appeared most beautiful to him. Consequently a slave of Phryne's came running to Praxiteles and told him that the greater part of his work had been ruined when a fire broke out at the workshop, but that not all his work had been destroyed. Praxiteles immediately began to rush through the door and said that there would be no satisfaction from all his work, if the flame had caught his Satyr or his Eros. But Phryne told him to remain and to cheer up, for he had suffered nothing grievous, but by a ruse she had trapped him and forced him to admit which of his works were the most beautiful. So it was that Phryne chose the Eros. In the temple of Dionysos nearby there is a Satyr, a boy who holds out a drinking cup.[16]

Tradition held that Phryne dedicated the Eros which she had been given in the sanctuary of Eros at Thespiai in Boeotia.

Pausanias IX, 27, 3-5 (at Thespiai): Lysippos later made an Eros in bronze for the Thespians, and prior to that Praxiteles had made one of Pentelic marble. As to the events concerning Phryne and the trick played by this woman on Praxiteles, I have already presented them in another place. They say it was Gaius [Caligula] who, when he became emperor, first moved the image of Eros to Rome; it is said that Claudius had it sent back to the Thespians and that Nero had it dragged back to Rome a second time. There a fire finally destroyed it. . . . The statue of Eros which exists in Thespiai in our own time was made by the Athenian Menodoros, copying the work of Praxiteles. There is also an Aphrodite and a portrait of Phryne by Praxiteles himself; both Phryne and the goddess are of stone.

Strabo, IX, 410: The Thespians formerly were famous for the Eros of Praxiteles, which he himself carved, and the courtesan Glykera [17] set up in Thespiai; she was a native of that place by birth and received the statue from the artist as a gift. Therefore, some people formerly

16. It is not clear whether Pausanias is referring to Praxiteles' Satyr in the last sentence or simply to another work in the area of the street of the tripods. A series of Roman copies representing a satyr pouring wine is frequently connected with a Praxitelean original; cf. Rizzo, *op. cit.,* Figs. XIX-XXVI; Richter, *Sculpture and Sculptors,*2 Figs. 682-684. Another well-known type representing a satyr relaxing against a tree stump is also associated with Praxiteles and seems more typical of his style. Cf. Rizzo, *op. cit.,* pls. XLVIII-LV; Richter, *op. cit.,* Fig. 51.

17. Glykera is presumably the same as Phryne.

used to go up to Thespiai in order to see the Eros, there being other-wise not much worth seeing. . . .

Athenaeus XIII, 591A: And on the base of the Eros beneath the stage building of the theatre he [Praxiteles] wrote:

> Praxiteles rendered precisely the love which he suffered,
> Drawing the archetype from his own heart.
> Phryne received me as a gift; love philtres no longer
> Do I shoot with any bow, but love is stirred by looking at me.

Many other less well-known figures of gods and goddesses by Praxiteles were seen by Pausanias in his travels. The passages which follow describe works for which there is some sort of corroborating archaeological evidence.

Pausanias VIII, 9, 1 (in Mantineia):   The Mantineians have a two-part temple which is divided right down the middle by a wall. In one sec-tion of the temple there is an image of Asklepios, the work of Alkamenes; in the other there is a sanctuary of Leto and her children. Praxiteles made the images in the third generation after Alkamenes. On the base of these figures are [reliefs of] the Muses and Marsyas playing the flute.[18]

Pausanias I, 44, 2 (at Megara):   Going from the Agora on the road which is called "the Straight" there is on the right a sanctuary of Apollo called *Prostaterios* ["Standing before the doors" or "Protecting"]. This is found by turning just a little away from the road. In it there is an Apollo which is worth seeing, an Artemis, a Leto, and other images; the Leto and her children were made by Praxiteles.[19]

Pausanias II, 21, 8-9 (in Argos):   The sanctuary of Leto is not far from the trophy, and the image is the work of Praxiteles. The figure of the maiden who is next to the goddess they call Chloris, saying that she was a daughter of Niobe, and that she was originally called Meli-boia.[20]

Pausanias X, 37, 1 (at Antikyra in Phokis):   On the right about two stades from the city itself, there is a high rock—the rock is a spur of the mountains—and on it a sanctuary of Artemis has been established. The

18. This base still exists and is now in the National Museum in Athens; cf. Richter, *Sculpture and Sculptors,*[2] Figs. 679-681; Rizzo, *op. cit.,* pls. CXXX-CXXXII.
19. The group is represented on Roman coins from the time of Commodus and Septimius Severus; cf. Lacroix, *Reproductions,* pl. XXVII, 1. Rizzo identified it with a marble figure of Artemis (a Roman copy) in Dresden, cf. *op. cit.,* pls. XVI-XVIII.
20. These images are represented on Argive coinage of the Roman Imperial period, cf. Lacroix, *Reproductions,* pl. XXVII, 2-4.

statue, which is one of the works of Praxiteles, holds a torch in the right hand and has a quiver over the shoulders. By her on the left is a dog. In size the image is taller than the tallest woman.[21]

Pausanias V, 17, 3 (at Olympia):   . . . at a later time still other works were set up in the Heraion, among them a Hermes of stone, who carries the infant Dionysos, the work of Praxiteles. . . .[22]

Pausanias, I, 2, 4, mentions a group in Athens representing Demeter, Persephone, and Iacchos. This work had an inscription in Attic letters, which went out of use in Athens in 403 B.C. *Therefore, some would ascribe the statues to an Elder Praxiteles. The inscription seen by Pausanias might, however, have been (as Frazer, Stuart Jones, and others have pointed out) a Hadrianic restoration which was intentionally carved in the old-fashioned manner.*

Pausanias (IX, 11, 6) also ascribes the pedimental sculptures of the temple of Herakles at Thebes to Praxiteles. Here again it is possible that we deal with an Elder Praxiteles, since such a commission would be unique among the works of the younger sculptor.

Demetrios of Alopeke (in Attica)

Although our information about Demetrios is limited to a few brief references, and no known Roman copy of any of his works exists, he must have been one of the most distinctive of the fourth century sculptors. In the late Hellenistic canon of sculptors preserved by Quintilian (see Chapter 6, p. 221) he is classified as the arch-realist of Greek sculpture, and ranks with Praxiteles and Lysippos as one of the three most important artists of the fourth century.[23]

Pliny, N.H. XXXIV, 76:   . . . Demetrios made a statue of Lysimache,[24] who was a priestess of Athena for sixty-four years, and also an Athena,

21. A figure fitting this description is found on the coins of Antikyra, cf. Richter, *Sculpture and Sculptors*,[2] Fig. 677. Rizzo, however, doubts that this Artemis was actually a work of Praxiteles; cf. *op. cit.,* p. 13.

22. This is the famous Hermes of Praxiteles which was found in the *Heraion* by the German excavators at Olympia in 1877. Cf. Lullies, Hirmer, *Greek Sculpture,* pls. 220-223.

23. On the probable style and influence of Demetrios, see Picard, *Manuel* III, 1, pp. 125-145. Four signed bases from statues by Demetrios are known: *I.G.*, II,[2] 3828, 4321, 4322, and 2895. These appear to date from the early fourth century. Demetrios' career may have begun even in the late fifth century.

24. D. M. Lewis has suggested that this Lysimache was the inspiration for Aristophanes' *Lysistrata* (produced in 411 B.C.). Cf. *Annual of the British School at Athens,* L, 1955, pp. 1 ff. If true, the association would suggest a date for Demetrios early in the fourth century.

which is called "the Musical" [25]—the serpents on its Gorgon echo with a tinkling sound at the stroke of a *kithara*. He also made a statue of the cavalryman Simon, who wrote the first treatise on horsemanship.

Lucian, *Philopseudes*, 18: "Did you not notice," he said, "upon coming into the courtyard the beautiful statue standing there, a work of Demetrios *Anthropopoios* ['Maker of Men']?" "Surely you don't mean the one throwing the discus?" I said. . . . "Not that one," he said, "since that is one of the works of Myron, the *Diskobolos*, of which you speak. Nor do I mean the one next to it, the one binding his head with a fillet, a beautiful statue, for this is a work of Polykleitos. . . . Perhaps you saw a certain figure which was beside the running water, the one with a pot-belly, a bald head, half exposed by the hang of his garment, with some of the hairs of his beard blown by the wind, and with his veins showing clearly, just like the man himself—that is the one I mean; it is reputed to be Pellichos the Corinthian general."

Leochares of Athens

For Leochares' work on the Mausoleum at Halikarnassos, cf. p. 183.

Pliny, *N.H.* XXXIV, 79: Leochares made an eagle [26] which is aware of just what it is abducting in Ganymede and for whom it carries him, and therefore refrains from injuring the boy with its claws, even through his clothing; [he also made] an Autolykos who was a victor in the *Pankration,* in honor of whom Xenophon wrote his *Symposium,* and the Zeus the Thunderer, praised before all others, on the Capitoline; also an Apollo wearing a diadem, and Lykiskos,[27] the slave dealer, and a boy who is endowed with a crafty and deceitful servility.

Pausanias V, 20, 9 (at Olympia): Within the *Altis* is a *Metroön* and a round building called the *Philippeion*. On the peak of the roof of the Philippeion is a bronze poppy, which serves as a binding point for the beams. . . . The building is made of burnt brick, and is circled by columns. It was made by Philip after the fall of Greece at Chaironeia (338 B.C.). There stand statues of Philip and Alexander, and with them

25. *Musica* is the reading of the poorer manuscripts. Another suggested reading is *mycetica*, "bellowing."

26. The Zeus and Ganymede, also mentioned by Tatian, *Adv. Graecos*, 56, is perhaps reflected in a small Roman copy in the Vatican; cf. Richter, *Sculpture and Sculptors,*2 Fig. 737. The Apollo mentioned by Pliny is sometimes associated with the famous "Apollo Belvedere" in the Vatican; cf. Richter, *op. cit.*, Fig. 736.

27. It is not clear from the text whether this Lykiskos is a work of Leochares or the name of another sculptor.

Amyntas the father of Philip. These works are by Leochares and are of ivory and gold, as are the portraits of Olympias and Eurydike.

Vitruvius II, 8, 11 (at Halikarnassos):   At the highest point of the citadel there is, in the middle, a sanctuary of Ares which has a colossal statue, which is "acrolithic," [28] by the hand of the noted artist Leochares. At least some think that this statue is by Leochares; others think it is by Timotheos.

Plutarch, *Lives of Ten Orators, Isocrates*, 27:   There is a bronze portrait of him [Isocrates] set up in Eleusis before the first colonnade, dedicated by Timotheos the son of Konon, which bears the inscription: "Timotheos for the sake of friendship, and respecting hospitality, set up this portrait of Isocrates to the goddesses. A work of Leochares."

Pseudo-Plato, *Epistle XIII*, 361 A (a letter purporting to be from Plato to Dionysios II of Syracuse):   Concerning the things about which you wrote asking me to send you, I bought the Apollo, and Leptines is bringing it to you; it is by a young and noble artist named Leochares; there was another work there by him which was very elegant, I thought. Therefore I bought it with the intention of giving it to your wife. . . .

Other works by Leochares included: A Zeus and Demos in Peiraeus (Pausanias I, 1, 3); A Zeus on the Acropolis in Athens (Pausanias I, 24, 4); An Apollo near the temple of Apollo Patroös in Athens (Pausanias I, 3, 4); see also Loewy, Inschriften, 77-83, for the signed statue bases by Leochares.

Bryaxis

Bryaxis was also one of the sculptors who worked on the Mausoleum at Halikarnassos (cf. p. 183).

Pliny, *N.H.* XXXIV, 73:   Bryaxis made an Asklepios [29] and a Seleukos.[30]

Pliny, *N.H.* XXXIV, 42 (in Rhodes):   "There are other colossal statues in the same city, one hundred in number, smaller than this one [the colossus of Rhodes, see p. 198], but each one of which, had it stood alone somewhere, would have made that place famous; and besides these there were five [colossal statues] of gods, which Bryaxis made.

---

28. *Acrolithic*—having the face and the extremities done in marble. Cf. p. 75.
29. Pliny probably refers to the Asklepios (with Hygieia) by Bryaxis seen by Pausanias (I, 40, 6) at Megara.
30. King Seleukos I of Syria, 312-280 B.C.

Pliny, *N.H.* XXXVI, 22: In Knidos there are other marble statues by illustrious artists, a Dionysos by Bryaxis . . . .

Kedrenos, *Compendium Historiarum*, 306 B (ed. Paris): Julian, crossing over into Antioch and continuing up to Daphne and worshipping the idol of Apollo—for in that place there stood a marvellous work by the sculptor Bryaxis, which no one else was capable of imitating—sought an oracular response about himself. . . .

This statue is further described by the rhetorician Libanios of Antioch.

Libanios, *Orat.*, 61: And a mental effort makes the apparition [of the Apollo] stand before my eyes—the gentleness of its form, . . . the offering bowl, the *kithara,* the tunic reaching to the feet, the softness in the stone which constitutes the neck, the belt around the chest which holds the gold tunic [31] in place, so that some of it is held in tight and some of it billows out . . . he seemed like one who was singing a melody.[32]

Another statue ascribed to a sculptor named Bryaxis was the great cult statue of Serapis at Alexandria.

Clement of Alexandria, *Protrept.* IV, 48 (after discussing several versions of the origin of the cult and where the statue came from): . . . the sculptor Bryaxis made it, not the Athenian, but another sculptor with the same name as that Bryaxis. He made use of mixed and varied materials for the work. There were filings of gold on it and of silver; also of bronze, iron, and lead, and, in addition to that, tin; nor did it lack any of the Egyptian gems—fragments of sapphire, haematite, and emerald, and others of topaz. Having ground all these to a powder and mixed them together, he colored the mixture to a dark blue shade (and owing to this, the color of the image is rather dark) and, blending all these things in with the dye left over from the worship of Osiris and Apis, he modelled the Serapis.[33]

Other works by Bryaxis were a Pasiphaë (Tatian, Adv. Graecos, 54, 117) and perhaps also a Zeus and Apollo with lions at Patara in

31. From Theodoretus, *Historia Ecclesiastica* III, 10, we learn that the statue was made of wood and gold.
32. The statue was probably the prototype for the Apollo represented on a Seleukid tetradrachm. Cf. Lacroix, *Reproductions,* XXVIII, 7.
33. A number of Roman copies of the Serapis exist. In spite of Clement's remark to the contrary, the statue was probably by the same Bryaxis who is mentioned in the other passages. He was perhaps a Karian who made Athens his headquarters. For a review of the whole Serapis question, cf. Picard, *Manuel,* IV, 2 (1963), pp. 871-890 (with illustrations).

Lycia (Clement of Alexandria, Protrept. IV, 47). A base in Athens with reliefs representing horsemen and tripods is signed by Bryaxis.³⁴

Silanion of Athens

Pliny, N.H. XXXIV, 51:   In the 113th Olympiad [327 B.C.] . . . was Silanion; in connection with whom there is the remarkable fact that he became famous without the benefit of a teacher.

Pliny, N.H. XXXIV, 81:   Silanion cast a [portrait of] Apollodoros, who was a modeller himself, but who was among all artists the most meticulous in his art and also a harsh critic of himself, frequently smashing his finished statues, as long as he was unable, owing to his zeal for his art, to be satisfied; and who therefore was given the surname "the Madman." This quality Silanion expressed in his portrait and made out of bronze not a man but anger itself. He also made a famous Achilles and a trainer exercising athletes.

Diogenes Laertius III, 25:   In the first chapter of the *Records* of Favorinus it is said that Mithridates the Persian set up a statue of Plato in the academy and inscribed on it: "Mithridates, son of Rhodobates, dedicated to the Muses this portrait of Plato, which Silanion made." ³⁵

Plutarch, De Aud. Poet. III, 30:   We are delighted when we see the Philoktetes of Aristophon and the Jokasta of Silanion represented as both wasting away and dying.

Plutarch, Quaest. Conviv. V, 1, 2:   We find pleasure in and we marvel at the modelled statue of Jokasta, in whose face, they say, the artist mixed silver, so that the bronze might take on the surface color of a human being whose life is slowly being snuffed out.

Cicero, Verrine, II, IV, 57, 125-126:   For the Sappho, which was carried off from the *Prytaneion* [in Syracuse], gives you such a just excuse that it is almost to be viewed as something which can be conceded and ignored. For this work of Silanion is so perfect, so elegant, so elaborate, that I ask if it would not be better off in the hands of a private citizen or even a whole people, rather than in the hands of that most refined and elegant man Verres?

Other works by Silanion include: A Theseus in Athens (Plutarch, Life of Theseus, 4); The Boxers Satyros of Elis (Pausanias VI, 4, 5),

34. Cf. Picard, *op. cit.,* pp. 858-863; Richter, *Sculpture and Sculptors,²* Figs. 723, 724.

35. The portrait is known through an extensive series of Roman copies; cf. R. Boehringer, *Platon, Bildnisse und Nachweise* (Breslau, 1935).

Telestas of Messenia (Pausanias VI, 14, 4), and Demaretas of Messenia (Pausanias VI, 14, 11).

Silanion was also the author of a treatise on symmetria *(see Chapter 6, p. 233).*

Euphranor

Euphranor worked primarily in Athens [36] *and was both a sculptor and a painter (see pp. 172-174). He also wrote on art theory (see pp. 173, 233). Pliny (N.H. XXXIV, 50) dates Euphranor in the 104th Olympiad (364 B.C.).*

Pliny, N.H. XXXIV, 77:   The Alexander Paris [37] is a work of Euphranor which is praised because it conveys all these [aspects of his personality] simultaneously—the judge of the goddesses, the lover of Helen, but also the killer of Achilles. His also was an Athena, which at Rome was called the *Catuliana,* and was dedicated below the Capitoline by Q. Lutatius Catulus, and also a statue of "Bonus Eventus," [38] holding an offering-bowl in the right hand and an ear of corn and some poppies in the left; also a Leto after childbirth, holding up the infants Apollo and Artemis,[39] [a group which is] in the temple of Concord. He also made four-horse chariots, two-horse chariots, a very beautiful "Key-bearer," [40] a "Virtue" and a "Greece," both colossal figures, a woman represented as wondering and worshipping, and also [portraits of] Alexander and Philip in four-horse chariots.

Euphranor also did a statue of Apollo for the temple of Apollo Patroös in the Agora at Athens. (Cf. Pausanias I, 3, 3.) This figure (minus the head, arms, shoulders) now stands in the Stoa of Attalos in Athens.[41] *A statue of Hephaistos by Euphranor is mentioned by Dio Chrysostom (Or. XXXVII, 43).*

36. Pliny refers to him as *Isthmius* (*N.H.* XXXV, 128). Perhaps he was from Corinth. On this question see Picard, *Manuel* III, 2 (1948), p. 854.
37. Possibly reflected in a Roman copy in the Lansdowne Collection. Cf. Picard, *op. cit.,* Fig. 391.
38. "Bonus Eventus" may be the Greek *Agathos Daimōn,* of which Praxiteles also did a figure, see p. 129. The attributes of the figure, however, as Furtwängler pointed out, are those of Triptolemos. Cf. *Meisterwerke der Griechischen Plastik* (Leipzig: 1893), p. 281 (Eng. trans. E. Sellers, New York, 1895).
39. This group seems to be represented on coins and in a Roman copy in the Museo Torlonia in Rome. Cf. Picard, *Manuel,* III, 2, Fig. 390.
40. Key-bearer—*kleidouchos.* This term is also used in connection with a work of Pheidias, see p. 68.
41. Cf. Picard, *op. cit.,* Fig. 385.

The Younger Kalamis, Praxias, and Androsthenes

Pausanias X, 19, 4 (the temple of Apollo at Delphi):   The figures in the pediments are Artemis, Leto, Apollo, the Muses, the setting sun, and Dionysos with the Thyiad women. The artist who executed the first of them was the Athenian Praxias, a pupil of Kalamis.[42] But since the temple was under construction for some time, fate, as was inevitable, carried off Praxias, and the remainder of the decoration of the pediments was done by Androsthenes, who was also an Athenian by birth and a pupil of Eukadmos.

Up to this point we have dealt with sculptors who were either Athenians or who were closely associated with Athens. A number of the most influential sculptors of the century, however, were unconnected with the Athenian school and developed styles uniquely their own. The two most important of these were Skopas and Lysippos.

Skopas of Paros

Skopas was one of the sculptors who worked on the Mausoleum of Halikarnassos (see p. 183), and he was also a distinguished architect.

Pliny, N.H. XXXVI, 25-26:   The fame of Skopas rivals that of these [Praxiteles and his relatives]. He made an Aphrodite and a "Pothos" ["Desire"],[43] which are worshipped with extremely sacred ceremonies at Samothrace; also an Apollo which is on the Palatine,[44] and a much-

---

42. On Kalamis the Younger, see p. 59. The Temple of Apollo at Delphi referred to in this passage was built c. 360-330 (this was the sixth and last temple). Overbeck, and, following him, Stuart Jones associated Pausanias' description of the pediments with the description of architectural (metope?) sculptures in Euripides' *Ion*, lines 190 ff., but the two passages are surely unconnected. Euripides would have known the fifth (or "Alkmaionid" temple); Pausanias would have seen the sixth one. If Praxias was active c. 360, the younger Kalamis can be placed in the early fourth century. He is probably the same as Kalamis the silversmith (see Chapter 6, p. 233). The story that Praxiteles made the charioteer for a chariot group by Kalamis may also refer to the younger sculptor (see p. 130). Perhaps too the Apollo in the Gardens of Servilius in Rome which Pliny (*N.H.* XXXVI, 36) ascribes to Kalamis the *caelator* was by him.

43. Roman copies exist. Cf. Picard, *Manuel* III, 2 (1948), pp. 653-662; P. Arias, *Skopas* (Rome, 1952), pp. 131-135, pls. XIII-XIV.

44. This statue was originally in Rhamnous. It was brought to Rome to be used as a cult statue in a new temple of Apollo on the Palatine, which commemorated the battle of Actium and was dedicated in 28 B.C. It is represented on Roman coins; cf. Picard, *op. cit.*, pp. 640-641.

praised seated Hestia [45] in the gardens of Servilius with two pillars [46] flanking her, pillars for which there are duplicates among the monuments collected by Asinius, where there is also a *Kanephoros* ["Basketbearer"] by him. But the greatest value is attached to those works in the shrine built by Cn. Domitius in the Flaminian Circus—Poseidon [47] himself and Thetis and Achilles, along with Nereids riding dolphins, huge fish and sea-horses, and also Tritons, the chorus of Phorkys, sea-monsters and many other creatures of the sea, all by his hand; a distinguished achievement, even if it had occupied his whole life. But the truth is that there also exists at present, in addition to the works mentioned above and those which we do not know about, a colossal seated Ares executed by his hand in the temple of Brutus Callaecus [48] also in the Circus, and in addition to this a nude Aphrodite, in the same place, a work which precedes the one by Praxiteles and would make any other place [but Rome] famous. . . .

Pliny, *N.H.* XXXVI, 28: There is equal doubt as to whether the "Dying Children of Niobe" in the temple of Apollo *Sosianus* were made by Skopas or Praxiteles; [49] and likewise there is doubt as to which of the two did the father Janus, which was dedicated by Augustus in its [or his?] own temple after being brought from Egypt; and now its identity is further concealed by a gilt covering.

Pausanias VIII, 45 4 (at Tegea in Arcadia): Aleos made the ancient sanctuary of Athena *Alea* for the Tegeans. At a later time the Tegeans built for the goddess a great temple, well worth seeing. A fire which spread suddenly destroyed that temple, when Diophantos was the Archon at Athens in the second year of the 96th Olympiad, the same year in which Eupolemos of Elis was the victor in the one-stade foot race [395 B.C.].[50] The temple which stands in our own time is superior to all the other temples in the Peloponnesos, in, among other things, its artistic adornment and in its size. The first ornamental colonnade in it is Doric, and the one after that is Corinthian. Also, outside the temple,

45. Hestia—Latin "Vesta." On this work see Picard, *op. cit.*, pp. 667-671.

46. Pillars—*kamptēras*, a Greek word for the pillars at the turning point of an ancient "hair-pin" shaped race course.

47. Stuart Jones, *Ancient Writers on Greek Sculpture*, p. 168, notes that Cn. Domitius Ahenobarbus may have brought these figures from Bithynia where he was governor c. 40-35 B.C. and where there was a famous temple of Poseidon at Astakos Olbia. Domitius probably completed the temple of Neptune in Rome in 32 B.C. when he was consul. For the works which may be associated with this group, cf. Picard, *op. cit.*, pp. 673-689.

48. This temple, dedicated to Mars, was built in 132 B.C.

49. On this question cf. Picard, *op. cit.*, pp. 751-762.

50. Although the old temple was burned in 395 B.C., the new one seems not to have been built until about 360 B.C. The main period of Skopas' artistic activity must be placed around the middle of the fourth century.

stand columns in the Ionic order.[51] The architect of it, I learned, was Skopas the Parian, who made images in many places in ancient Greece and also made some in Ionia and Karia. The figures in the pediment on the front represent the hunt for the Kalydonian boar. The boar is placed exactly in the middle of it and to the side of it are Atalanta, Meleager, Theseus, Telamon, Peleus, Polydeukes [Pollux], Iolaos (who undertook most of the labors with Herakles), the children of Thestius, and the brothers of Althaia, Prothoüs and Kometes. By the boar on the other side is Epochos holding up Ankaios who already has wounds and has dropped his axe; by him is Castor and Amphiaraos, the son of Oikles; after them is Hippothoös, the son of Kerkyon, the son of Agamedes, the son of Stymphalos. The last figure represented is Peirithoös. Represented in the pediment on the back of the temple is the battle of Telephos against Achilles on the plain of the river Kaïkos.[52]

Pausanias VIII, 47, 1 (in the sanctuary of Athena *Alea* at Tegea): Beside the image of Athena on one side stands a statue of Asklepios and, on the other side, one of Hygieia [Health], both of Pentelic marble, works of Skopas the Parian.

Pausanias VI, 25, 1 (in Elis):   The precinct of Aphrodite is enclosed by a fence; inside the precinct a base has been made and on the base is a bronze image of Aphrodite seated upon a goat, also of bronze. This is a work of Skopas and they call it Aphrodite *Pandemos*.[53] The significance . . . of the goat I leave to those who wish to guess.[54]

Scholiast on Aeschines, *Against Timarchos*, p. 747 (ed. Reiske):   There were three female deities called the "Holy Goddesses" or the "Eumenides" or the "Erinyes" ["Furies"]. Of them the two on each side were made by Skopas of Paros from *lychnites;* [55] the one in the center was by Kalamis.

---

51. The outer colonnade of the temple was Doric and engaged columns in the interior of the cella were Corinthian. Where the Ionic columns stood is not known; they may have belonged to another building in the sanctuary.

52. Fragments of these pedimental figures have been found and are now in the Museum at Tegea. They may not be by the hand of Skopas, but they must certainly reflect his artistic influence. The fully developed use of excited, dramatic facial expressions reflects a new interest in the representation of pathos in Greek sculpture. See C. Dugas, *Le Sanctuaire d'Aléa Athéna à Tégée* (Paris, 1924), pls. XCVI-CXII; Picard, *Manuel* IV, 1 (1954), pp. 153-190.

53. *Pandēmos*—"Common," "For everybody." The statue forms a contrast with the Aphrodite *Ourania* of Pheidias (see p. 75) which Pausanias describes immediately before this.

54. This Aphrodite is represented on the coinage of Elis during the time of the Roman Empire and in the minor arts. Cf. Lacroix, *Reproductions,* pl. XXVIII, 5; Picard, *Manuel* III, 2, pp. 698-703.

55. *Lychnitēs*—a term for Parian marble; cf. Pliny, *N.H.* XXXVI, 14.

Pausanias is probably describing the same works in the following passage.

Pausanias I, 28, 6 (in Athens): Nearby is the sanctuary of those gods which the Athenians call "the Holy ones" but which Hesiod in the *Theogony* calls the "Erinyes." Aeschylus first represented them as having snakes on their head along with their hair. But there is nothing fearful in these images. . . .

Strabo XIII, 604: In this town of Chryse [in Asia Minor near Troy] there is a sanctuary of Apollo Smintheus, and the symbol which preserves the etymology of the name, the mouse, is placed at the foot of the statue. These are works of Skopas the Parian.[56]

A famous work by Skopas was a figure of a Bacchante (Maenad), a frenzied female devotee of Dionysos.[57]

Anth. Graec. III, 57, 3 (Anth. Pal. IX, 774) by Glaukos the Athenian:

> This is a Parian Bacchante; the sculptor breathed life
> Into the stone; she leaps up as if in frenzied revel.
> O Skopas, the god-creating art of your hand has wrought
> A goat-slaying wonder, a raving Thyiad.

On Skopas' architectural sculptures other than those mentioned above, see p. 183 (Mausoleum) and p. 37 (Artemision at Ephesos). Another work by Skopas which is perhaps preserved in Roman copies was his Herakles at Sikyon (cf. Pausanias II, 10, 1).[58]

Lysippos of Sikyon

Pliny, N.H. XXXIV, 61: Douris[59] says that Lysippos of Sikyon was not a disciple of any other artist, but that he was at first a bronze-worker and undertook a career in the fine arts[60] upon hearing a re-

56. Perhaps represented on the coins of Kyzikos and Alexandreia in the Troad; cf. Arias, *op. cit.*, pl. VI, nos. 19, 20; Picard, *op. cit.*, pp. 690-691; Lacroix, however, doubts the identification, cf. *Reproductions*, p. 318.

57. The work is possibly represented by a type of raving maenad known in Roman copies. Cf. Arias, *op. cit.*, pl. X, Figs, 34-37. Cf. also Kallistratos, *Eikones*, 2.

58. This work is frequently connected with the Lansdowne Herakles in London; cf. Arias, *op. cit.*, pl. 1, nos. 3, 4; for other types which may be associated with it see Picard, *op. cit.*, pp. 703-711.

59. See Introduction, p. xv.

60. "Undertook a career in the fine arts"—*rationem cepisse*. The Latin term *ratio* refers essentially to the theoretical principles which formed the basis of any art. Lysippos, it will be seen, was an important innovator in the theory of sculptural proportions. This is probably what is implied by the tradition that he had no teacher—that is, he did not use the theoretical principles of any other artist.

sponse of the painter Eupompos. For when that man [Eupompos] was asked which of his predecessors he followed, he pointed to a crowd of men, and said that one ought to imitate nature itself, and not another artist. Lysippos made more statues than any other artist, being, as we said, very prolific in the art; among them was a youth scraping himself with a strigil, which Marcus Agrippa dedicated in front of his baths, and which the Emperor Tiberius was astonishingly fond of. He [Tiberius] was, in fact, unable to restrain himself in its case (although at the beginning of his principate he had been master of himself), and had it moved to his own bedroom, substituting another statue in its place. When, however, the indignation of the Roman people was so great, that it demanded, by an uproar in the theatre, that the *Apoxyomenos* [61] be replaced, the Emperor, although he had fallen in love with it, put it back. Lysippos is also famed for his "Tipsy Flute-girl" and his "Hunt with Dogs," but most especially for his "Quadriga with the Sun" [that is, the god Helios] belonging to the Rhodians. He also made many portraits of Alexander the Great, beginning from his boyhood, [the portrait of Alexander as a boy was a work] which the Emperor Nero ordered to be gilded, so delighted was he with it. Afterwards however, since the artistic value of the statue vanished with the [increase in] monetary value, the gold was taken off, and it was considered more precious in that state even though the scars left on the work and the cuttings into which the gold had been fastened remained. He also made a portrait of Hephaistion, the friend of Alexander the Great, which some ascribe to Polykleitos, although he lived about a hundred years earlier. He also made "Alexander's Hunt" which was consecrated at Delphi, a Satyr at Athens, and "Alexander's Squadron," in which he executed portraits of all Alexander's friends with the utmost exactitude. Metellus, after subduing Macedonia, transferred this work to Rome [148 B.C.]. He also made quadrigas of various types. He is said to have contributed much to the art of casting statues by representing the hair in detail, by making the head smaller than earlier sculptors had, and by making the bodies slenderer and more tightly knit, as a result of which the height of his statues seems greater. There is no Latin term for [the Greek word] *symmetria* which he observed with the utmost precision by a new and previously unattempted system which involved altering the "square" [62] figures of the older sculptors; and he used commonly to say that by them [that is, the earlier sculptors] men were represented as they really

61. A well-known marble statue in the Vatican Museum representing an athlete scraping himself with a strigil is thought to be a copy of Lysippos' *Apoxyomenos;* cf. Richter, *Sculpture and Sculptors,*[2] Figs. 739, 742, 743; also the standard monograph on Lysippos: F. P. Johnson, *Lysippos* (Durham, N. C.: 1927), pls. 12, 13.

62. "Square figures"—*quadratas staturas.* It will be remembered that Polykleitos' statues were *quadrata;* on the meaning of the term see p. 89, n. 100.

were, but by him they were represented as they appeared. What seems to be especially characteristic of his art are the subtle fluctuations of surface which were apparent even in the smallest details.[63]

Pliny, *N.H.* XXXIV, 37:   . . . Lysippos is related to have made 1,500 works, all of them of such artistic quality that any single one could have given him fame; this number came to light upon his death, when his heir broke open his strong-box. For it was his cusotm to put in it one gold coin, worth a denarius, from the fee which he received for each statue.

Pliny's discussion of Lysippos makes it clear that his career was closely associated with the Macedonian royal family. He was perhaps originally employed by Philip II (ruled 359-336 B.C.) and later served Alexander (ruled 336-323 B.C.) as his court sculptor. His portraits of Alexander seem to have established a type of heroic portrait which was imitated throughout the rest of Classical antiquity.[64]

Plutarch, *De Alexandri Fortitudine seu Virtute*, II, 2, 3:   When Lysippos first modelled a portrait of Alexander with his face turned upward toward the sky, just as Alexander himself was accustomed to gaze, turning his neck gently to one side, someone inscribed, not inappropriately, the following epigram:

> The bronze statue seems to proclaim, looking at
> Zeus: I place the earth under my sway; you
> O Zeus, keep Olympos.

For this reason, Alexander decreed that only Lysippos should make his portrait. For only Lysippos, it seems, brought out his real character in the bronze and gave form to his essential excellence. For others, in their eagerness to imitate the turn of his neck and the expressive, liquid glance of his eyes, failed to preserve his manly and leonine quality.

Plutarch, *De Iside et Osiride*, 24:   Lysippos the modeller did well to find fault with the painter Apelles because the latter, in painting a portrait of Alexander put a thunderbolt in his hand. He himself repre-

---

63. The sections of this passage which deal with the contributions of Lysippos to the art of sculpture are very probably derived from the "Xenokratic tradition" of ancient art criticism; see Introduction, pp. xii, xviii.

64. The "Azara Herm" in the Louvre has Lysippos' name inscribed on it and is almost certainly a Roman copy of one of his Alexander portraits. Cf. Johnson, *op. cit.*, pp. 43-44; on the portraits of Alexander in general see M. Bieber, *The Portraits of Alexander the Great, Proceedings of the American Philosophical Society*, 93, 5 (1949), pp. 373-427; on the portraits which are usually connected with Lysippos see Picard, *Manuel* IV, 2 (1963), pp. 689-753.

sented Alexander with a spear, which time would never rob of its glory, being a true and proper attribute.[65]

The ideas contained in these two passages from Plutarch are repeated in passages from many other writers.[66] In addition to single portraits of Alexander, Lysippos also represented him in two large monumental groups. One of these, the "Granikos Monument," was set up to commemorate Alexander's victory at the river Granikos in 334 B.C. It is probably identical with the "Squadron of Alexander" mentioned by Pliny.

Arrian, *Anabasis* **1, 16, 4:** Of the Macedonians, twenty-five of the "Companions" died in the first assault, and bronze portraits of them stood in Dion [in Macedonia], made by Lysippos at the command of Alexander. . . .[67]

The group mentioned by Pliny representing "Alexander's Hunt" at Delphi is further described by Plutarch.

Plutarch, *Life of Alexander,* **40:** Krateros [68] set up a memorial of this hunt at Delphi and had bronze statues made of the lion and of the dogs, and also of the king engaged in combat with the lion, and of himself coming to give aid; some of these were made by Lysippos, others by Leochares.[69]

Another interesting aspect of Lysippos' artistic production was the apparently playful use which he made of the effects of scale in sculpture. A number of his famous statues were colossal and at least one was a miniature. The impressions which were produced in both cases seem to have been surprising.

65. A statuette in the Louvre, sometimes called the "Alexander with a Lance" is probably a diminutive copy of Lysippos' work; cf. Johnson, *op. cit.,* pl. 47; Picard, *op. cit.,* pl. XVII.

66. These passages are collected by Johnson, *op. cit.,* pp. 299-307, where translations are also provided.

67. According to Velleius Paterculus, *Historia Romana* I, 11, 3-4, the group contained a portrait of Alexander himself; he also says that when the group was moved to Rome, it was set up in front of the temples of Jupiter Stator and Juno Regina in Rome (later surrounded by the porticoes of Octavia). The portrait of Alexander in this group is thought by some to be represented by a bronze equestrian statuette in Naples. Cf. Picard, *op. cit.,* p. 713, Fig. 302; Johnson, *op. cit.,* pl. 48, Fig. A.

68. Krateros (c. 370-332 B.C.) was one of Alexander's generals.

69. This group must have formed the prototype for the hunting scene on the so-called "Alexander Sarcophagus" in Istanbul; cf. Richter, *Sculpture and Sculptors,*2 Fig. 748.

Pliny, *N.H.* XXXIV, 40:   Of such a sort [that is, colossal] also is the statue in Tarentum made by Lysippos, forty cubits high. A remarkable fact about this statue is that, although it can be moved, as they say, by hand, the system by which its weight is distributed is such that it cannot be dislodged by storms. In fact the artist is said to have provided against this possibility by a column which was placed opposite it a short distance away in the direction from which it was most necessary to break the blast of the wind. Therefore, on account of its size and the difficulty of removing it, Fabius Verrucosus [70] did not touch it when he transferred from that place the Herakles which is now on the Capitoline.[71]

The Herakles mentioned in the passage above was also a colossal statue.

Strabo, VI, 278:   The acropolis [of Tarentum] has few remains of the offerings which were part of its ornamentation in the old days. The Carthaginians destroyed many of them when they took the city, and the Romans carried off others as booty when they conquered the city by force. One of these is the colossal bronze of Herakles which is on the Capitoline, the work of Lysippos, an offering of Fabius Maximus after he took the city. . . .

Apparently this Herakles was the one which was subsequently transferred to Constantinople and was destroyed by the Franks who attacked the city in 1204 A.D.

Niketas Choniates, *De Signis Constantinopolitanis*, 5:   The great Herakles, begotten in a triple night, is now cast down and stretches over a great space, he who was seated on a basket with a lion's skin stretched out over it. . . . He sat there with no quiver slung upon him, neither bearing a bow in his hands, nor brandishing a club before him, but rather stretching out his right foot and also his right hand as much as was possible, while bending his left leg at the knee and leaning on the elbow of his left arm, with his forearm stretched upward, thus gently supporting his head in the palm of his hand, a figure full of despondency. His chest was wide, his shoulders broad, his hair thick, his buttocks ample, his arms strong, and in size he was as great as, I

70. Fabius Verrucosus—Q. Fabius Maximus, a Roman consul general, and elected dictator, who conquered Tarentum in 209 B.C.

71. Strabo VI, 278, notes that this colossus represented Zeus and that it was second in size only to the Colossus of Rhodes (see p. 198).

suppose, the actual Herakles was imagined to have been by Lysippos,[72] the artist who wrought this most excellent work of bronze, the foremost and ultimate creation of his own hands, and a work of such great size that a cord which fit around its thumb could be used as a man's belt and the shin of its leg equalled the height of a man.

Lysippos seems to have had a particular fondness for representing Herakles, and these representations offered a challenge to his powers of invention. One Herakles type created by him represented the muscle-bound hero leaning on his club in exhaustion. The original was apparently over life-sized and is known in a number of Roman copies, of which the most famous is the "Herakles Farnese" in Naples.[73] It formed the subject for a display of descriptive rhetoric by the rhetorician Libanios (fourth century A.D.*).*

Libanios, *Ekphraseis,* **XV:**   It was not possible for Herakles, when he ceased from his labors, to stand without praise nor to avoid being an object of wonder as he took respite from his achievements, but rather, by being represented in sculpture, he was preserved so that people could see him both laboring and after a labor. It was with a form of this sort that the artist set him up in a conspicuous place. For Herakles rested there, not undergoing danger as he was when Nemea saw him, but rather as Argos received him after he destroyed the lion. Thus he stood there bearing tokens of his exploits, but at the same time having passed the high-point of his trials. To begin with his head bends toward the earth and he seems to me to be looking to see if he can kill another opponent. Then his neck is bent downward along with his head. And his whole body is bare of covering, for Herakles was not one to care about modesty when his attention was directed toward excellence. Of his arms, the right one is taut and is bent behind his back, while the left is relaxed and stretches toward the earth. He is supported under the arm-pit by his club which rests on the earth, experiencing the same leisure [as he]. And so the club supports him while he rests, just as it saved him when he fought. The artist has done well, it seems to me, in arranging the disposition of the club. For while laboring he [Herakles] uses his right hand, while in pausing for a moment of peace he uses his left. And he has also given him an idle hand. The lion skin is draped upon the club, and this covers both the lion and that by which

72. The text says "Lysimachos," which is almost certainly a corruption of "Lysippos."

73. For the Herakles Farnese cf. Johnson, *op. cit.*, pl. 37; Richter, *op. cit.*, Fig. 749; Picard, *op. cit.*, Fig. 249; a small copy of the type in the Palazzo Pitti in Florence bears the inscription: "The work of Lysippos"; cf. Brunn-Bruckmann, *Denkmäler*, no. 284.

it was destroyed. Of Herakles' two legs the right one is beginning to
make a movement, while the left is placed beneath and fitted firmly on
the base, and this arrangement makes it possible for the onlookers to
learn just what sort of man Herakles is, even though he has ceased
from his labors.

*By contrast to these colossal works, another of Lysippos' most
famous representations of Herakles was a miniature table-piece. This
Herakles* Epitrapezios *("On the table") is also known in a number of
Roman copies.*[74]

Martial IX, 44: He who, being seated, mitigates the hardness of the
stone with a stretched out lion's skin, a great god [compressed] in a
small bronze, and who with his face turned upward beholds the stars
which he once bore; whose left hand glows with the strength of oak,
and his right with unmixed wine; his fame is not something recent, nor
is his glory from our [Roman] chisel. It is the well-known gift and work
of Lysippos that you see. This divine power was once held by the table
of the tyrant of Pella, the victor who now lies in the earth which he
had quickly tamed; by this [statue] Hannibal, as a boy, took an oath
at the Libyan altars; it was this god who commanded savage Sulla to
give up his rule; offended by the tumid terrors of various rulers' courts,
he rejoices now to dwell at private hearths, and as he was once the
convivial guest of placid Molorchus, so now he has decided to be the
god of learned Vindex.[75]

Vindex's art collection and especially the Herakles Epitrapezios
*are also described at length by Statius. The following passage is an
excerpt from that description.*

Statius, *Silvae* IV, 6, lines 32-47: Among these [Vindex's treasures] was
the genius and tutelary deity of his pure table, the son of Amphitryon
[Herakles], who greatly captured my heart; nor was my eye satiated
by looking at him long. So great was the dignity enclosed within the
narrow borders of the work; so great its majesty. A god he was, a god!
He granted, Lysippos, that the impression of himself which was produced by your art should be this—to be seen as small but to be thought
of as enormous. And although this marvellous work is contained within
the measure of a foot, nevertheless there will be an urge to cry out, as

74. Johnson, *op. cit.*, pl. 15-16; Richter, *op. cit.*, Fig. 751; Picard, *op. cit.*, Fig.
241.
75. Martial traces here some of the owners of the statue from Alexander the
Great down to Novius Vindex in his own day.

you cast your glance over his body: "On this chest the Nemean ravager was throttled; those the arms which bore the deadly oak-club and broke the Argo's oars!" And its size! How great is the deception in that small form! What controlled skill! How great was the experience that learned artist had in the details of art, in that he had the ingenuity to fashion a table ornament but at the same time to conceive a colossus.

Another work by Lysippos which illustrated his characteristic inventiveness was his allegorical statue of "Kairos" ("Opportunity").

Anth. Graec. II, 49, 13 (*Anth. Pal.* XVI, 275), an epigram by Poseidippos: Questioner—"Who was the sculptor and where was he from?" Statue—"He was a Sikyonian." Q.—"And what was his name?" S.—"Lysippos." Q.—"And who are you?" S.—"Opportunity, the all conqueror." Q.—"Why do you stride on the tips of your toes?" S.—"I am always running." Q.—"Why do you have pairs of wings on your feet?" S.—"I fly like the wind." Q.—"Why do you carry a razor in your right hand?" S.—"As a sign to men that my appearance is more abrupt than any blade [is sharp]." Q.—"And your hair, why does it hang down over your face?" S.—"So that he who encounters me may grab it." Q.—"By Zeus,[76] and why is the back of your head bald?" S.—"Because nobody, once I have run past him with my winged feet can ever catch me from behind, even though he yearns to." Q.—"For what reason did the artist fashion you?" S.—"For your sake, stranger. And he placed me before the doors as a lesson."

The "Kairos," with its obvious "content" or "message," became a common subject for the ancient art of ekphrasis, the rhetorical description of works of art. Two late antique descriptions of the statue, those of Himerios (Eclogae, XIV, 1) and Kallistratos (Eikones, VI), are also extant. Himerios recounts that the statue had a scale in its left hand; Kallistratos says that it stood in Sikyon and that its feet rested on a globe. In these late antique writings one must allow for a certain exaggeration. That the "Kairos" stood in Sikyon, however, seems likely, and the scale in the left hand seems to be justified by the representations of "Kairos" on late gems and reliefs. For a review of the whole complex question see Picard, op. cit., pp. 553-565.

Other works by Lysippos receiving brief mentions which are possibly preserved in Roman copies are: a bronze Poseidon [77] in Corinth

---

76. This oath could belong either to this question, or with the preceding answer. The punctuation of the original text is uncertain.

77. For the possible Roman copies cf. Johnson, *op. cit.*, pls. 24-25; Picard, *op. cit.*, pp. 491-513.

(Lucian, Jup. Trag. *9); an Eros* [78] *in Thespiai (Pausanias IX, 27, 3); and a portrait of Socrates* [79] *(Diogenes Laertius II, 43).*

Lysistratos, Brother of Lysippos

Pliny, *N.H*. XXXV, 153:   The first of all artists to mould an image of a man in plaster taken from the surface [of the body] itself [80] and to institute the method of making corrections on that work after pouring wax into the resulting mould was Lysistratos of Sikyon, the brother of Lysippos, of whom we have spoken. It was this man who introduced the method of making realistic likenesses; before him they sought to make statues as beautiful as possible.[81] He also invented the technique of taking casts from statues, and this practice increased to such an extent that no figures or statues were made without clay [that is, a clay model].[82]

Timotheos

Since he was one of the sculptors hired to do a major portion of the sculptures on the Mausoleum, Timotheos was apparently one of the more successful sculptors of the fourth century (see p. 183). He also worked on sculptures connected with the temple of Asklepios at Epidauros (c. 370 B.C.) as is attested by an inscription which records the expenses for the temple.

I.G. IV, 1484, line 36 and line 90:   Timotheos contracted to make and to furnish a *typos* [83] for 900 drachmas. Pythokles was his surety. . . .

78. For Roman copies see: Johnson, *op. cit.*, pls. 17-19; Picard, *op. cit.*, pp. 534-552.

79. A series of related portrait types representing Socrates is known in Roman copies. Cf. Johnson, *op. cit.*, pp. 231-233 and pl. 50; J. J. Bernoulli, *Griechische Ikonographie*, I (Munich, 1901), pp. 184-205; M. Bieber, *The Sculpture of the Hellenistic Age*,2 (New York, 1961), Figs. 124-139.

80. "Surface of the body itself"—*e facie ipsa*. The Latin *facies* refers to the whole surface of the body, not simply to the face. Thus the passage does not necessarily refer to the rise of "veristic" portraiture. Cf. Rhys Carpenter, "Observations on Familiar Statuary in Rome," *Memoirs of the American Academy in Rome*, XVIII (1941), pp. 74-76.

81. The contrast is perhaps between the newer statues made from casts and the earlier tradition, apparently beginning to die out at this time, of making them according to a canon of *symmetria*.

82. This was one of the first steps in the development of the copying industry in ancient sculpture. Cf. G. M. A. Richter, *Ancient Italy* (Ann Arbor: University of Michigan Press, 1955), p. 113.

83. The term *typos* apparently means "relief," although some scholars still adhere to an earlier interpretation of the term as meaning "models" for a pediment. On the interpretation of *typos* see Richter, *Sculpture and Sculptors*,2 pp. 276-280. For bibliography on the question cf. Lippold, *Die Griechische Plastik* (Munich, 1950), p. 220, n. 2.

(line 90) Timotheos contracted [to make] *akroteria* [84] for one of the pediments for 2240 drachmas. Pythokles was his surety.

Other works by Timotheos were an image of Asklepios at Troizen (Pausanias II, 32, 4) and a statue of Artemis which was on the Palatine at Rome in Pliny's day (N.H. XXXVI, 32).

Thrasymedes of Paros

Thrasymedes was both an architect and a sculptor and applied these skills on the temple of Asklepios at Epidauros. (See also under architecture, p. 182).

Pausanias II, 27, 2: The image of Asklepios [in the temple at Epidauros] is half the size of that of Olympian Zeus in Athens [85] and is made of ivory and gold. An inscription indicates that it was fashioned by Thrasymedes the son of Arignotos, a Parian. He [Asklepios] is seated on a throne and holds in one hand a staff; he holds the other hand over the head of the serpent, and a dog is also represented lying beside him. On the throne there are wrought the exploits of the Argive heroes—Bellerophon against the Chimaira and Perseus carrying off the head of Medusa.

The Relatives and Descendants of Polykleitos

The family of Polykleitos has been discussed previously, pp. 93-94.

Daidalos of Sikyon

Pliny, *N.H.* XXXIV, 76: Daidalos, who is also mentioned with praise among the sculptors in marble, made [statues in bronze of] two boys scraping themselves with strigils. . . .

Pausanias VI, 2, 8 (at Olympia): In the *Altis* . . . are statues of Timon and of Aisypos, the son of Timon, who is represented as a boy mounted on a horse. For the fact is that the boy's victory was in the horse race, while Timon claimed victory in the chariot race. The artist who fashioned the portraits for Timon and for his son was Daidalos of Sikyon, who also made the trophy in the *Altis* for the Eleans, commemorating their victory [86] over the Spartans.

84. Substantial portions of the *akroteria* and fragments of the pedimental sculptures from the temple of Asklepios are extant. Cf. Richter, *op. cit.,* Figs. 710-719; J. Crome, *Die Skulpturen des Asklepios-Tempels von Epidauros* (Berlin: 1951).
   85. Presumably the image in the *Olympieion* in Athens; on this temple see pp. 213-214.
   86. The victory took place c. 400 B.C.; cf. Pausanias V, 4, 8.

Daidalos was also one of several sculptors who worked on a monument set up by the Tegeans at Delphi to commemorate a victory over the Spartans. Cf. Pausanias X, 8, 5.

Polykleitos the Younger

Pausanias VI, 6, 2 (at Olympia): Polykleitos the Argive, not the artist who made the image of Hera,[87] but rather the pupil of Naukydes, made a statue of the boy wrestler, Agenor the Theban.

Pausanias VIII, 31, 4 (in the sanctuary of Demeter and Kore at Megalopolis)[88]: Within the sanctuary there is a temple of Zeus *Philios* ["of Friendship"]; the image is by Polykleitos the Argive and resembles [an image of] Dionysos. For as footwear it has high boots, and it holds a drinking cup in one hand and a *thyrsos* in the other; an eagle, however, is seated on the *thyrsos,* and this, to be sure, is not in agreement with the things which are recorded about Dionysos.

Alypos of Sikyon

Alypos was a pupil of Naukydes (see p. 92) and was one of the sculptors who worked on the great Spartan victory monument at Delphi (see p. 94). He also executed statues of victorious athletes at Olympia (cf. Pausanias VI, 1, 3; VI, 8, 5).

Sthennis of Olynthos

Pliny (N.H. XXXIV, 51) dates Sthennis in the 113th Olympiad (328 B.C.). Olynthos, which (according to Pausanias) was his native city, was destroyed in 348 B.C. by Philip of Macedon. An inscribed statue base (Loewy, Inschriften, no. 103a) indicates that Sthennis subsequently obtained Athenian citizenship.

Pliny, N.H. XXXIV, 90: Sthennis made the Demeter, Zeus, and Athena, which are in the temple of Concord in Rome; and also the "Weeping Matrons" and figures of worshippers and sacrificers.

Plutarch, *Life of Lucullus*, XXIII, 3-4: It seemed that some person stood by him [Lucullus] in his sleep and said: "Go forward a little, Lucullus. For Autolykos has come and wishes to meet you." Waking up at that moment he was not able to figure out what the vision meant, but took the city [Sinope] on that very day, and as he was pursuing

---

87. The image of *Hera* in the Argive *Heraion* by the Elder Polykleitos is referred to here. Cf. p. 90.

88. Megalopolis was founded in 370 B.C. Assuming that the statue was made expressly for the sanctuary, it would have to be the work of the Younger Polykleitos.

those of the Cilicians who were sailing away, he saw a statue lying on the shore, which the Cilicians had been carrying off but had not had time to put on board. This was one of the most beautiful works of Sthennis. Someone informed him thereupon that it was a statue of Autolykos, the founder of Sinope.[89]

The other known works by Sthennis were portraits of victorious athletes at Olympia (Pausanias VI, 16, 8; VI, 17, 5).

PAINTING

Judging by the literary sources the fourth century B.C. was the great age of Greek painting, but with the exception of a few possible echoes in Italian painting and on a few early fourth century vases, no archaeological evidence survives to show us what this painting was like. The leading painters of this era seem to have been strong personalities; personal ambitions, rivalries, and eccentricities are more apparent here than in any other period.

Zeuxis of Herakleia

See also Chapter 6, pp. 219, 221, 223.

Pliny, *N.H.* XXXV, 61:   After the portals of the art of painting were opened by him [Apollodoros], Zeuxis of Herakleia entered them in the fourth year of the 95th Olympiad [397 B.C.], and he led the paintbrush, which now would dare to undertake anything, onward to great glory. His prime is placed falsely by some writers in the 89th Olympiad [424 B.C.], since he was a disciple of either Demophilos of Himera or Neseus of Thasos (it is uncertain which) who, it is certain, flourished at that time.[90] Apollodoros, who was discussed above [see p. 111] wrote this verse about him: "Zeuxis stole the art from his very teachers, and carried it off with him." He also acquired such great wealth that he showed it off at Olympia by exhibiting his name woven into the checks of his cloaks in gold letters. Afterwards he decided to give away his works as gifts, since he said that no price could be considered equal to their value—works such as the *Alkmene* [which he gave] to Akragas, and the *Pan* to Archelaos. He also did a *Penelope* in which he seems to have painted morality itself, and an athlete; in the case of the last mentioned

89. Lucullus captured Sinope c. 70 B.C.
90. This is a free translation of an enigmatic sentence. Pliny's meaning may also be that, since Zeuxis was a disciple of Demophilos and Neseus, his prime could not have come at the same time as theirs.

work he was so pleased with himself, that he wrote beneath it the verse which, as a result, became famous: "One could criticize it more easily than one could imitate it." [91] A magnificent work is his *Zeus on a Throne* with the gods standing by and also his *Herakles Strangling the Snakes* in the presence of his mother Alkmene, who is quaking with fear, and Amphitryon. He is criticized, however, for having made the head and the limbs too large, although in other respects he was so attentive to precision of detail that, when he was about to make a picture for the people of Akragas, which they were going to dedicate in the temple of Hera *Lakinia* at public expense, he made an inspection of the virgins of the city, who were nude, and selected five in order that he might represent in the picture that which was the most laudable feature of each. He also painted monochromes in white.[92] His contemporaries and rivals were Timanthes, Androkydes, Eupompos, and Parrhasios. The last is reputed to have entered into a contest with Zeuxis, and when the latter depicted some grapes with such success that birds flew up to the scene,[93] he [Parrhasios] then depicted a linen curtain with such verisimilitude that Zeuxis, puffed up with pride by the verdict of the birds, eventually requested that the curtain be removed and his picture shown, and, when he understood his error, conceded defeat with sincere modesty, because he himself had only deceived birds, but Parrhasios had deceived him, an artist. It is said that afterwards Zeuxis painted a picture of a boy carrying grapes, and when the birds flew up to them, he approached the work and, in irritation with it, said, "I have painted the grapes better than the boy, for if I had rendered him perfectly, the birds would have been afraid." He also made statues in clay, which were the only works left behind in Ambrakia when Fulvius Nobilior transferred the statues of the Muses from there to Rome [189 B.C.]. There is also in Rome a *Helen* by the hand of Zeuxis which is in the porticoes of Philippus, and a *Marsyas Tied Up* in the temple of Concord.

The picture of Helen which Pliny mentions above appears to have been the same as the picture which he mentions in connection with the temple of Hera Lakinia *at Akragas. According to Cicero and Dionysios of Halikarnassos* [94] *this picture was actually at Kroton in south Italy, where there was a famous temple of Hera* Lakinia.

91. The epigram is also preserved in its Greek form by Plutarch, who ascribes it to Apollodoros, see above, p. 112.

92. Perhaps line drawings on a white ground similar to the example from Herculaneum, now in Naples, cf. A. Maiuri, *Roman Painting* (Geneva: 1953), p. 104; or perhaps paintings done in white paint on a dark ground.

93. "Up to the scene"—*in scaenam,* probably indicating that the paintings were part of the stage setting, unless *scaenam* refers to the "scene" within the painting itself.

94. Dionysios of Halikarnassos, *De Vet. Script. Cens.,* 1—Overbeck, *Schriftquellen* 1669.

Cicero, *De Inventione* II, 1, 1:   At one time, the people of Kroton, when they were at the height of their resources and were counted among the first cities of Italy in wealth, wanted to enrich the temple of Hera, which they cared for with the utmost conscientiousness, with outstanding pictures. Therefore they hired for a large fee Zeuxis of Herakleia, who at that time was thought to excel by far all other painters. He also painted many other pictures, of which a portion has been preserved from his time down to our own owing to the sanctity of the shrine, and, in order that his mute image would contain within itself the preeminent beauty of the feminine form, he said that he wanted to paint a *Helen*. This statement the people of Kroton, who had often been informed that he surpassed all others in painting the female body, heard with pleasure. For they thought that if he should apply his utmost efforts to that genre in which he was most capable, an outstanding work would be left behind for them in that sanctuary. Nor did their opinion prove to be a deception. For Zeuxis immediately questioned them as to which were the most beautiful virgins which they had in the city. They immediately took him to the *palaestra* [wrestling court] and showed him many youths . . . [when] he marvelled greatly at the forms and the bodies of these boys, they exclaimed: "Their sisters are our virgins; so you can guess just what their quality is from these youths." "I beg you to provide me," he said, "with the most beautiful of these virgins, while I paint the picture which I promised you, in order that the truth may be transferred to the mute image from the physical model." Thereupon the citizens of Kroton by a resolution of the public council gathered the virgins into one place and gave the painter the power to choose whichever ones he wanted. And so he chose five, whose names many poets have handed down to posterity because they were approved by the judgment of him who is supposed to have had the most reliable judgment about beauty. For he did not believe that it was possible to find in one body all the things he looked for in beauty, since nature has not refined to perfection any single object in all its parts. [Consequently Zeuxis selected the best feature of each of the virgins whom he had chosen to serve as models for his painting.]

The painting by Zeuxis which is most clearly described was his picture of a Centaur Family. In an essay entitled Zeuxis or Antiochos, Lucian pretends to be worried about the fact that his speeches are being praised only for their novelty and not for their technique. He then draws a parallel to the Centaur Family of Zeuxis.

Lucian, *Zeuxis or Antiochos*, 3:   Zeuxis, that best of painters, did not paint popular and common subjects, or at least as few as he could, that is subjects such as heroes or gods or wars; but rather he always tried to do something new, and whenever he conceived of something unusual and strange, he demonstrated the precision of his art in [representing] it. Among his other daring innovations Zeuxis represented a female centaur, who in turn was feeding twin centaur children, mere infants. A copy of this picture now exists in Athens which duplicates the original in precision of line. The Roman general Sulla is said to have sent off the original to Italy along with other things, but I think that everything, including the painting, was destroyed when the cargo-ship sank while rounding Cape Malea. Be that as it may, I have seen the "picture of the picture" and to the degree that I am capable, I will give you a verbal description of it, although, by Zeus, I am not a connoisseur of the graphic arts; however, I remember it quite well, since it was not long ago that I saw it in the house of one of the painters in Athens. And the great admiration which I had for its artistry at that time may now be of help to me in describing it more clearly.

The centaur herself is represented as lying on rich grass with the horse part of her on the ground, and her feet stretched out behind. The human womanly part of her is raised up slightly and is supported by her bent arm. Her fore-legs are not placed in front of her and stretched out at length as would be normal with one lying on her side, but one foot is bent, like one who is kneeling, with the hoof tucked underneath, while the other foot, on the contrary, is stretched forward and takes hold of the ground, just as horses do when they are trying to get up. She holds up one of the two newborn children in her cradled arms and nurses it in the human manner by holding it up to her woman's breast; the other child she suckles from her horse's teat in the manner of a foal. In the upper part of the picture, as if placed on some kind of lookout post, is a male centaur, obviously the husband of her who is nursing the infants in two ways; he leans over, laughing, and is not completely visible but [can be seen only up to a point] in the middle of his horse body; he holds up in his right hand a lion's whelp and waves it above his head as if he were frightening the children with this joke.

As for the other aspects of the painting, those which are not wholly apparent to amateurs like us but which nevertheless contain the whole power of the art—such as drawing the lines with the utmost exactitude, making a precise mixture of the colors, and an apt application of them, employing shading where necessary, a rationale for the size of figures [that is, perspective], and equality and harmony of the parts to the whole—let painters' pupils, whose job it is to know about such things, praise them. As for me, I particularly praised Zeuxis for this achievement, namely that in one and the same design he has demonstrated the greatness of his artistic skill in a variety of ways. For, on the one hand, he has made the husband completely terrifying and quite wild, with impressively frightful hair, and shaggy all over, not just in the horse part of his body but also on his human chest and most of all on his shoulders, and the look on his face, even though he is laughing, is thoroughly bestial, with a wildness belonging to the hills.

He, then, is as I have described. The horse part of the female, on the other hand, is extremely beautiful, just like the Thessalian fillies, when they are as yet untamed and chaste; the upper part of her is that of a very beautiful woman except for the ears—these alone of her features are satyr-like. The combination and the junction of the bodies, by which the horse part is connected with and bound to the womanly part changes softly, without any harshness, and makes the transition so gradually that it escapes notice and deceives the eye as it goes from one part to another. As for the young ones there is a certain wildness in them in spite of their infancy, and there is already something frightening even in their tenderness—yes, this too struck me as something marvellous—and also how, in their babyish way, they look up at the lion's whelp, while each of them clutches the nipple and presses close to the body of their mother.

Now when Zeuxis put these things on exhibition he thought that the viewers would be astounded at his artistry—and they, to be sure, shouted their approval—for what else could they say when they came upon so beautiful a sight? But they praised all the things which those people have lately praised in me, such as the strangeness of the conception, and how the subject of the painting was new and previously unknown to them. The result was that Zeuxis, when he perceived that the newness of the subject was engaging them and drawing their attention away from its artistic quality, and that the precision of its details was being treated as a by-product, said to his pupil: "Come, Mikion, cover up the picture and the rest of you pick it up and take it home. For they are praising only the clay of my work, but as to the lighting effects, and whether these are beautifully executed and of artistic merit, these questions they treat as if they were not of much importance; rather the new-fangled quality of the subject surpasses in renown the precision of its workmanship."

Parrhasios of Ephesos

Pliny, *N.H.* XXXV, 67: Parrhasios who was born in Ephesos contributed much to the art. He first gave *symmetria* to painting, and was the first to give liveliness to the face, elegance to the hair, and beauty to the mouth; and it is acknowledged by artists that he was supreme in painting contour lines, which is the most subtle aspect of painting. For

to paint corporeal forms and the mass of things is no doubt a great
achievement, but it is one in which many have achieved fame; but to
make the contour lines of bodies and to include just the right amount
when establishing the limits of a painted figure, is an artistic success
rarely achieved. For the outline ought to round itself off and establish
such limits that it suggests other things behind it and thus reveals even
what it hides. This is the glory which Xenokrates and Antigonos, who
wrote about painting, conceded to him,[95] proclaiming their opinion
with pride rather than simply confiding it. And there are many other
remnants of his drawing among his tablets and parchments, from which,
they say, artists derive great benefit. In conveying the spatial mass [96]
of bodies, however, his success was inferior to his achievement elsewhere. He painted a picture of the *Dēmos* [*Populace*] *of the Athenians*,
a work which is especially ingenious in its presentation of the subject
matter; for he represented it as changeable, irascible, unjust, and unstable, but also placable, clement, and full of pity; boastful and . . .[97],
illustrious and humble, ferocious and fearful—all at the same time. He
also painted a *Theseus* which was on the Capitoline in Rome, a *Naval
Commander* armed with a breastplate, and, in a single picture which
is in Rhodes, Meleager, Herakles, and Perseus; this last has there been
scorched three times by lightning but not obliterated, a fact which adds
to its miraculous quality. He also painted an *Archigallus*,[98] a picture
which the emperor Tiberius fell in love with and shut up in his bedroom; the value of the picture, according to Deculo, was estimated at
6,000,000 [99] sesterces. He also painted a *Thracian Nurse* with an infant
in her arms, a *Philiskos*, a *Dionysos with Virtue Standing by*, and two
children in whom the carefree and uncomplicated quality of childhood
is observable; and also a priest attended by a boy with an incense box
and a wreath. There are two extremely well-known pictures by him, one
representing a man engaged in the race in soldier's armor who is running so hard that he appears to be dripping with sweat, and another
representing a man taking off his armor [and who is so exhausted]
that he is perceived to be gasping for breath. Also praised are his *Aeneas
and Castor and Pollux*, all in the same picture, and likewise [in a single
picture] his *Telephos, Achilles, Agamemnon, and Odysseus*. He was a

95. On the background of this passage see Introduction, p. xi.
96. Spatial mass—*in mediis corporibus*, which could simply refer to the linear
details within an outline, but which more likely refers to the technique of conveying
bodily mass through shading; in this regard Zeuxis perhaps surpassed Parrhasios.
97. A lacuna is suggested here by Mayhoff. Perhaps a word like *modestum* was
paired with *gloriosum* (boastful).
98. *Archigallus*—the chief priest among the priests of the goddess Kybele, who
were called *galli*.
99. The manuscripts read 60 (LX) and 60,000 ($\overline{\text{LX}}$); present reading was suggested by Ian.

prolific artist, but no one ever made use of the fame of his art more insolently than he, for he even adopted certain surnames, calling himself the *Habrodiaitos* ["He who lives in luxury"] and, in some other verses, the "Prince of Painting," claiming that the art had been brought to perfection by him; above all, he maintained that he was sprung from the lineage of Apollo and that his *Herakles,* which is in Lindos, was painted by him, just as he had often seen him in his dreams. And when, by a large majority of votes, he was defeated at Samos by Timanthes in [a competition for a painting of] *Ajax and the Award of the Armor,* he said in the name of his hero that it was a great vexation to him that he should have been defeated for a second time by an unworthy opponent. He also painted some small obscene pictures, apparently refreshing himself by a wanton joke of this sort.

The verses mentioned by Pliny which Parrhasios wrote about himself are preserved by Athenaeus.

Athenaeus XII, 543 D (translated in prose):   A man who loves luxury but respects virtue painted this: Parrhasios, whose renowned fatherland was Ephesos, nor do I forget my father Euenor, who begat me, his legitimate child, and the foremost practitioner of art among the Greeks.

XII, 543 E: And if they harken to the unbelievable, I say this. I say that already, the clear limits of this art have been revealed, by my hand. A boundary not to be surpassed has been fixed; but there is nothing which is completely flawless among mortal men.

In the Memorabilia *Xenophon records what purports to be an actual discussion of painting between Socrates and Parrhasios. Whether such a conversation ever actually took place is a debatable question, but the passage is nevertheless important as a reflection of the interest among the artists of the fourth century in representing* ēthos *and* pathos, *"character" and "emotion."*

Xenophon, *Memorabilia* **III, X, 1:**   . . . Coming one day to the house of Parrhasios, he [Socrates] said, in the course of a discussion: "Well, Parrhasios, is painting the representation of visible things? Certainly by making likenesses with colors you imitate forms which are deep and high, shadowy and light, hard and soft, rough and smooth, and young and old."

"What you say is quite true," he [Parrhasios] said.

"Moreover, in making a likeness of beautiful forms, since it is not easy to find one man who is completely faultless in appearance, you take the most beautiful features from each of many models and thus you make the whole body appear beautiful."

"That is just what we do," Parrhasios said.

"Well what about this?" Socrates said, "do you not imitate the character of the soul, the character which is the most persuasive, the sweetest, the most friendly, the most longed for, and the most beloved? Or are these things inimitable?"

"But how could a thing be imitated, O Socrates, which has neither proportions, nor color, nor any of the things which you mentioned just now, and which, in fact, is not even visible?"

"Well," Socrates said, "is it not natural for a man to look at certain things with either affection or hostility?"

"I suppose so," he said.

"Therefore this much must be imitable in the eyes?"

"Yes certainly," he said.

"And does it seem to you that people keep the same expression on their faces when they behold the good and evil fortunes of their friends, so that people who are concerned behave just like those who are not?"

"No indeed," Parrhasios said, "for they beam with joy at their good fortune, and they display a sad countenance at their evil fortunes."

"And is it not possible," Socrates said, "to imitate these?"

"Yes, of course," he said.

"And likewise grandeur and liberality as well as lowliness and illiberality, moderation and thoughtfulness as well as insolence and vulgarity—these too are revealed through the expression of the face and through the attitudes of the body both stationary and in movement."

"You are right," he said.

"Therefore these too can be imitated?"

"Yes, of course," he said.

"And which," Socrates said, "do you think it is more pleasant to look at, men in whom beautiful and noble and lovable natures are revealed or those in whom shameful, villainous, and hateful natures reveal themselves?"

"By Zeus, there is a great difference, Socrates," he said.

Timanthes [100]

Pliny, *N.H.* XXXV, 73: As for Timanthes, he was an artist of great ingenuity. Particularly famous owing to the praise given to it by ora-

---

100. Quintilian, *Inst. Or.* II, 13, 12, says that Timanthes was from the island of Kythnos. Eustathius, *Comm. ad Il.* p. 1313, 60, calls him a Sikyonian.

tors [101] is his *Iphigeneia*,[102] whom he depicted as she was about to perish standing at the altar while all who are with her are gloomy, especially her uncle [Menelaos]; he [Timanthes] has exahusted every expression of sadness and has veiled the face of her own father [Agamemnon], whom he could not represent adequately. And there are other examples of his ingenuity, such as the *Sleeping Cyclops* which he painted in a small panel, but wishing even so, to express its great size, he painted next to the Cyclops some satyrs who are measuring its thumb with a *thyrsos*. Moreover, in the works of this artist only, more is suggested than is actually painted, and, although the art is of the highest quality, nevertheless the ingenuity is greater than the art. He also painted a *Hero*, a work of the utmost perfection, in which he has included the art of painting men itself. This work is now in Rome in the temple of Peace.

The Schools of Classical Painting: Eupompos of Sikyon and Pamphilos of Amphipolis

The painters mentioned up to this point were thought of as belonging to a mainland or "Helladic" school (Zeuxis, and before him, Aglaophon and Apollodoros) and an Asiatic school (Euenor, Parrhasios, and Timanthes). With Eupompos and the growing influence of the artists of Sikyon, a new division was made.

Pliny, *N.H.* XXXV, 75: It was at this time [103] that Euxinidas was the teacher of Pamphilos, who was in turn the preceptor of Apelles. One work by Eupompos represents a victor in a gymnastic contest holding a palm branch. His influence was so great that he effected a [new] division of the art of painting: the schools, which before him were counted as two—called the "Helladic" and "Asiatic"—were on account of this artist, who was a Sikyonian, made into three [new schools] by subdividing the Helladic—the Ionic, the Sikyonian, and the Attic. By Pamphilos are a *Family Group*, a *Battle of Phlios*, and a *Victory of the Athenians;* [104] also an *Odysseus on his Raft*. He was himself a Macedonian by birth . . . and he was the first painter who was erudite in all branches

101. These orators could be Cicero, *Orator*, 74, and Quintilian, *Inst. Or.* II, 13, 12, from whom we learn that Odysseus and the prophet Kalchas were also represented in the picture.

102. Timanthes' *Iphigeneia* is perhaps freely copied in a wall painting representing the same scene from the house of the tragic poet in Pompeii, now in Naples. Cf. A. Maiuri, *Pompeian Wall Paintings* (Berne: 1960), no. VI.

103. That is, the early fourth century B.C., contemporary with Zeuxis, Parrhasios, and Timanthes.

104. The battles referred to may be the capture of Phlios by the Spartans in 379 B.C. and Athens' naval victory over Sparta at Naxos in 376 B.C.

of knowledge, especially arithmetic and geometry, without which, he held, an art could not be perfected; he taught no pupil for less than a talent, charging 500 drachmas a year,[105] a fee which both Apelles and Melanthios paid him. As a result of his prestige, it came about that, first in Sikyon and then in all Greece, free-born boys were given lessons in drawing on wooden tablets, although the subject had previously been omitted, and thus painting was received into the front rank of the liberal arts. And indeed it has always been an honorable feature of it, that it was practiced by free-born men, and subsequently by distinguished people, while there has been a standing prohibition against slaves being instructed in it. Hence neither in this art nor in the sculptural arts [*toreutikē*] are there any renowned works done by someone who was a slave.

The Sikyonian School

Plutarch, *Life of Aratos,* **12-13** (Plutarch describes the artistic interests of Aratos of Sikyon [271-213 B.C.], the leader of the Achaean League, and goes on to discuss the Sikyonian school in general):   From Karia, Aratos came after a long time to Egypt and went to the king [Ptolemy III] who happened to be amicably disposed toward him, since his favor had been cultivated by drawings and paintings from Greece; for this was a subject in which Aratos was not without good taste, and, constantly collecting works which were of high artistic skill and great refinement, especially those of Pamphilos and Melanthios, he would send them [to the king]. For the fame of the Sikyonian school and the success of its painting was then still at its height, because this painting alone had a beauty which did not fade. As a result of this, Apelles, who was then already much admired, came there and became a member of the school for the fee of one talent, desiring to partake of its reputation rather than because he was lacking in artistic skill.

Apelles of Kos

Apelles seems to have been the most renowned of the Greek painters. Pliny's long and colorful account of his career is an amalgamation of information derived from every variety of ancient art criticism, including the writings of Apelles himself.

Pliny, *N.H.* **XXXV, 79 ff.:** Nevertheless the painter who surpassed all those who were born before him and all those who came later was Apelles of Kos, who was active in the 112th Olympiad [332 B.C.]. He

---

105. A talent was reckoned at 6000 drachmas; hence Pamphilos' course took twelve years.

alone contributed almost more to the art of painting than all other painters combined and also produced volumes, which contain his doctrine [concerning painting]. The "grace" [*venustas*] of his art was outstanding, even though other very great painters were active at that time. Apelles admired the work of these other artists, and bestowed praise on all, but held that they lacked his artistic grace [*venerem*], which the Greeks call *charis;* he held that the rest of the artists attained every other quality, but in this one alone nobody was his equal. And he made still another claim to fame, when he admired a work of Protogenes which involved immense labor and an anguishing, unlimited attention to detail; for he said that by every standard Protogenes' achievements were either equal to his own or superior but that in one quality he [Apelles] was outstanding, and that was in knowing when to take his hand away from a painting, a memorable warning that too much detail can be harmful. His candor, however, was no less impressive than his art; for he used to admit his inferiority to Melanthios in *dispositio,* and to Asklepiodoros in *mensurae,* that is, how much distance should be left between one thing and another.[106]

An instructive incident occurred involving him and Protogenes. The latter lived in Rhodes, and Apelles at one time sailed there, eager to get to know at first hand the works of that artist who was known to him only by the extent of his reputation, and immediately sought him out in his studio. He was absent at the time, but a panel of considerable size was set up on the easel and one old woman was the custodian of it. She informed him that Protogenes was out and asked by whom she should say he was being sought. "By this person," answered Apelles, and picking up the paintbrush he drew in color across the panel a line of the utmost fineness. When Protogenes returned, the old woman showed him what had been done. They say that the artist immediately contemplated the subtlety of the line and said that it was Apelles who had come, for such a perfect piece of work could not be fittingly ascribed to anyone else. Then he himself, with another color, drew an even finer line over the first one, and, absenting himself again, instructed the old woman that if the visitor returned she should show him the line and add that this was the person whom he was seeking. And this is just what occurred. For Apelles returned and, blushing with shame at the thought of being defeated, he split the [first two] lines with a third color, thus leaving no room for any further display of subtlety. At this Protogenes, admitting that he was defeated, flew down to the port in search of his guest. And he resolved that the panel should be handed

106. *Dispositio* (—Greek *diathesis?*) probably refers to the grouping of figures. *Mensurae* may refer to the distance between groups, or it may refer to measurements by which perspective is achieved.

down to posterity just as it was, a marvel which, to be sure, would impress everyone, but especially other artists. I am informed that it was consumed in the first conflagration of the house of Caesar on the Palatine; [107] prior to that it was much admired by us [that is, the Romans], since it contained on that extensive surface nothing other than those lines which almost eluded one's vision; among the outstanding works of many artists it seemed to be a blank panel, and by that very fact it attracted attention and was better known than any other work there.

In general it was a standing practice with Apelles never to be so occupied with carrying out the day's business, that he did not practice his art by drawing a line, and the example which he set has come down as a proverb. He also used to place finished works in a shop in view of passers-by, and, hiding behind a panel himself, he would listen attentively to the faults which they noticed, holding that the public was a more astute judge than himself. They say that he was criticized by a shoemaker because he had made one too few lace-holes in the sandals, and that on the following day, the same man, proud that a correction had been made on the basis of his previous criticism, made fun of the leg, whereupon the artist peered out and denounced him, saying a shoemaker should not presume to judge anything higher than a sandal; and this too has come to be a proverb. He was also gifted with a courteous nature and, on account of this, was on quite good terms with Alexander the Great who frequently came to his studio—for, as we said, he forbade by an edict that his portrait should be made by any other artist—but when Alexander used to discourse upon many aspects of painting even though he was not well informed, Apelles would politely advise him to be quiet, saying that he was being laughed at by the boys who were grinding the colors. So confident was he in the power of his privileged position even with a king who was otherwise of an irascible nature. And Alexander, notwithstanding, bestowed honor on him in one very conspicuous case. For when he gave orders that the woman named Pankaspe, who was his principal favorite among all his concubines, should, owing to his admiration for her beauty, be painted in the nude by Apelles, and when he learned that Apelles, while working on the picture, had fallen in love with her, he gave her to him; for he [Alexander] was great in spirit and even greater in his power over himself; he made this into a victory no less great than his other victories, because he conquered himself and gave to the artist not only his bed but also his affection; nor was he even moved by consideration of [the feelings of] his favorite, who had once belonged to a king, but now belonged to a painter. There are those who believe that she was

107. Caesar—Augustus; this fire occurred in 4 A.D.

the model from whom the *Aphrodite Anadyomenē* ["Rising from the Sea"] was painted. It was also Apelles who, being kindly disposed toward his rivals, first established the reputation of Protogenes at Rhodes. Protogenes was treated with contempt by his own people, as is the case with many artists who are domestic products, and when Apelles inquired of him about what sort of prices he asked for his completed works, Protogenes mentioned some small sum (I am not sure how much). Thereupon Apelles made an offer of fifty talents and spread the word around that he was buying the paintings in order to sell them as his own works. This ruse aroused the Rhodians to an appreciation of their artist, and Apelles would not give up the pictures except at an increased price.

He also painted portraits which were such exact likenesses that—incredible as it is to say—the grammarian Apio has recorded in his writings that a certain one of those men who read the future from the features of the face (whom they call *metoposcopoi*) told from these portraits either the time of [the subjects'] death in the future or the number of years of life which had already elapsed. Apelles had not been in the good graces of Ptolemy [108] when the latter was in Alexander's retinue; when Ptolemy was reigning in Alexandria and Apelles was driven there by the force of a storm, a royal jester was suborned, through a plot of Apelles' rivals, to carry to him a dinner invitation. Apelles came to the dinner and Ptolemy, with great indignation, put his social secretaries on display in order that Apelles might say from which of them he had received the invitation. Apelles picked up a piece of extinguished charcoal from a brazier and drew a portrait on the wall, whereupon the king immediately recognized the face of the jester, even when it was unfinished. He also painted a portrait of King Antigonos,[109] one of whose eyes was missing, and first devised the technique for concealing this defect. For he made a three-quarter view of the king so that the part which was actually lacking in the body might rather seem only to be lacking in the picture, and he showed only that part of the face which he could show as flawless. There are also among his pictures portraits of people who are expiring. Which is the most renowned of his works, however, is not easy to say. His *Aphrodite Rising from the Sea*, which is called the *Anadyomenē*, was dedicated by Augustus in the shrine of his father [Julius] Caesar. . . . The lower part of it was damaged, and it was impossible to find anyone who could restore it; thus the injury itself contributed to the fame of the artist.

108. Ptolemy son of Lagos (c. 367-283 B.C.) became Ptolemy I, King of Egypt after Alexander's death.
109. Antigonos *Monophthalmos*, "the one-eyed" (c. 382-301 B.C.) was one of Alexander's generals and later king of Macedonia.

This picture decayed from age and rottenness, and Nero, in his principate, substituted for it another painting by the hand of Dorotheus. Apelles also began an Aphrodite at Kos, which was to be superior even to his earlier one. But death grew envious of him when the work was only partly finished, nor was anyone found who could complete it according to the sketch-lines which he had drawn beforehand. He also painted for twenty gold talents an *Alexander the Great Holding a Thunderbolt* in the temple of Artemis at Ephesos. The fingers [in this painting] seem to stand out and the thunderbolt also seems to project out of the picture—my readers will remember that all this was done with only four colors.[110] He received the fee for this picture in gold coin measured by weight, not by number. He also painted a *Procession of the Megabyzus,* the priest of Artemis at Ephesos, a *Kleitos* [111] with his horse hastening into battle, and an armor-bearer holding out a helmet to a man who has asked for it. How many times he painted Alexander and Philip would be superfluous to enumerate. Greatly admired are his *Habron* at Samos, his *Menander King of the Karians,* and his *Antaios;* at Alexandria his *Gorgosthenes* the tragic actor; and at Rome his *Castor and Pollux with Victory and Alexander the Great,* and his representation of *War* with his hands tied behind his back along with Alexander riding in triumph on a chariot. Both of these pictures the divine Augustus dedicated with modest restraint in the most frequently visited parts of his forum. The divine Claudius, however, thought it better to cut out the face of Alexander from both pictures and to add portraits of Augustus. People are also of the opinion that the *Herakles with his Face Turned* in the temple of Diana is by Apelles' hand and that the painting actually displays Herakles' face more truly than it suggests it, which is a very difficult feat. He also painted a *Nude Hero,* and in this picture he challenged nature itself. There is, or at least was, a horse by him painted in a competition which he presented for judgment to dumb quadrupeds rather than to men. For becoming aware that his rivals were prevailing against him by bribery, he had some horses led in and showed them the pictures one by one, and they neighed only at the horse of Apelles. And this always happened again in later trials, so that it was shown to be a valid test of artistic quality. He also made a *Neoptolemos* fighting against the Persians from horseback, an *Archelaos with his Wife and Daughter,* and *Antigonos* armed with a breastplate and marching along with his horse.[112] Those who are con-

110. See pp. 221, 228.
111. Several Macedonian soldiers of the time of Alexander bore this name. The best known of them was Kleitos the son of Dropides whom Alexander killed in a fit of anger in 328 B.C.
112. Neoptolemos and Archelaos, as well as Antigonos, were officers in Alexander's army.

noisseurs of the art prefer before all his other works a portrait of the same king [Antigonos] seated on a horse and his *Artemis Mingling with a Group of Virgins* who are offering sacrifice, a work which seems to surpass the verses of Homer describing the same subject.[113] He also painted things which [supposedly] cannot be represented in painting— thunder, lightning, and thunderbolts, which they call [in Greek] *brontē, astrapē,* and *keraunobolia.*

His inventions in the art were useful to others as well. There was one, however, which no one could imitate; this was that he coated his finished works with a black varnish so thin that while it accentuated the reflection of the brightness of all the colors and protected the painting from dust and dirt, the varnish was visible only to one inspecting it close at hand; but this also involved considerable theoretical calculation, lest the brightness of the colors offend the eye, as in the case of those who look through a transparent colored stone, and also so that from a distance the same device might, though hidden, give somberness to the colors which were too bright.

Although Apelles is frequently mentioned elsewhere in ancient literature, there are only a few references which add anything to the information given in Pliny's long commentary. One of these is Lucian's description (ekphrasis) of an allegorical painting apparently called the Calumny. *Apelles was accused by his rival Antiphilos of having participated in a plot to overthrow Ptolemy I. Before he was acquitted he painted the picture to express the predicament in which the slander had put him. Lucian's ekphrasis later became the basis for Botticelli's* Calumny of Apelles *in the Uffizi in Florence.*

Lucian, *Calumniae Non Temere Credendum,* 4: Apelles, mindful of dangers which surrounded him, defended himself against the slander with a picture of the following sort. On the right is a man with huge ears, which are only just short of being like those of Midas, stretching out one hand from afar to "Calumny" who is still coming forward. Flanking him stand two women, who seem to me to be "Ignorance" and "Suspicion." On the other side "Calumny" comes forward, a small woman of extreme beauty, heated with passion and in a state of great excitement, the sort of woman who puts madness and rage on display; in her left hand she holds a lighted torch and in her right she drags along a certain youth by the hair who stretches out his hands to heaven and bears witness before the gods. A man who is sallow and ugly leads them, glancing around sharply and wearing that look which people get when they have been withered by a long disease. One would sup-

113. *Odyssey,* VI, 102 ff. seems to be referred to.

pose that this was "Jealousy." There are also two other female figures who accompany "Calumny" and are in the act of exhorting, protecting, and adorning her. According to the guide who explained the features of the picture to me, one of these women was "Treachery" and the other was "Deception." Behind them comes another figure, represented as if in mourning, and dressed in black raiment which is torn in shreds; she, I think, is said to be "Repentance." She turns around in tears and with a great sense of shame toward "Truth" who looks up to heaven as she approaches. Thus did Apelles reproduce his own danger in the painting.

Melanthios of Sikyon

As has already been indicated, Melanthios, a pupil of Pamphilos, was the artist to whom Apelles acknowledged his inferiority in dispositio. *He was also one of the "four-color painters" (see p. 228) and wrote a book about painting.*

Diogenes Laertius IV, 18: And he [Polemon] [114] was just such a man as Melanthios describes in his book on painting. For he says that one should strive to put a ceratin willfulness and harshness into one's paintings, just like that which exists in the characters.[115]

Plutarch, *Life of Aratos,* **13** (continuing the passage given above, p. 163): And when he freed the city [Sikyon], Aratos immediately took down all the other portraits of the tyrants, but in the case of a portrait of Aristratos, who was in power in the time of Philip, he deliberated for a long time. For Aristratos, standing by a chariot which bore a figure of Victory, had been painted by Melanthios and his circle, and, according to the geographer Polemon, Apelles even had a hand in the painting. It was a work of remarkable quality, so much so that Aratos was tempted to spare it because of its artistry; again, however, led on by his hatred for the tyrants, he ordered that it be taken down. They say that the painter Nealkes, who was a friend of Aratos, entreated him not to do it and even wept, but when he could not persuade him, he said: "The battle should be against the tyrants, not those with the tyrants. Let us save therefore the chariot and the Victory. I will take charge of getting Aristratos out of the picture for you." When Aratos gave him permission, Neakles erased the figure of Aristratos and painted in its place a single palm tree, but he did not dare to vie with the original by adding anything else. They say, however, that the feet of the

---

114. Polemon—a follower of Plato and head of the Academy from 314 to 267 B.C.
115. The meaning of the statement is probably that portraits should reflect the real nature, even though harsh, of the subject.

erased Aristratos which showed beneath the chariot escaped notice [and hence were not erased].

Pausias of Sikyon

Pliny, *N.H.* XXXV, 123-127: There is also a tradition that Pamphilos, the teacher of Apelles, not only painted in encaustic but also taught it to Pausias of Sikyon, who was the first to become well-known in this technique. He was the son of Bryetes and was at first a disciple of his father. He himself also did some brush paintings [116] on walls at Thespiai, at a time when some paintings of Polygnotos were being restored, and he was deemed, when compared [with Polygnotos], to have been far surpassed, since he had competed in a category which was not his strong point. Pausias also first introduced the practice of painting paneled ceilings, for before his time it was not the custom to decorate vaulted chambers in this way; he also used to paint small panels, mostly of children. The interpretation of his rivals was that he did this because his method of painting was very slow. On account of this charge and to give himself a reputation for speed, he finished in one day a panel, with a boy painted on it, which is called the *Hēmerēsios* [*One-day Boy*]. In his youth he was in love with a girl from his home-town named Glykera, who was the inventrix of garlands, and in competing with and imitating her, he introduced a great many varieties of flowers into the art [of painting]. Eventually he painted a picture of this girl herself seated within a garland, which is one of his best-known pictures and is called the *Stephanoplocos* [*Girl Weaving a Garland*], or, by others, the *Stephanopolis* [*The Girl Selling Garlands*] because Glykera had eked out a poor living by selling garlands. A copy of this painting, which is called in Greek an *apographon* was bought by L. Lucullus for two talents . . . [the copy was made by] [117] Dionysios of Athens. Pausias, however, also made large pictures such as that which was to be seen in the portico of Pompey representing the *Immolation of an Ox,* a work which many later imitated, but none equalled. For the most remarkable feature of all was that, although he wished to show the longitudinal extension of the ox, he painted it in a facing position, rather than sideways, and yet its full size is clearly conveyed. Thereupon, whereas all other artists make the things which they wish to appear prominent in bright colors, and those which they wish to suppress in dark, he painted the whole ox black and gave body to this dark shade from shade itself, an achievement of great artistic skill which conveys a formal projection

116. As compared with encaustic paintings which were done with a *cestrum,* a kind of spatula used in applying wax.

117. There is a lacuna in the text which should probably be filled by *quod fecit* or a similar phrase.

even on a flat plane and on a surface which is broken up in patches [of color] makes everything seem solid. This artist spent his life in Sikyon, which was for a long time the homeland of the art of painting. But eventually all the pictures were confiscated from public ownership because of a debt and were transferred from there [Sikyon] to Rome during the aedilship of Scaurus [56 B.C.].

Pausanias II, 27, 3 (at Epidauros): There has been built nearby a circular building of white marble called the *Tholos*,[118] a building worth seeing. In it there is a picture painted by Pausias of *Eros* who has put aside his bow and arrows and holds a lyre which he has taken up instead of them. Also there is a picture of *Drunkenness* drinking from a glass cup, this too being a work of Pausias. You may see in this painting both the glass cup and the woman's face showing through it.

The Sikyonian School in the Later Fourth Century: Nikophanes, Aristolaos, Socrates, Perseus, and Ktesilochos

Pliny, N.H. XXXV, 111: . . . Nikophanes [was a painter] whose style was so elegant and harmonious, that few artists may be compared to him for beauty. But in the dramatic and serious aspect of art he was much inferior to Zeuxis and Apelles. Perseus, who was Apelles' disciple and the person to whom Apelles addressed his writings about painting, belonged to the same period.

Pliny, N.H. XXXV, 137: Aristolaos, the son and disciple of Pausias, was among the most severe of painters. By him are an *Epaminondas*, a *Pericles*, a *Medea*, a *Virtue*, a *Theseus*, an image of the *Athenian Populace*, and an *Immolation of an Ox*. There are also some to whom Nikophanes, a disciple of the same Pausias, is pleasing because of his precision [*diligentia*] which is of a sort which only artists appreciate; he was otherwise rather hard in his use of color and free in his use of yellow ochre. As for Socrates, he is rightly pleasing to all. By him there are such pictures as *Asklepios with his Daughters Hygieia* ["Health"], *Aiglē* ["Brightness"], and *Panacea and Iaso* ["Cure"], and also his picture of a slothful man called *Oknos*, who is twisting a grass rope on which an ass is chewing.

Pliny, N.H. XXXV, 140: Ktesilochos, the disciple of Apelles, became famous for his impudent picture, representing *Zeus Suffering Labor Pains over Dionysos*, and wearing a woman's headdress and moaning like a woman among the goddesses, who are acting as midwives.

---

118. The architect was Polykleitos the Younger; see p. 182.

The Attic School

The earliest painters connected with this school were Euxeinides and the Elder Aristeides. Aristeides the Elder had two prominent pupils —his son Nikomachos and Euphranor of Isthmia.

Nikomachos, son of Aristeides

See also pp. 228-229.

Pliny, N.H. XXXV, 108-110: Nikomachos, the son of Aristeides, should be numbered among these artists. He painted a *Rape of Persephone,* which was once in the shrine of Minerva on the Capitoline just above the chapel of Iuventas ["Youth"]; also on the Capitoline was a painting which the general Plancus [119] put there, representing *Victory Hurrying Aloft in a Quadriga.* He was the first to add a felt cap to the representa- ation of Odysseus. He also painted an *Apollo and Artemis* and a *Mother of the Gods Seated on a Lion,* also a well-known picture of *Baccantes with Satyrs Creeping up to Them,* and a *Skylla* which is now in Rome in the temple of Peace. No other artist ever worked more rapidly in this art. For there is a tradition that he took a commission from Aristratos,[120] the tyrant of Sikyon, to paint a monument which Aris- tratos was erecting to the poet Telestes, and agreed that it should be finished on a predetermined date; he did not arrive, however, until shortly before that date, and the tyrant, incensed, threatened punish- ishment, but he finished off the work in a few days with remarkable rapidity and artistic skill. He had as his disciples his brother Ariston and his son Aristeides and also Philoxenos of Eretria.[121]

Euphranor

Euphranor, as we have already seen, was also a well-known sculptor (see p. 139).

Pliny, N.H. XXXV, 128: After him [Pausias] by far the most dis- tinguished painter was Euphranor the Isthmian, who was active in the 104th Olympiad [364 B.C.] and whom we have already mentioned among

119. Plancus—Lucius Munatius (consul in 42 B.C.), Roman soldier and politician who served under both Julius Caesar and Augustus.

120. Aristratos, as has been indicated, was a contemporary of Philip of Macedon, and hence active in the middle of the fourth century B.C.

121. On these artists see pp. 174-175 and p. 229. Aristeides, the son of Niko- machos, is usually called "Aristeides the Younger" and is, of course, the grandson of the Elder Aristeides.

the sculptors. He made colossal statues and works in marble, and also carved reliefs; he was the most intellectual [*docilis*] and industrious of artists, excelling in every genre of art and always maintaining his artistic standard. He seems to have been the first to express the dignified qualities of heroes and to have made *symmetria* his special province,[122] although [the proportions he used] for the whole body were too thin and those for the head and the limbs [123] were too large. He also wrote volumes about *symmetria* and about colors. Works by him are a *Cavalry Battle, The Twelve Gods,* and a *Theseus,* in connection with which he said that the *Theseus* by Parrhasios had been fed on roses, but his own was fed on meat. There is a well-known panel by him in Ephesos representing Odysseus simulating insanity and yoking together an ox and a horse, while some men who are cloaked in mantles contemplate the scene and their leader conceals his sword.

The Theseus *and the* Cavalry Battle *mentioned by Pliny were seen by Pausanias on a wall of the* Stoa Basileios *in the Agora in Athens.*

Pausanias I, 3, 3-4: A stoa is built behind which has paintings of the gods which are called *The Twelve.* On the wall adjacent a *Theseus* is painted, along with "Democracy" and *Dēmos* ["The People"]. The picture indicates that it was Theseus who established political equality among the Athenians. . . . Also depicted is the exploit of the Athenians around Mantineia, when they were sent to give aid to the Lakedaimonians.[124] . . . In this painting there is a cavalry battle, in which the most prominent figures are, among the Athenians, Grylos the son of Xenophon, and amidst the Boeotian cavalry, Epaminondas the Theban. These pictures were painted for the Athenians by Euphranor. . . .

The following anecdotes, perhaps contradictory, are told about Euphranor's painting of the Twelve Gods *mentioned above.*

Valerius Maximus VIII, 11, ext. 5: For when he [Euphranor] painted the *Twelve Gods* in Athens, he composed the image of Poseidon with color of the most extraordinary splendor, and afterwards in the same way he intended to make the image of Zeus considerably more august. But all the inspiration behind his conception had been spent on the

123. *Usurpasse symmetrian.* Parrhasios, as we have seen, was credited with having first introduced *symmetria* into painting. Euphranor must have refined and developed it.

123. Limbs—*articuli.* The word can also mean "joints."

124. This occurred in 362 B.C., when Epaminondas and the Thebans invaded the Peloponnesos.

earlier work, and his later attempts were not able to rise to the level for which he was striving.

Eustathius, *Comm. ad Il.*, p. 145, 11: There is a story that Euphranor, when he was painting the *Twelve Gods* in Athens and was at a loss as to what model he should paint his Zeus from, happened to pass by a poetry class. And hearing the following verses: "His ambrosial locks" and so on, he said that he now had the model. And, going on his way he proceeded to paint it accordingly.[125]

Aristeides the Younger

Pliny, *N.H.* XXXV, 98-100: Contemporary with him [Apelles] was Aristeides the Theban. He first depicted the character and mental sensibilities of man, which the Greeks call *ēthē*, and also the emotions,[126] but he was a little hard in his use of colors. His works include a picture showing the capture of a town, with an infant crawling toward the breast of its mother who is dying from a wound, and one is made to feel that the mother is conscious of it and is afraid lest, with her milk failing as she dies, the child may suck blood. Alexander the Great transferred this picture to Pella in his fatherland. The same artist also painted a battle against the Persians, and after incorporating into it one hundred men, he drove a bargain for it with Mnason, the tyrant of Elateia, for ten minae per figure. He also painted *Quadrigas Racing*, a *Suppliant* who almost seems to have a voice, *Hunters with Captured Game*, *Leontion [the mistress] of Epicurus*, an *Anapauomenē [a Woman Expiring]* [127] on account of her love for her brother, also a *Dionysos and Ariadne*, which could once be seen in the temple of Ceres in Rome, and a *Tragic Actor and a Boy* in the temple of Apollo, a painting of which the grace was destroyed by the ignorance of a painter whom M. Iunius, the praetor, commissioned to clean it in preparation for the day of the festival games of Apollo. Also once on display in the temple of Faith on the Capitoline was his picture of an *Old Man with a Lyre Teaching a Boy*. He also painted an *Invalid* which is praised endlessly, and he was so proficient in this art that King Attalos is reputed to have bought one of his pictures for a hundred talents.

Philoxenos of Eretria (Pupil of Nikomachos)

Pliny, *N.H.* XXXV, 110: . . . Philoxenos of Eretria painted a picture for King Kassander,[128] which must be considered inferior to none; it

125. The verses Euphranor is said to have heard were from the *Iliad*. Compare the story about Pheidias' inspiration for the Zeus at Olympia, p. 73.

126. "Emotions"—Greek *pathē*. See pp. 160-161 and Chapter 6, p. 229.

127. Possibly a reference to the myth of Kanake and Makareus (cf. Ovid, *Heroides*, 11), or that of Biblis and Kaunos (cf. Ovid, *Metamorphoses*, IX, lines 454 ff.).

128. Kassander—king of Macedonia c. 319-297 B.C.

contained the *Battle of Alexander Against Darius*.[129] He also painted a lascivious picture in which three Satyrs revel riotously. This artist followed the rapidity of his teacher and invented certain even more rapid short cuts [130] in painting.

Antidotos and Nikias (Son of Nikomedes)

Pliny, *N.H.* XXXV, 130-133: Antidotos, however, was a pupil of Euphranor. Works by him are an *Armed Fighter with a Shield* at Athens, a *Wrestler,* and a *Trumpeter,* which is particularly praised. He emphasized precision rather than varieties of composition [131] and was severe in his colors; his chief claim to fame was his disciple Nikias the Athenian, who painted women in a most detailed manner. He kept a careful watch on light and shade and took great care so that the painted figures should stand out from the panel.[132] Works by him are a *Nemea* which was brought from Asia to Rome by Silanus and . . . placed in the *Curia* [Senate House], also a *Dionysos* in the temple of Concord, a *Hyakinthos,*[133] which Augustus Caesar took delight in and brought back with him after he took Alexandria (because of this Tiberius Caesar dedicated this picture in his [Augustus'] temple), and a *Danaë;* at Ephesos there is a *Sepulchre of a Megabyzus,* the priest of Artemis at Ephesos, and at Athens the *Nekyomanteia* [*Prophecy of the Dead*] after Homer. This picture he refused to sell to King Attalos for 60 talents and gave it rather to his home town, since he had plenty of money already. He also did some large pictures, among which are a *Calypso,* an *Io,* and an *Andromeda;* also the very excellent *Alexander* in the porticoes of Pompey and a *Seated Calypso* are ascribed to him.

Of four-footed animals he rendered dogs best. It was this Nikias of whom Praxiteles used to say when asked which of his own works he valued the most, "Those to which Nikias has applied his hand"; so greatly did he pay tribute to the way he [Nikias] applied paint to a surface. It is not quite clear whether this refers to another artist of this

129. It has often been suggested that this painting was the original from which the famous Alexander Mosaic (from Pompeii, now in Naples) was copied. Cf. H. Fuhrmann, *Philoxenos von Eretria* (Gottingen: 1931); B. Andreae, *Das Alexandermosaik* (Bremen: 1959) (with bibliography).

130. Short cuts—*compendiariae.* The term has sometimes been interpreted as referring to an impressionistic technique, but it may equally well refer to technical innovations in preparing the paint, the painted surface, etc.

131. "Precision . . . composition"—*diligentior quam numerosior; diligens* was the translation of the Greek *akribēs; numerus* was used to translate the Greek *rhythmos.*

132. A. Rumpf suggests that Nikias' achievement was to apply the technique of *skiagraphia* to the female figure; cf. "Diligentissime Mulieres Pinxit," *Jahrbuch der Deutschen Archäologischen Instituts,* 49 (1934), pp. 6-23.

133. See also Pausanias III, 19, 4.

name or the same one [which we have been discussing], whom some place in the 112th Olympiad [332 B.C.].[134]

The Nemea *mentioned above is further elaborated upon by Pliny,* N.H. XXXV, 27:

Augustus also had imbedded into the wall in the *Curia* which he consecrated in the *Comitium,* a *Nemea,* seated on a lion and carrying a palm branch, by whom stands an old man with a staff, over whose head hangs a picture of a two-horse chariot—a picture on which Nikias wrote that he did it in the encaustic technique. . . .

Another work seen by Pausanias is probably by the same Nikias.

Pausanias VII, 22, 6 (at Triteia in Achaia):   Before you enter the city there is a grave monument of white marble which is worth seeing, especially for the paintings on the gravestone which are by Nikias. There is a chair of ivory and on it sits a young woman of fair appearance, by whom stands a maid carrying a parasol. There is also a young man who stands upright and does not yet have a beard; he is dressed in a tunic and has a purple travelling cloak thrown over it. By him is a servant who has some javelins and leads dogs of the sort with which men hunt. I was not able to learn the names of these people; but anyone would be able to surmise that a husband and wife are buried here together.

The grave of Nikias was seen by Pausanias on the road from Athens to the Academy. It was placed near those of such famous men as Miltiades, Kimon, Zeno the Stoic, and Harmodios and Aristogeiton.

Pausanias I, 29, 15:   Here too is buried . . . Nikias the son of Nikomedes, the best of all the painters of his day in painting living figures. . . .

The Ionic School

Protogenes of Rhodes

Aspects of Protogenes' career have already been discussed in connection with Apelles.

134. Some modern editors feel that the Nikias who painted the statues of Praxiteles was an "Elder Nikias," who should be distinguished from Nikias the pupil of Antidotos. That this need not necessarily be the case is convincingly argued by H. Brunn, *Geschichte der Griechischen Künstler,*2 II (Stuttgart: 1889), p. 111.

Pliny, *N.H.* XXXV, 101-106:   Protogenes, as was said, flourished in the same period [as Apelles and Aristeides]. His home was in Kaunos [in Karia], a city belonging to people subject to the Rhodians. At the beginning of his career he was extremely poor and very intent about his art with the result that he was not very prolific. Whoever it was who taught him was not, they think, well-known. Indeed up to his fiftieth year he is thought to have painted ships; the argument for this conclusion is that when he was doing some paintings in an extremely famous place in Athens, the Propylon of the sanctuary of Athena, where he painted the well-known *Paralos* and the *Hammonias*,[135] which some call the *Nausikaa,* he added some small pictures of warships next to these (the sort of pictures which they call *parergia*) [136] in order that it would be apparent from what sort of beginning his works had risen to the pinnacle of prominence. Among his pictures the first prize must go to his *Ialysos*,[137] which is dedicated at Rome in the temple of Peace; there is a tradition that while he was painting this, he lived on wet lupines and thus sustained his hunger and thirst but did not blunt his senses by too much sweet food. On this picture he used four layers of color so that there would be three sub-layers to guard against injury and old age, for as the outer layer disappeared the one below would succeed it. In this painting there is a dog which was done in a miraculous manner, as if art and chance had painted together. For he judged that he had not successfully expressed in this work the foam of the panting dog, although in the other parts he had satisfied himself, which was extremely difficult. The artistry itself, however, displeased him; nor was he able to tone it down and it seemed to diverge too much and too far from what was true—the foam appeared only to be painted and not actually to have originated in the dog's mouth. Tormented by this anxiety in his mind (since he wanted reality to exist in his picture and not simply verisimilitude), he frequently wiped off the paint and changed to another brush, but he could not get himself to approve of the work by any method. Finally, irritated with his art because it was so obvious, he dashed a sponge against the hated spot in the picture. And this sponge put back the colors which he had removed in the way that all his effort had striven for, and thus chance produced nature in the picture.

It is said that, following this example, Nealkes achieved a similar success in painting the foam on a horse, that is, by throwing a sponge

135. These were the flagships of the city of Athens and were used for various diplomatic and ritual functions.

136. *Parergia*—a Latin form of the Greek term *parerga,* literally "side products."

137. Ialysos—a mythical Rhodian hero, founder of the city of Ialysos on the island of Rhodes.

in the same way, when he was painting a picture of a man making a clucking noise while he restrained his horse.

It was on account of this *Ialysos* that King Demetrios,[138] when he could only capture Rhodes from that part of the city [where the picture was], did not set fire to the city, and thus, in sparing the picture, lost his chance for victory. Protogenes was then in his suburban garden, which was within the area of Demetrios' encampment; he was not disturbed by the battles in progress nor did he abandon his incomplete works for any reason until he was summoned by the king and asked what he trusted in when he continued to go about his business outside the walls; he responded that he knew the king was at war with the Rhodians but not with the arts. The king then stationed guards for his protection, rejoicing that he could safeguard the hands which he had spared; also, lest he call him [Protogenes] away from his work too often, he, an enemy, came of his own accord to visit him; and with the prayers for his own victory forgotten amidst the defense and the attack on the walls, he gazed at [the work of] the artist. The story survives in connection with a picture done at that time, that Protogenes painted it beneath a sword. This was a picture of a *Satyr*, which they call the *Anapauomenon* [*Resting*]; and lest it be felt that there was something lacking from the security which he felt at that time, the satyr holds flutes.

He also made a *Kydippe and Tlepolemos,* a *Philiskos, the Writer of Tragedies, in Meditation,* an *Athlete, King Antigonos,* and *The Mother of the Philosopher Aristotle;* it was Aristotle who used to advise him that he should paint the exploits of Alexander the Great because of their eternal influence. The natural bent of his mind and a certain sensuality about art led him rather to do work of the sort mentioned above. His latest work was an *Alexander and Pan.* He also made statues in bronze.

Plutarch elaborates on the Ialysos *and on Demetrios' appreciation of Protogenes.*

Plutarch, *Life of Demetrios,* 22: It happened that Protogenes the Kaunian was painting the story of Ialysos for the Rhodians and that the picture was little short of completion when Demetrios seized it in one of the suburbs. Sending a herald, the Rhodians begged him to spare the picture and not to destroy it, to which he replied that he would sooner burn the portraits of his father rather than this great labor of art. For

138. Demetrios *Poliorkētēs* (336-283 B.C.), son of Antigonos. As a part of his father's scheme to reunite Alexander's empire, he laid siege to Rhodes in 305 B.C. He became king of Macedonia in 294 B.C.

it is said that Protogenes worked on the painting for seven years. And they say that when Apelles saw the work he was so astounded that his voice left him; but later he said that although the labor was great and the work was marvellous, it did not have his own *charis* through which the figures painted by him touched heaven itself.

Other Painters of the Fourth Century

Asklepiodoros

See also above, p. 164.

Pliny, N.H. XXXV, 107: In the same period [as Apelles, Protogenes, and others] lived Asklepiodoros, who was admired by Apelles for his ability in *symmetria*.[139] For his picture of the *Twelve Gods* the tyrant Mnason gave him 300 minae for each god.

Antiphilos

Pliny, N.H. XXXV, 114: . . . Antiphilos. For he painted a well-known picture of *Hesione* and an *Alexander and Philip with Athena* which are now in the school in the Porticoes of Octavia; in those of Philippus [140] there is a *Dionysos*, an *Alexander as a Boy*, and a *Hippolytos Greatly Dreading the Unleashed Bull;* while in those of Pompey there are a *Cadmus* and a *Europa.* He also painted a figure in a ridiculous garb which had the humorous name *Gryllos*, and it is after this that there is a genre of pictures called *Grylloi.* He himself was born in Egypt and was taught by Ktesidemos.

Pliny, N.H. XXXV, 138: Antiphilos is praised for his *Boy Blowing on a Fire,* in which the beautiful room as well as the boy's face are illuminated [by the fire]; also for his *Spinning of Wool,* in which the tasks of all the women are being briskly attended to; also his *Ptolemy Hunting,* but, most famous of all, his *Satyr with a Panther Skin,* which they call the *Aposkopeuonta.*[141]

Athenion of Maroneia (in Thrace)

Pliny, N.H. XXXV, 134: Athenion of Maroneia, a pupil of Glaukion of Corinth, is compared and sometimes preferred to Nikias; he was more austere in his colors but in this austerity he was more pleasing so that

139. Pliny's index to Book XXXV indicates that Asklepiodoros wrote a book about *symmetria.*
140. That is, the porticoes built either by L. Marcius Philippus, the step-father of Augustus, or by his son.
141. *Aposkopeuonta*—One who shades his eyes as he looks at something.

his erudition glittered within the picture itself.[142] He painted a *Phylarchos* [143] in the temple at Eleusis, and at Athens an *Assembly of Relatives* which they call the *Syngenikon,* also an *Achilles Disguised in the Garb of a Virgin Being Discovered by Odysseus,* a group of six figures in one picture, and a *Groom with a Horse,* by which he became very well known. Had he not died in his youth, no one would have been comparable to him.

Kydias

Pliny, *N.H.* XXXV, 130:   Active at the same time [as Euphranor] was Kydias, whose picture of *The Argonauts* [144] was bought for 144,000 sesterces by the orator Hortensius who made a temple for it in his [estate] in Tusculum.

Aëtion (and Therimachos)

Pliny, *N.H.* XXXV, 78:   Aëtion and Therimachos were outstanding artists in the 107th Olympiad [352 B.C]. Well-known paintings by Aëtion are his *Dionysos,* his *Tragedy and Comedy,* his *Semiramis Ascending to the Throne from Being a Maid-Servant,* and an *Old Woman Leading the Way with a Wedding Torch and a New Bride,* [the latter] notable for her shyness.

Lucian also gives a detailed ekphrasis of a picture by a painter named Aëtion representing the Marriage of Alexander and Roxane. *Although Lucian seems to imply that the picture had been executed in his own time (that is, in the second century* A.D.*) most modern scholars ascribe the picture to the fourth century Aëtion. Perhaps he had recently seen the picture in Italy and assumed that it was a recent work. The subject of the painting is certainly appropriate to the late fourth century* B.C.

Lucian, *Herodotus sive Aëtion,* 4 (Lucian has been discussing how Herodotus and the early philosophers and sophists gained fame for their works by giving public recitations of them at festivals):   But why

142. This sentence seems to reflect the technical and critical terminology of an ancient theory of color in painting. *Austeritas* refers to the choice of certain groups of colors (see p. 228), and *iucundus* ("pleasing") probably refers to the style used in applying these colors.

143. Phylarchos—the commander in charge of the cavalry furnished by each Athenian tribe.

144. A. Rumpf, *Malerei und Zeichnung* (Munich: 1950), p. 129, suggests that the Argonaut episode on the famous Ficoroni Cista in the Villa Giulia in Rome is a copy of this work.

do I speak to you of those old sophists and historians and other prose writers when, as a last example,[145] they say that the painter Aëtion, after painting a picture of the wedding of Alexander and Roxane, took it to Olympia and put it on display, with the result that Proxenidas, who was then one of the *Hellanodikai* [judges at the Olympic Games] and was pleased with the art, made Aëtion his son-in-law.

And what was the marvellous quality in this painting of his, one might ask, which had the result of making an Olympic judge give his daughter in marriage to a man who was not even from the same region? The picture is in Italy and I have seen it and hence I am able to describe it to you. There is a very beautiful chamber and a marriage bed, and on it Roxane is seated, represented as a virgin of great beauty, whose eyes are cast down toward the ground in modesty since Alexander stands nearby. There are also some smiling Cupids. One of them, standing behind her, draws the veil from her head and shows Roxane to the bridegroom; another, in the manner of a true servant, is taking the sandal from her foot as if he were already preparing her for bed; still another figure, this one also being a Cupid, has taken hold of Alexander's mantle, and is pulling him toward Roxane, using all his strength to drag him. The king himself holds out a kind of garland to the girl, while Hephaistion, who drove the bridal chariot and brought the bride from her house, stands by holding a flaming torch, and leans on a very handsome lad who, I think, is Hymenaios [the god of marriage], although the name is not inscribed. On the other side of the picture are more Cupids who are playing with the armor of Alexander; two of them are carrying his spear and are represented like men who are weighed down with a great burden as they are when they bear the weight of a beam. Two others are dragging one of their own group who reclines on the shield—he must be their king I suppose—holding on to the shield by the handle. Another one has gotten into the corselet, which is lying there with the chest part facing upward, and seems to be waiting in ambush, in order to frighten the others when they reach that point as they drag the shield.

These features are not simply childish amusements, nor has Aëtion wasted his time on them; on the contrary he makes clear by them Alexander's love of military pursuits and indicates that while he loved Roxane, he was not unmindful of his armor. But besides all this, the picture was conspicuous for having had another connection with an actual marriage, since it courted the daughter of Proxenidas for Aëtion. And so he himself came away with a wife, a by-product of the marriage of Alexander, with the king himself serving as the man who escorted

---

145. "As a last example"—Greek *ta teleutaia* could also mean "last of all" or "the last time," which would imply a recent event.

the bride, thus getting a real marriage as payment for the one which had been represented by imagination.

ARCHITECTURE

Works by Polykleitos the Younger at Epidauros

Pausanias II, 27, 5:   The Epidaurians have a theatre in the sanctuary which in my opinion is well worth seeing. The theatres of the Romans are much superior to those anywhere in their ornamentation, and that of the Arcadians of Megalopolis is superior in size. But for harmony and beauty what architect is there who would be worthy to compete with Polykleitos? For it was Polykleitos who made this theatre and also the round building.[146]

The Temple of Asklepios at Epidauros

The large inscription recording the expenses involved in the building of the temple of Asklepios at Epidauros (c. 370 B.C.) has already been mentioned in connection with Timotheos (see above, p. 151). The following excerpt conveys the character of the inscription and provides an impression of the type and number of the jobs involved in building a Greek temple. Note that among the artists and contractors mentioned in this passage is Thrasymedes, who also did the cult image of Asklepios (see above, p. 152). Also mentioned is Theodotos the architect, whose annual wage is recorded.

I.G. IV,² 102, lines 44-67:   Sotairos contracted to provide the elm and the lotus-wood and box-wood for the doors and also for the workshop: [147] 840 drachmas. Thrasymedes contracted to make the roof above and the inner doorway and also [the doorway] between the columns: 9800 drachmas. His sureties being Pythokles, Theopheides, and Agemon. Eukleon contracted to put the tile roof on the temple: 263 drachmas, 4 obols; 5 drachmas, 3 obols.[148] Eudamos contracted to finish the thresholds: 700 drachmas, his surety being Thiares. For the block and tackle equipment to Archedamas: 260 drachmas. Binding materials for the

146. The theatre at Epidauros is well-preserved; the foundations of the *tholos* may still be seen and some of its architectural members, most notably its splendid inner Corinthian columns, are in the Museum at Epidauros. Cf. A. W. Lawrence, *Greek Architecture*, rev. ed. (Harmondsworth/Baltimore: 1952), pls. 88a, 147-148, 151.

147. A workshop, to be used by all the artists working on the temple, was apparently built at the same time.

148. 5 drachmas, 3 obols is apparently a correction for the 3 drachmas, 4 obols originally written.

doors and for the wood up above: 803 drachmas, 2 obols. For the encaustic painting on the *akanthoi* to Dorkon, Anaxilas, Xenophon, and Protagoras: 311 drachmas. Echetimos contracted to make the pavement for the temple: 749 drachmas, his sureties being Kallias and Atlatidas. To Theodotos [149] for another year: 353 drachmas. Mnasikleidas contracted for the tiles: 798 drachmas, his surety being Aristomedes. Timastheos contracted for the polishing of the *prodomos* [= *pronaos*]: 275 drachmas. To Axiochos for the coffer slabs with faces: [150] 128 drachmas. To Kleinias, Protagoras, and Aristomachos for the cymas, mouldings, and coffer slabs without faces: 272 drachmas, 5 obols. Protagoras contracted to do the encaustic painting on the beam-support and on the cyma: 747 drachmas, his surety was Sotimos. Phrikon contracted to work the iron for both doors: 708 drachmas, his surety being Aristomidas. Damophanes contracted for the nails and the hinge sockets and the handles and hinge pins for the doors between the columns: 1,400 drachmas, his surety being Aristophylos. Sotairos contracted to furnish the ivory, as much as is needed for the door: 3,070 drachmas. Marsyas contracted for the polishing of the columns both outside and inside: 1,336 drachmas, his surety being Antikritos and Aristophylos. . . .

The Mausoleum at Halikarnassos

Pliny, *N.H.* XXXVI, 30-31: The rivals and contemporaries of Skopas were Bryaxis, Timotheos, and Leochares, whom we must discuss at the same time since they too did carvings for the Mausoleum. This was the tomb built by Artemisia, the wife of Mausolos, the governor of Karia, who died in the second year of the 107th Olympiad [351 B.C.].[151] These artists put their utmost effort into this work with the result that it came to be included among the Seven Wonders of the World. Along the south and north sides it extends for a length of 63 feet, but it is shorter on the front side, the total length of the circuit being 440 feet; [152]

149. Theodotos the architect received this sum as an annual wage. The temple took roughly four and one-half years to complete. Five regular payments were made to the architect, the last being for six months of work.

150. The technique of painting coffered ceilings in encaustic was an invention which Pliny ascribes to the painter Pausias (see p. 170). This and other details of the temple mentioned in the inscription are discussed in G. Roux, *L'Architecture de l'Argolide aux IVᵉ et IIIᵉ Siècles avant J.C.* (Paris: 1961), pp. 84-130; see especially pp. 123-129.

151. Mausolos was a Satrap (regional governor) under the Persian kings Artaxerxes II and Artaxerxes III; he actually died in 353 B.C.

152. If the building itself was 440 feet in circumference, 63 feet could quite obviously not be the length of the longest side. Perhaps the term *circumitus*, translated here as "circuit," refers to the dimensions of the platform of the Mausoleum, not to the building itself. Others take the 63 feet to refer to the *cella* of the Mausoleum.

the tomb is 25 [153] cubits high and is surrounded by 36 columns. They call these surrounding columns a *pteron* [in Greek]. Skopas did the carving on the east side, Bryaxis on the north, Timotheos on the south, and Leochares on the west, but before they had completed the work the Queen died. They did not stop working, however, until it was complete, having already decided that it would be a monument both to their own glory and to that of their art; and even today their hands rival one another. A fifth artist also worked on it. For above the *pteron* there is a pyramid which is equal in height to the lower part and tapers toward the top in pyramidal fashion with 24 steps; at the top there is a marble quadriga which Pythis [154] made. With this added, the total height of the building comes to 140 feet.[155]

Vitruvius, VII, praef. 12-13: . . . concerning the Mausoleum [the architects] Satyros and Pythios [wrote a treatise]. On these men good fortune conferred the highest tribute. For their works of art are judged to have praiseworthy qualities which are renowned and possess a sempiternal freshness in all ages; for having planned them with deep thought they produced outstanding works. An example [of their planning] is that individual artists undertook separate portions of the facade, competing with one another in ornamenting the work and assuring its quality—Leochares, Bryaxis, Skopas, and Praxiteles, or as some think, Timotheos,[156] and the outstanding excellence of their art created a reputation for the work which caused it to be classed among the Seven Wonders of the World.

Pythios

In addition to being one of the architects of the Mausoleum, Pythios also built, and wrote about, the Ionic temple of Athena at Priene (c. 335 B.C.). It was apparently in this treatise that he criticized the Doric order (cf. Vitruvius IV, 3, 1) and also recommended that an architect should be trained in all the arts.

153. The manuscripts read 25; whether this is accurate or not depends upon what elements Pliny included as part of "the tomb."

154. The correct form of the name is probably Pythios, which is given by Vitruvius.

155. Many reconstructions of the appearance of the building have been attempted on the basis of the surviving fragments. The attempts at reconstruction up to the year 1942 are summarized and illustrated in J. Van Breen, *Het Reconstructieplan voor het Mausoleum te Halikarnassos* (Amsterdam: 1942). For an excellent recent study of the problems of reconstruction, cf. K. Jeppesen, *Paradeigmata* (Aarhus: 1958); illustrations of the sculptures may be found in all standard handbooks of Greek art; on the attribution of the sculpture, cf. B. Ashmole, *J.H.S.*, LXXI (1951), pp. 15 ff.

156. Most modern scholars would accept Timotheos rather than Praxiteles as the fourth sculptor of the Mausoleum.

Vitruvius I, 1, 12: So those who from a tender age are instructed in all the different branches of learning recognize the same qualities in all sciences and recognize the interrelationship of all disciplines, and by this very fact they understand all of them more easily. Thus one of the old architects, Pythios, who was the renowned builder of the temple of Athena at Priene, says in his *Commentaries* that an architect should be able to do more in all the arts and sciences than those who, by their industry and exertions, bring single disciplines to the highest renown.

Philon of Eleusis

Philon was active in the second half of the fourth century. His two known projects were a grandiose porch which he added to Iktinos' Telestērion at Eleusis and a famous "arsenal" (skeuothēkē) in Peiraeus, a storage building for the sails, rigging, and the like of the Athenian fleet. He was apparently a theoretician as well as a practicing architect. His treatise on the proportions of temples and a commentary on his arsenal at Peiraeus are both mentioned by Vitruvius (see below, p. 233), who also mentions the porch at Eleusis.

Vitruvius VII, praef. 17 (following the passage on Iktinos and the *Telestērion,* see above, p. 117): Afterwards, however, when Demetrios of Phaleron was in charge of affairs at Athens [c. 317-307 B.C.], Philon placed columns in front of the temple along its facade and thus made it into a prostyle structure; by expanding the building with a porch he provided increased space for the initiates and caused it to be held in the highest esteem.

Philon's arsenal achieved a considerable reputation in antiquity, possibly as a result of his book about it. According to Plutarch (Life of Sulla, 14) and Strabo (IX, 395) the building was burned by Sulla when he sacked Athens in 86 B.C.

Cicero, *de Oratore* I, 14, 62: For if the architect Philon, who made the arsenal for the Athenians, is agreed to have explained the theory of his work to the people with great eloquence, this eloquence must be ascribed not so much to his skill as an architect as to his skill in oratory.

More important than these literary sources, however, is a very well-preserved inscription found in Peiraeus which gives in minute detail the specifications for the arsenal which were agreed upon before it was built. As Dinsmoor has pointed out,[157] we learn more about the

157. *The Architecture of Ancient Greece,* p. 241.

building from this inscription than could have been learned by an excavation of its remains. It provides a step by step account of how an ancient building was constructed from its foundation through its interior supports to the roof and the final interior details.

I.G. II,² 1668 (347-346 B.C.):   The Gods: Specifications of Euthydemos, son of Demetrios of Melite, and Philon, son of Exekestides of Eleusis, for the stone *skeuothēkē* to be used for storage of sailing equipment. To construct the *skeuothēkē* [storage building] for storing the sailing equipment in Zeia,[158] beginning from the *Propylaia* of the Agora and running behind the ship sheds which have a common roof, to have a length of four *plethra* [about 405 feet], a width of 55 feet including the walls; having dug a trench to a depth of three feet from the surface at the deepest point, and having thoroughly cleared the rest of the area, one will pave the space with a stone foundation and will erect the structure upright and level in accordance with a stonemason's rule, and will extend the pavement over to the piers from each wall covering [a space of] 15 feet, including the thickness of the pier, from each wall. The number of the piers of each row shall be 35, leaving a passageway for the public through the middle of the *skeuothēkē*. The space between the piers shall be 20 feet. One will make the pavement four feet thick, placing the stones alternately crosswise and lengthwise. And one shall build the walls and the piers of the *skeuothēkē* of stone from the promontory, having established a *euthynteria* for the walls with blocks three feet in width, a foot and a half thick, and four feet long, but at the corners four feet and three palms. And on the *euthynteria* one shall place orthostates around the middle of the *euthynteria*, with a length of four feet and a thickness of two and a half feet and one finger, and a height of three feet, with those at the corners deriving their length from the measurement of the triglyphs, leaving doorways at the ends of the long axis of the *skeuothēkē*, two on each, nine feet wide. And one shall construct a center wall on each end between the doors, two feet wide and running ten feet into the interior. And one shall make angles in the wall running up as far as the first of the piers, against which each door shall open. On top of the orthostate course one shall build the walls with squared blocks, four feet long, two and a half feet wide (but at the corners of a length taken from the measurement of the triglyph), and one and a half feet thick. One shall make the height of the wall from the *euthynteria* 27 feet including the triglyph beneath the geison, with the height of the doors 15½ feet. And one shall set

158. An area near one of the smaller harbors of Peiraeus.

into position lintels of Pentelic marble, 12 feet long, with a width equal to the walls, and a height of two courses, doing this after having put in door jambs of Pentelic or Hymettian marble, and thresholds of Hymettian marble. One will also place gutters over the lintels, one and a half feet high. And one shall place windows all around opposite each intercolumniation, and three along the width at each end, three feet high and two feet wide. And into each window there shall be fitted bronze shutters of the proper size. And one shall place cornices all around the walls and shall make pediments and put cornices on the pediments. One shall also set up the piers on a stylobate level with the *euthynteria* [with blocks] one and a half feet thick, three feet and one palm wide, and four feet long. The thickness of the columns below shall be two feet and three palms, the length, including the capital, 30 feet, each with seven drums, four feet long except the first which will be five feet long. One shall place capitals on the columns of Pentelic marble. And one shall put in place wooden epistyle blocks fastening them to the top of the piers, two and a half feet in width with the height of the upper part being nine palms, 18 in number, over each row [of piers]. And one shall place cross-beams on the piers, over the aisle, of a width and height equal to the epistyle blocks. One shall then put in place ridge supports, seven palms in width, and five palms and two fingers in height without the sloping surface, after having put a base in each cross-beam, three feet in length and one and a half feet wide. One shall also fit the ridge supports with iron dowels on the crossbeams, and shall put on rafters, ten fingers thick, three palms and three fingers wide, spaced at an interval of five palms. And having put planks on top of them, half a foot in width and two fingers thick, placing them at intervals of four fingers from one another, and having put sheathing planks on these, a finger thick and six fingers wide, and fastening them in place with iron nails, and having coated these, one shall make the roof with Corinthian tiles, fitting them together. One shall also place over the doors on the walls that separate them on the inside a stone ceiling of Hymettian marble. And one shall put doors on the *skeuothēkē* fitting the doorways, making them of bronze on the outside. And one shall pave the floor on the interior with stones which all fit together with one another and make it level and even on the top. . . . [A section giving specifications for interior storage facilities is omitted.] And so that there may be coolness in the *skeuothēkē* when one builds the walls of the *skeuothēkē*, one shall leave an interval in the joints of the plinth-stones, as the architect may direct. All these things shall be executed by those who are hired according to the specifications and the measurements and the model, as the architect advises, and they will make delivery at the times which were arranged by contract for each of the jobs.[159]

Temple of Apollo at Branchidai near Miletos

The oracular temple of Apollo at Branchidai had been destroyed by the Persians when they sacked Miletos in 494 B.C. *When the Persians were driven out of Asia Minor by Alexander in 333* B.C., *a rebuilding of the temple was begun. Although work on it continued for centuries, the original conception for the temple belongs to the fourth century.*

Strabo XIV, 634:   Next after the Milesian Poseidion, as you go inland for 18 stades, is the oracular shrine of Apollo *Didymaios* at Branchidai. This was burned down by Xerxes, as were all the other sanctuaries except Ephesos. The *Branchidai* [the priests of the temple] betrayed the treasures of the gods to the Persian king and accompanied him when he withdrew, lest they be required to pay the penalty for temple-robbing and treason. Later the Milesians built the largest[160] of all temples, although on account of its size it remained without a roof.[161] For the circuit wall of the sacred enclosure is large enough to hold a village settlement and there is a lavish grove both inside and out. The other sacred enclosures contain the oracle and other shrines. The myth of Branchos and the love of Apollo is set here. The sanctuary is adorned with offerings of ancient works of art, very expensive ones.

THE MINOR ARTS

For the Younger Kalamis and other practitioners of toreutikē *in the fourth century see Chapter 6, p. 233.*

159. On the restoration of the *skeuothēkē* cf. A. Choisy, *Etudes épigraphiques sur l'architecture greque* (Paris: 1884), pp. 1-42, Pls. I, II; W. Dörpfeld, "Der Skeu-otheke Philons," *Ath. Mitt.* VIII (1883), pp. 147-164; V. Marstrand, *Arsenalet i Piraeus* (Copenhagen: 1922); one of Marstrand's drawings is reproduced by Lawrence, *op. cit.,* Fig. 147, p. 260. For a complete translation of the inscription and a more recent study of both the arsenal and the porch of the *Telestērion,* cf. Jeppesen, *Paradeigmata.*

160. This is a slight exaggeration, unless Strabo is referring to the total area of the sanctuary. The *Heraion* at Samos, the temple of Artemis at Ephesos, and the *Olympieion* at Agrigento were larger.

161. Actually the design of the *Didymaion* consisted of a "temple within a temple." Within a huge Ionic dipteral and hypaethral outer temple (167 x 358 feet) there was a small tetrastyle *naïskos.* Cf. D. S. Robertson, *A Handbook of Greek and Roman Architecture,*[2] pp. 152-153, Fig. 66, Pl. VI; A. W. Lawrence, *Greek Architecture,* pp. 202-206, Figs. 110-113, pl. 98-100A.

The Funeral Carriage of Alexander the Great

This chapter may fittingly end with the description preserved by Diodorus of the funeral vehicle in which Alexander's remains were transported from Babylon (where he died) to Alexandria. The lavishness of the monument, its oriental features, and its emphasis on monarchical grandeur, all point to the spirit of the coming Hellenistic age.[162]

Diodorus Siculus XVIII, 26, 3 ff.:   First a hammered gold sarcophagus, fitting the body, was made, and they placed inside of it spices which could both give the body fragrance and preserve it. On top of the casket a gold cover was placed, fitting it exactly and connecting with it all around its upper periphery. On top of this was placed a splendid purple robe embroidered with gold, beside which they placed the armor of him who had passed away, wishing that the whole impression be in keeping with the deeds which he had performed in his lifetime. After this they placed it beside the carriage that was to carry it, over which a vaulted gold roof decorated with scales studded with jewels was constructed, eight cubits wide and 12 cubits long; beneath the roof and running around the whole work was a gold cornice, rectangular in design, with goat-stag protomes done in high relief, from which gold rings two palms wide were hung, and through which, in turn, there ran a processional garland splendidly decorated with flowers of all sorts of colors. At the ends there was a tassel made of netting holding good-sized bells, so that the sound would reach those who were approaching it from a great distance. At the corners of the vault on each side there was a gold Nike bearing a trophy. The peristyle which supported the vault was of gold, and had Ionic column capitals. Inside the peristyle there was a gold net made from woven strands which had the thickness of a finger and [on this] were pictures hung adjoining one another on the same level and equal in length to the walls.[163]

Of these pictures, the first represented a chariot with embossed decoration and in it was seated Alexander, holding a splendid sceptre in his hands. Around the king there was one fully armed retinue of Macedonians and another of Persian "Apple-bearers," [164] and in front of these there were weapon bearers. The second picture showed the ele-

---

162. For a reconstruction of the funeral carriage and an examination of the textual problems involved in Diodorus' description, see K. F. Müller, *Der Leichenwagen Alexanders des Grossen* (Leipzig: 1905); also H. Bulle, "Der Leichenwagen Alexanders," *Jahrbuch der Deutschen Archäologischen Instituts*, XXI (1906), pp. 53-73.

163. The gold netting apparently served as walls.

164. The honor guard of the Persian king had spears topped with golden apples. Cf. Herodotus VII, 41.

phants which followed the retinue, arrayed in a warlike manner; mounted on them were Indian drivers in front and Macedonians, armed with their customary equipment, behind. The third picture had troops of cavalry represented as being drawn up into their battle formations; the fourth picture showed ships fitted out for a sea battle. By the entrance to the vaulted chamber there were golden lions which looked at those who were entering. Along the middle of each column there was a gold acanthus which extended from the bottom, going from one stage to the next, up to the capitals. Atop the vaulted roof, in the middle of its crowning ridge, there was displayed beneath the open sky a purple flag, having on it a gold olive wreath of good size, on which the sun, when it struck it with its rays, made such a radiant and shimmering glow that, from a great distance, its appearance was like that of a lightning bolt.

The platform of the vehicle beneath the vaulted chamber had two axles, on which turned four Persian wheels; the naves and spokes of these were gilded, but the part which struck against the ground was of iron. The hubs of the axles were gold and had lion protomes which held hunting spears in their teeth. Half-way down their length the axles had a bearing which was mechanically connected to the center of the vaulted chamber, the purpose being that through this device the vaulted chamber would be cushioned from the shocks caused by the uneven places. There were four poles on each of which four teams of animals were yoked, four mules being in each team so that altogether there were sixty-four mules, chosen for their strength and stature. Each of them was crowned with a gilded garland, and by their jaws on either side there hung a golden bell, and around their necks the harnesses were studded with jewels.

This then was what the construction of the carriage was like and the impression made by the actual sight of it was even more impressive than its description; it attracted many sightseers because of its far-flung renown. For the whole population from every city along its route always turned out to meet it and again escorted it as it moved on, nor were people even satiated with the delight of looking at it. As an appropriate accompaniment to its grandeur, a crowd of road-workers and technicians followed it, as well as the soldiers who were sent along as its escort.

Arrhidaios,[165] having spent nearly two years in the preparation of the work, brought the body of the king from Babylon to Egypt. Ptolemy, as a mark of respect for Alexander, came with a force as far as Syria to meet it, and, receiving the body, deemed it worthy of the greatest

165. Arrhidaios—one of Alexander's generals, who was assigned the task of transporting the king's body to the oracle of Zeus Ammon.

attention. He decided for the time being not to send it to Ammon,[166] but rather to put it to rest in the city founded by Alexander himself [Alexandria], which came close to being the most illustrious city of the inhabited world. He constructed there a sanctuary which was worthy of the glory of Alexander in its size and elaborateness. . . .

166. Ammon—the Egyptian god Amun was called Zeus Ammon by the Greeks. There was an oracle of the god at the oasis of Siwa in the Libyan desert. Tradition held that when Alexander visited the oracle the priests greeted him as the god's own son. Cf. Plutarch, *Life of Alexander*, XXVII, 3-4.

5

The
Hellenistic
Period

Modern historians apply the term "Hellenistic" to the period between the death of Alexander the Great in 323 B.C. and the rise of the Roman empire after Augustus' victory at Actium in 31 B.C.

The first phase of the Hellenistic period was marked by bitter and extended struggles between Alexander's Macedonian officers for control of his Eastern and African conquests. The result of these wars was the formation of three sizable kingdoms ruled by Macedonian dynasties—the Ptolemies in Egypt, the Seleukids in the Near East, and the Antigonids in Macedonia. A less extensive but equally important kingdom was that of the Attalids centered at Pergamon in Asia Minor. Amid the frequent struggles and depredations of these powers some of the old Greek cities, such as Athens, managed to maintain a nominal independence, while others joined into federalized leagues. But the political influence of the individual Greek cities was naturally of little account in this greatly expanded world.

The cities of the Hellenistic kingdoms, Alexandria and Antioch, for example, consisted of a privileged and educated upper class of Macedonians and Greeks served by a series of lower classes—merchants, laborers, serfs, and slaves—composed, for the most part, from the subject non-Greek populations. The attitude of the Macedonian rulers to these subject populations varied. The Seleukids for a time undertook with missionary zeal to instill the Greek language and culture into them and thus create a truly Hellenized kingdom. The Ptolemies, on the other hand, were content to accept much of the political structure of Pharaonic Egypt and brought few changes into the life of the Egyptian population.

The third century B.C. is characterized by the aggressive consolidation of these kingdoms. In the second century a decline becomes apparent, fostered both by a rebirth of ethnic pride among the non-Greek populations and by the rising political influence of Rome. During the later second century and throughout the first, the Hellenistic kingdoms, like the rest of the Mediterranean world, were gradually absorbed into the growing Roman Empire, of which they became tax-paying provinces.

The artistic history of the Hellenistic age mirrors its political history in many respects. Its early phase (c. 323-250 B.C.) is characterized by ambitious experimentation; in its middle phase (c. 250-175 B.C.) national consolidation and royal propaganda become a subject for art; and in its late phase (after 175 B.C.) the neo-classic taste of the Roman nobility becomes increasingly influential.

In order to function effectively in the expanded social horizons of the Hellenistic world, the artist was compelled to produce an art which was either more generalized or more particular than that of the Classical *artist. While the Classical artist, working within the tightly knit frame-work of the Greek city-states, could assume that his patrons and his audience shared many common cultural, social, and religious traditions, the Hellenistic artist worked for men with varied ethnic, social, and political backgrounds. He was thus forced to appeal either to the indi-vidual sensitivities of his patron or to the basic human emotions shared by all men. Among the significant results of these new appeals was, in the first case, the increased popularity of private portraiture in the Hellenistic period, and, in the second case, an emphasis on dramatic pathos in sculpture and painting.*

SCULPTURE

The Early Hellenistic Phase (c. 323-250 B.C.)

The School of Lysippos

Among the most active artists of the early Hellenistic period were the sons, pupils, and followers of Lysippos. Like Lysippos himself, the school is characterized by a fondness for colossal figures and by the frequent use of torsion in composition. The principal period of the school's influence seems to have been in the late fourth century and in the first half of the third.

Pliny, N.H. XXXIV, 66: Lysippos left behind sons and pupils who were renowned artists—Daippos, Boedas, and above all Euthykrates, al-though the last-mentioned, having imitated the *constantia* of his father rather than his elegance, chose to find favor through the austere genre [of sculpture] rather than the pleasant.[1] Thus he portrayed best a *Herakles,* at Delphi, an *Alexander Hunting* at Thespiai,[2] and a *Cavalry Battle;* likewise his image of *Trophonios* at the oracle [in Lebadeia], several quadrigas, a horse with baskets,[3] and a pack of hunting dogs.

1. The language of this passage seems to reflect the critical terminology of rhetoric, which included an "austere genre" of rhetorical style and an "elegant (Greek *glaphyros*) genre." Cf. Dionysios of Halikarnassos, *De Compositione Verborum,* 22; Demetrios, *De Elocut.,* 128. *Constantia* is probably an aspect of the austere style. It is usually taken to mean "conscientiousness" or "harmoniousness" in the general sense, al-though S. Ferri has suggested that it refers to Lysippos' formulas for proportion and composition (cf. *Riv. del R. Ist. d'Arch. e Storia d. Arte,* 7 (1940), pp. 139-140). Pliny seems to suggest, however, that Euthykrates' *austeritas* lay in the choice of masculine, martial subjects.
2. Some of the manuscripts add "Thespiadas" here, that is "the Muses," but this is probably a textual corruption. It is not in keeping with the virile subjects which Pliny is emphasizing.
3. Baskets—*fiscinis;* some manuscripts read *fascinis,* "forked poles."

Tisikrates, also from Sikyon, was in turn his disciple, but was closer to the school of Lysippos—to the extent, in fact, that several of his statues can scarcely be distinguished [from those of Lysippos] as, for example, his *Aged Theban,* his *King Demetrios,* and his *Peukestes,* the man who saved Alexander's life and was hence worthy of such an honor.

Pliny, *N.H.* XXXIV, 80: Phanis, the disciple of Lysippos, made an *Epithyousa.*[4]

Pliny makes several other brief references to some of these artists.

Pliny, *N.H.* XXXIV, 73: Boedas made a figure who is worshipping. *N.H.* XXXIV, 87: Daippos[5] made a *Perixyomenon* ["man scraping himself all around with a strigil"]. *N.H.* XXXIV, 89: Tisikrates made a two-horse chariot in which [the artist] Piston placed a woman.

Xenokrates, the sculptor and writer on art (see the introduction) was a pupil of Tisikrates or Euthykrates.

Pliny, *N.H.* XXXIV, 83: Xenokrates, the disciple of Tisikrates, or according to others of Euthykrates, surpassed both of them in the number of his statues, and wrote volumes about his art.

Another of the outstanding pupils of Lysippos was Eutychides of Sikyon, known especially for his statue of the Tyche *(Fortune) of Antioch on the Orontes, which survives in a number of Roman copies.*[6] *Antioch was founded in 300* B.C., *and the statue must date from a time shortly thereafter.*

Pausanias VI, 2, 6-7 (at Olympia): By the portrait of Thrasyboulos stands one of Timosthenes the Elean, who won a victory in the footrace for boys. . . . The statue of Timosthenes was made by Eutychides of Sikyon who was taught by Lysippos. This Eutychides made the image of Tyche for the Syrians, a work which is held in great honor by the local people.[7]

4. *Epithyousa*—"girl assisting at a sacrifice." The famous "Girl of Anzio' in the Terme in Rome has been thought to be a copy of this work. Cf. M. Bieber, *The Sculpture of the Hellenistic Age,* rev. ed. (New York: 1961) (hereafter cited as "Bieber"), p. 40, Figs. 97-100.

5. On Daippos cf. also Paus. VI, 12, 6; VI, 16, 5.

6. Cf. Bieber, Fig. 102; Richter, *Sculpture and Sculptors,*[2] Figs. 753-755.

7. An additional piece of evidence is provided by the Byzantine historian John Malalas, XI, p. 276 (ed. Bonn), who states that the Tyche was seated above a figure of the river Orontes, a detail which is born out by the Roman copies.

Personifications seem to have been one of Eutychides' specialties.

Pliny, N.H. XXXIV, 78:   Eutychides made a river Eurotas in which many have said that the art is more liquid than the water.

(Pliny's description of the Eurotas apparently derives its phraseology from a poem by Philippos in the Palatine Anthology, *IX, 709.)*

Eutychides also did a statue of Dionysos which was in the collection of Asinius Pollio at Rome (cf. Pliny, N.H. XXXVI, 34).
The most famous statue executed by a follower of Lysippos was the "Colossus of Rhodes," executed by the sculptor Chares of Lindos. The statue represented Helios, the god of the sun.

Pliny, N.H. XXXIV, 41:   But the work which surpassed all in admiration was the colossal statue of the Sun of Rhodes, which was made by Chares of Lindos, a disciple of Lysippos who was mentioned above. This statue was 70 cubits high [c. 105 feet]; after standing 56 years [8] it was thrown down by an earthquake, but even as it lies on the ground it is a marvel. Few people can get their arms around its thumb, and the fingers are larger than most statues. Vast caves yawn within the limbs which have been broken off, and in them are seen great masses of rock, with the weight of which he [Chares] stabilized it as he was setting it up. The tradition is that the work on it took twelve years and cost 300 talents, which they raised from [the sale of] the siege machinery left behind by King Demetrios when he gave up the long siege of Rhodes in disgust.

Many other references are made to the colossus in ancient literature, but these add little to the information given by Pliny. According to Strabo (XIV, 652) the Rhodians were forbidden by an oracle to set the statue up again. Sextus Empiricus (Adv. Math. VII, 107) tells the unlikely story that Chares committed suicide because the expenses for the statue were greater than the fee upon which he had agreed.
The only other known work by Chares was a colossal head dedicated on the Capitoline in Rome by the Consul P. Lentulus in 57 B.C. *(cf. Pliny, N.H. XXXIV, 44).*
Another sculptor who was not a member of the school of Lysippos but who appears to have been influenced by it was Doidalsas (of Bithynia?). Pliny (N.H. XXXVI, 35) mentions a statue of Aphrodite bathing herself by Doidalsas in the portico of Octavia in Rome; this work is

---

8. The earthquake is thought to have occurred in 224 B.C. The colossus was thus made c. 280 B.C.

thought to survive in the "Crouching Aphrodite," a statue type known through several Roman copies.[9]

Attic Sculpture

THE SONS OF PRAXITELES: KEPHISODOTOS AND TIMARCHOS

Pliny dates these two sculptors in the 121st Olympiad (295 B.C.).

Pliny, *N.H.* XXXVI, 24: Kephisodotos was the son of Praxiteles and was his artistic heir. A work by him which is much praised is his *Symplegma,*[10] notable for the way the fingers seem to press on flesh rather than marble. Works by him at Rome are a Leto in the temple on the Palatine, an Aphrodite in the collection of Asinius Pollio, and, in the temple of Juno within the portico of Octavia, an Asklepios and Artemis.

Pliny also notes that Kephisodotos made portraits of "philosophers" (N.H. XXXIV, 87).

Plutarch, *Lives of the Ten Orators: Lykourgos,* 38: There are wooden portraits of Lykourgos and his sons, Habron, Lykourgos, and Lykophron, which were made by Timarchos and Kephisodotos, the sons of Praxiteles.

Other works by the sons of Praxiteles were an image of Enyo in the temple of Ares in Athens (Pausanias I, 8, 4) and a portrait of Menander from which the identifying inscription is preserved (Loewy, 108).[11]

In addition to his sons, Praxiteles had a pupil named Papylos who made a statue of Zeus Xenios (Jupiter Hospitalis) which was in the collection of Asinius Pollio in Rome (cf. Pliny, N.H. XXXVI, 33).

POLYEUKTOS

This artist is known only for his great portrait of Demosthenes which survives in good Roman copies.[12]

9. Cf. Richter, *Sculpture and Sculptors,*[2] Figs. 135, 764; Bieber, pp. 82-97, Figs. 290-295. Note also that a sculptor named "Daedalus," perhaps originally "Doidalsas," made the statue of Zeus *Stratios* for King Nikomedes of Bithynia when the cult was instituted in 264 B.C. (Cf. Eustathius, *Comm. ad Dionys. Perieg.,* 793.) Doidalsas appears to be a Bithynian name, cf. Strabo XII, 563.

10. *Symplegma*—a group of intertwined figures.

11. For other portrait signatures and literary references involving one or both of the sons of Praxiteles, cf. Loewy, nos. 109-112; Tatian, *Adv. Graecos,* 52; and Pausanias IX, 12, 4.

12. Cf. Bieber, pp. 66-67, Figs. 214-229.

Plutarch, *Lives of the Ten Orators: Demosthenes,* **44:** [Demosthenes himself] wrote . . . the elegiac couplet which was later inscribed on his portrait statue by the Athenians:

> If you had strength equal to your conviction, Demosthenes,
> The Macedonian Ares never would have ruled the Greeks.

This portrait stands near the roped-off area and the Altar of the Twelve Gods [in the Agora in Athens] and was made by Polyeuktos.

Plutarch, Life of Demosthenes, *31, also mentions this statue and notes that: "It stood there with the fingers interlaced . . ."*

The Middle Hellenistic Phase (c. 250-150 B.C.)

The School of Pergamon

The kingdom of Pergamon came into political and artistic prominence under King Attalos I (ruled 241-197 B.C.*). In 238* B.C. *Attalos' armies defeated a host of Gallic tribes which had settled in Asia Minor and had been exacting tribute from some of the Greek cities. The fruits of this first victory were reinforced by a second, this time over the Seleukid ruler Antiochos Hierax, who had hired the Gauls as mercenaries. To commemorate these successes Attalos subsidized at least two victory monuments which represented the Pergamenes as standard-bearers of Greek culture, defeating the Gauls and other opponents. The first of these was set up in Pergamon in the sanctuary of Athena. The famous group of a "Dying Gaul and his Wife" in the Terme in Rome is thought to be a copy of part of this monument.[13] Later, apparently in 201* B.C. *Attalos set up another group on the south slope of the Acropolis in Athens. The figures in this group—Gauls, Persians, Amazons, and even giants—were on a smaller scale and are thought to be reflected by copies in Naples, Venice, and elsewhere.[14]*

Under Attalos' successor Eumenes II (197-159 B.C.*) the great Altar of Zeus at Pergamon* [15] *was built. The gigantomachy frieze of this altar marks the culmination of the grandiose and dramatic traditions which had been developing for a century in the Pergamene school.*

Pliny, *N.H.* **XXXIV, 84:** A number of artists have represented the battles of Attalos and Eumenes against the Gauls—Isogonos, Phyromachos, Stratonikos, and Antigonos who wrote volumes about his art.

13. *Ibid.,* Figs. 281-3, 424.
14. *Ibid.,* Figs. 432-436.
15. The bibliography on the altar is extensive. Cf. *ibid.,* p. 114, n. 45, and for a general introduction pp. 113-118 and Figs. 458-470.

These artists probably worked on the group set up by Attalos I in Pergamon itself. Pliny also mentions a quadriga by Phyromachos (N.H. XXXIV, 80) and some philosophers by Stratonikos (N.H. XXIV, 90). On Antigonos of Karystos, see Introduction, p. xii.

Phyromachos also made an image of Asklepios which was in the sanctuary known as the Nikephorion *outside Pergamon.*

Diodorus Siculus XXXI, 35: . . . Prousias the Bithynian king [Prousias I], when his attack on Attalos [Attalos II] was unsuccessful [156 B.C.], sacked the sanctuary called *Nikephorion* which was outside the city, and plundered the temple. He took as booty both the votive statues and also the cult images of the gods including the famous image of Asklepios, which, they think, was the work of Phyromachos, an example of extraordinary workmanship.

The Pergamene sculptor Isogonos mentioned by Pliny is not otherwise known, and it has been suggested that this name may be a corruption of "Epigonos" whom Pliny mentions in the following passage.

Pliny, *N.H.* XXXIV, 88: Epigonos, who imitated almost all the subjects thus far mentioned, surpassed others with his Trumpeter [16] and with his Infant pitiably caressing its slain mother.

Pausanias I, 25, 2: By the south wall [of the Athenian Acropolis] Attalos dedicated [figures representing] the legendary war of the giants who lived in the area of Thrace and the isthmus of Pallene, the battle of the Athenians against the Amazons and their exploit against the Persians at Marathon, and the destruction of the Gauls in Mysia, each figure being about two cubits [in height].

This dedication in Athens demonstrates clearly that Attalos I sought to link his victory over the Gauls with all the great victories of "civilization over barbarism" in the Greek past.

The great Pergamene altar is mentioned in only one [17] scant reference.

Ampelius, *Liber Memorialis* VIII, 14: At Pergamon there is a great marble altar, 40 feet high, and with extremely large sculptures; it [the sculptural decoration] consists of the battle of the giants.

16. The "Dying Gaul" in the Capitoline is represented with a trumpet lying on the ground beside him and may be a copy of this work. Cf. *Ibid.*, Figs. 426-427.

17. Unless the mention of a "throne of Satan" at Pergamon in the Bible (*Revelation* II, 12) also refers to the altar.

The School of Rhodes

THE SCULPTORS OF THE LAOKOÖN

Pliny, *N.H.* XXXVI, 37:   Furthermore the fame of many is not great, for in certain instances the number of artists involved stands in the way of their achieving individual renown even in the case of outstanding works, since no single person received the glory and since many names cannot all be recognized equally. Thus it is with the Laokoön in the palace of the emperor Titus, a work which must be considered superior to all the products of the arts of painting and sculpture. From one stone the eminent artists Hagesandros, Polydoros, and Athenodoros of Rhodes, following an agreed upon plan, made him [Laokoön], his sons, and the marvellous intertwinings of the snakes.

The statue which Pliny describes is normally assumed to be the famous Laokoön in the Vatican Museum,[18] although that statue is made of five blocks, not one. It is now generally agreed that the statue dates from about the middle of the second century B.C.[19] *The names of Hagesandros and Athenodoros occur on inscriptions of a later date, but these names were not uncommon and the inscriptions probably refer to different sculptors.*

APOLLONIOS AND TAURISKOS OF TRALLES (IN KARIA)

Pliny, *N.H.* XXXVI, 33-34:   Asinius Pollio, being a man of great enthusiasm, naturally wanted his art collection to be seen. In it are . . . the *Hermerotes* [20] of Tauriskos (not the engraver [*caelator*], but rather an artist from Tralles) . . . and a Zethos and Amphion along with Dirke, the bull and the rope—all carved from the same piece of stone— a work by Apollonios and Tauriskos which was brought from Rhodes. These men caused a controversy about their parents,[21] professing that although Menekrates [22] appeared to be their father, their actual father was Artemidoros.

The famous "Farnese Bull" [23] *in Naples is probably a rather late copy of the group of Zethos, Amphion, etc. Judging by this work and*

18. Cf. Bieber, pp. 134-135, Figs. 530-533.
19. On the date see G. M. A. Richter, *Three Critical Periods of Greek Sculpture* (Oxford, 1951), pp. 48 and 300 ff.
20. *Hermerotes*—double busts with Hermes and Eros back to back.
21. *Parentum...certamen* might also be translated as a "competition of parents."
22. An artist named Menekrates is known from an inscription to have been the architect of the Pergamon altar. Possibly Menekrates adopted Apollonios and Tauriskos.
23. Cf. Bieber, Fig. 529; Richter, *Sculpture and Sculptors,*2 Fig. 772.

the Laokoön, the artistic tour de force *seems to have been a Rhodian specialty.*

ARISTONIDAS AND MNASTIMOS

An inscription from Rhodes dating c. 200 B.C. *(Loewy, no. 197) records the signature of Mnastimos the son of Aristonidas. We are also told by Pliny (N.H. XXV, 146) that Mnastimos, the "son and disciple" of Aristonidas, was a painter (as well as a sculptor). One work by Aristonidas is described by Pliny.*

Pliny, *N.H.* XXXIV, 140: The artist Aristonidas, when he wanted to represent the madness of Athamas subsiding into remorse after he had thrown his son Learchos over the precipice, made a mixture of bronze and iron, so that, when the rust shone through the sleek beauty of the bronze, a blush of shame would be expressed. This statue still exists today in Rhodes.

Other Artists of the Mid-Hellenistic Period

BOETHOS OF KALCHEDON (ON THE BOSPOROS)

There are several artists by the name of Boethos, but the one mentioned in the following passages was probably active in the first half of the third century B.C.

Pliny, *N.H.* XXXIV, 84: By Boethos, who was better known for working in silver, there is a child . . . strangling a goose.[24]

This boy strangling a goose may be the work mentioned, along with others, in the Fourth Mime *of Herondas. In this mime two women, Kynno and Kokkale, have entered the sanctuary of Asklepios at Kos and are admiring some of the statues set up there.*

Herondas IV, 20-34:

Kokkale: "Oh my, Kynno dear, what beautiful statues. Who was the artist who made this stone and who set it up?"

Kynno: "The children of Praxiteles! Don't you see those letters on the base? And Euthies and Prexon set it up."

Kokkale: "May Paion be gracious to such people and to Euthies for these beautiful works. Look, dearie, look at that child gazing upward toward the apple. Wouldn't you say that if she doesn't get the apple

---

24. The work is known through several Roman copies, cf. Richter, *Sculpture and Sculptors,*[2] Fig. 762; Bieber, Fig. 285.

she might expire on the spot? And look at that old man, Kynno—and by the Fates, look how that child strangles the Egyptian goose. If the stone weren't right in front of us, this work, you might say, would start talking. My, my! The time will come when man will put real life into these stones!"

Pausanias V, 17, 4 (at Olympia):   There is a gilt, nude child seated before Aphrodite [in the *Heraion* at Olympia]; this was wrought by Boethos of Kalchedon.

An original bronze group representing a winged boy leaning on a herm and signed by "Boethos of Kalchedon" has been found in the sea off the coast of Tunisia and is now in Tunis.[25]

Euboulides the Elder

Pliny (N.H. XXXIV, 88) states that "Euboulides is praised for his 'man counting with his fingers'." Many modern scholars associate this reference with a portrait of the Stoic philosopher Chrysippos, known through several copies, which dates from c. 225-200 B.C.[26]

The Rise of Classicism and the Late Hellenistic Period—
c. 175 B.C. and after

As the great art of the Classical period receded farther into the Greek past, it began to take on an aura of sanctity in the minds of both the later Hellenistic artists and their patrons (especially the Romans). A desire to imitate the masterpieces of the Classical period, and, subsequently through the use of newly invented machines, to copy it mechanically, characterizes much of the art of the late Hellenistic period; nevertheless, a few powerful artistic personalities continued to make their marks as individuals within the classicistic movement.

Damophon of Messene

Damophon was one of the earliest classicists. A group of original cult statues, which he made for the sanctuary of Despoina ("the Mistress") at Lykosoura in Arcadia were found in 1889, fragments of the group are in the small museum in Lykosoura, while others are in the National Museum in Athens.[27] *They are described by Pausanias.*

25. Bieber, p. 82, Figs. 287-289; Richter, *Sculpture and Sculptors,*2 p. 300, Figs. 762-766.

26. Cf. Bieber, pp. 68-70, Figs. 234-242.

27. For the latter see Richter, *op. cit.,* Figs. 758-759; see also Bieber, Figs. 665-668.

Pausanias VIII, 37, 3-5 (in the temple of Despoina): The images of Despoina and Demeter themselves, the throne on which they sit, and the stool beneath their feet are all of one stone. No part of the drapery, nor any of the parts carved around the throne, nor any other part of the stone is clamped by iron or cement, but all the parts are from one piece of stone. This stone was not brought [to the sanctuary] by them, but they say that, following a vision in a dream, they dug into the earth within the sanctuary and found it. The size of both of the images is about like that of the Mother in Athens. Demeter carries a torch in her right hand, while the other hand rests upon Despoina. Despoina holds a sceptre and has what is called "the *cista*" on her knees. Beside the throne by Demeter stands Artemis who is wrapped in the skin of a deer and has a quiver slung over her shoulders; in one of her hands she holds a torch and in the other two serpents. Alongside Artemis, a dog of the type which is suitable for hunting is reclining. Near Despoina stands Anytos, who was represented in the form of an armed warrior. Those around the sanctuary say that Despoina was brought up by Anytos, and that Anytos was one of those who are called Titans.

In the course of describing other works by Damophon at Messene, Pausanias mentions that the sculptor did an admirable job of repairing Pheidias' Zeus at Olympia. This assignment may have been the cause of or the result of his affinity for the Classical style.

Pausanias IV, 31, 6-10: A statue which is most worthy of mention is the image of the Mother of the Gods in Parian marble, a work of Damophon, who made refittings of the utmost precision on the Zeus at Olympia when the ivory on it cracked. For this service, honors have been bestowed on him by the Eleans. Also by Damophon is [the statue of the goddess] called *Laphria* by the Messenians . . . [a discussion of the cult of Artemis *Laphria* intervenes] . . . The greatest number of images and those which are most worth seeing are in the sanctuary of Asklepios. In one separate group there are images of the god and his children and in another are images of Apollo, the Muses and Herakles. Also represented are the city of Thebes, Epaminondas the son of Tyche, and Artemis *Phōsphoros* ["Light-bringer"]; Damophon made those of the statues which are made of stone [I know of no Messenian other than him who achieved importance as a maker of images]; the portrait of Epaminondas is of iron and is the work of some other artist, not him.

Pausanias VII, 23, 5-7: At Aigion [in Achaea] there is an ancient sanctuary of Eileithyia, and [the image of] Eileithyia is covered from head to foot with a fine woven garment; it is a wooden image except for the face, hands, and feet—these are made of Pentelic marble. One of her hands is stretched out straight, the other holds a torch. One might con-jecture that torches are an attribute of Eileithyia because the birth-pains of women are like fire.[28] The torches might also be explained by the fact that it is Eileithyia who brings children to the light. The image is the work of Damophon of Messene.

Not far from the sanctuary of Eileithyia is one of Asklepios with images of Hygieia and Asklepios. The iambic inscription on the base says that they were made by Damophon of Messene.

Pausanias VIII, 31, 1-6 (at Megalopolis in Arcadia):   At the other end of the stoa [of Aristander] toward the west there is a sanctuary of the Great Goddesses. The Great Goddesses are Demeter and Kore, as I have made clear in my chapter on Messenia. The Arcadians call Kore *Sōteira* ["Savior"]. Carved in relief before the entrance are Artemis on one side and Asklepios and Hygieia on the other. Of the Great God-desses Demeter is made completely of stone, while *Sōteira* has drapery made of wood. The height of each is about fifteen feet. [Damophon of Messene[29]] made these images and also the rather small maidens in front of them, who are dressed in tunics reaching to the ankles and each of whom carries on her head a basket filled with flowers. These are said to be the daughters of Damophon, but by those who incline to a more religious interpretation they are thought to be Athena and Artemis collecting flowers with Persephone. Next to Demeter there is a Herakles, about a cubit tall. Onomakritos says in his epic verses that this Herakles is one of those who are called "Idaian Daktyls." . . . [Pausanias then mentions a table carved with reliefs of Apollo, Pan, and the Nymphs, but it is not clear whether this is a work of Damophon] With-in the sanctuary of the Great Goddesses there is also a shrine of Aphro-dite. Before the entrance are ancient wooden images of Hera, Apollo, and the Muses (these, they say, were brought from Trapezos) while in the temple are images made by Damophon of Messene—a wooden Hermes and an Aphrodite made of wood except for her hands, face, and feet which are of stone. They ascribe the title *Machanitis* ["the Contriver"] to this goddess with considerable justification it seems to me, for on account of the works of Aphrodite there has been much devising and all sorts of discourses have been invented by men.

Pasiteles

Pasiteles, a Greek from south Italy, and a noted sculptor, silver-smith, and writer, was one of the most influential classicists. According

28. Eileithyia was the goddess of childbirth.
29. The name is missing in the text, but the reference to Damophon which fol-lows makes the restoration of it certain.

to Pliny (N.H. *XXXIII, 156*) *he lived "around the time of Pompey the Great," that is, c. 108-48* B.C.[30]

Pliny, *N.H.* XXXV, 156: [Varro] also praised Pasiteles who said that modelling was the mother both of working sculpture in metal [*caelaturae*] and of carving statues [*statuariae scalpturaeque*] and who, although he was outstanding in all these arts, never made anything unless he made a model [31] beforehand.

Pliny, *N.H.* XXXVI, 39: Varro . . . is also an admirer of Pasiteles who wrote five volumes on famous works throughout the world. He was born on the Greek coast of Italy and was given Roman citizenship along with the towns there [89/88 B.C.]; it was he who made the ivory statue of Jupiter in the temple of Metellus at the approach to the *Campus Martius*. It once happened that when he was on the dockyards where there were some wild African animals and was looking into a cage at a lion of which he was making an engraving, a panther broke out of another cage, and posed no slight danger to this most attentive artist. He is said to have made many works, but those which he made are not enumerated by name.

Cicero, *De Divinatione* I, 36, 79 (in the course of describing omens at the birth of famous men, Cicero refers to Roscius, a famous actor): . . . when he [Roscius] was in the cradle and was being brought up in Solonium, which is a field in the territory of Lanuvium, his nurse once woke up suddenly and perceived in the night by the light of a lamp the sleeping boy entwined in the embrace of a serpent. . . . Pasiteles engraved this scene on silver, and our own Archias expressed it in verse.

Neo-Attic Sculptors

POLYKLES, TIMOKLES, TIMARCHIDES, DIONYSIOS, AND POLYKLES II

According to Pliny (N.H. XXXIV, 51) Polykles and Timokles were among the sculptors who were active in the 156th Olympiad (156 B.C.*).*

30. On the style and the influence of Pasiteles see M. Borda, *La Scuola di Pasitele* (Bari: 1953). No work by Pasiteles himself has been positively identified, but works of his school are known. A statue of a youth signed by "Stephanos the pupil of Pasiteles" is in the Villa Albani in Rome. Cf. Richter, *Sculpture and Sculptors*,[2] Fig. 773; for other copies of the same figure see Bieber, Figs. 784-786; a group signed by "Menelaos the pupil of Stephanos," apparently representing Orestes and Electra, is in the Terme in Rome. Cf. Richter, *op. cit.*, Fig. 775; Bieber, Figs. 787-788.

31. "Made a model"—*antequam finxit*. Richter has suggested, however, that the phrase may refer to the taking of plaster models as part of a copying technique. Cf. *Ancient Italy*, pp. 112-116.

Pliny, N.H. XXXVI, 35: . . . Timarchides made the Apollo who holds a *kithara* in the same temple [the temple of Apollo near the Portico of Octavia], and in the temple of Juno within the Portico of Octavia the image of the goddess herself is by Dionysios; Polykles did still another one . . . Polykles and Dionysios, the sons of Timarchides, did the Jupiter which is in the adjacent temple. . . .

Pausanias VI, 4, 5 (at Olympia): Polykles, another of the Attic sculptors, and a pupil of Stadieus the Athenian, made a statue of the Ephesian boy pankratiast Amyntas, the son of Hellanikos.

Pausanias VI, 12, 8 (at Olympia): The portrait of [the boxer] Agesarchos [of Triteia] is the work of the sons of Polykles.

Pausanias X, 34, 7 (in the sanctuary of Athena *Kranaia* at Elateia): The image [of Athena] was also made by the sons of Polykles. It is armed as if for battle, and worked upon its shield are reliefs which are a copy of those in Athens on the shield of the statue called the Athena *Parthenos.*

Pausanias X, 34, 6 (also at Elateia):   A temple is built here to Asklepios, and there is an image which has a beard. The names of those who made the image are Timokles and Timarchides, who are natives of Attica.

Pliny also mentions that Timarchides did statues of hunters, athletes, armed warriors, and the like (N.H. XXXIV, 91), and Cicero mentions a Herakles by Polykles which came into the possession of Scipio (Ep. ad Att. VI, 1, 7). A statue of a Roman magistrate, found on Delos, is signed by Dionysios the son of Timarchides and Timarchides the son of Polykles.[32]

The classicistic strain in the work of these artists is supported not only by the fact that they made copies of famous works like the shield of the Athena Parthenos *but also that the torso of the one extant statue seems to imitate the style of Praxiteles.*

The genealogy of the "sons of Polykles" is difficult to disentangle. One possibility is:

156 B.C.   Polykles, pupil of Stadieus—Timokles, brother of Polykles
     |
     Timarchides (son of Polykles)

Dionysios   Polykles II

This would mean that the sculptors of the statue in Delos were father and son.

32. Cf. Richter, *Sculpture and Sculptors,*[2] p. 304, Fig. 767.

EUBOULIDES THE YOUNGER AND EUCHEIROS

Pausanias I, 2, 5 (in the "House of Poulytion" within the Gymnasium of Hermes near the gates leading into the *Kerameikos* in Athens):   Here there is an image of Paion, of Zeus, of Memory and the Muses, and an Apollo, the offering of and the work of Euboulides.

Pausanias VIII, 14, 10 (at Pheneos in Arcadia):   Among the gods, the people of Pheneos give the most honor to Hermes and celebrate an athletic festival called the *Hermaia;* they have a temple of Hermes and in it a stone image. This was made by an Athenian, Eucheiros, son of Euboulides.

Fragments of the sculpture mentioned by Pausanias in the "House of Poulytion" in Athens have been excavated along with an inscription bearing the name of Eucheiros. They date from the late second century B.C. *Euboulides and Eucheiros must have worked on the monument together.*[33]

PAINTING

Nealkes

This painter has already been mentioned in connection with Protogenes (see p. 177) and Melanthios (see p. 169). Since Nealkes was a contemporary of Aratos of Sikyon, his career must be assigned to the mid third century B.C.

Pliny, *N.H.* XXXV, 142: Nealkes painted an *Aphrodite* . . . he was an inventive and clever artist, as is confirmed by the fact that when he painted a *Naval Battle of the Persians and Egyptians* and wanted to indicate that it took place on the Nile (the waters of which look just like the sea), he expressed by the use of subject matter what he was unable to express by technique: for he painted a donkey drinking on the shore and a crocodile lying in wait for it.

Pliny (N.H. XXXV, 145) also mentions a pupil of Nealkes named Erigonos who began his career by grinding colors for Nealkes. He in turn had a disciple named Pasias.

Artemon

Pliny, *N.H.* XXXV, 139: Artemon painted a *Danaë* with pirates admiring her, a *Queen Stratonike*,[34] and a *Herakles and Deianeira;*

---

33. Cf. *ibid.*, pp. 303-304, Fig. 765.

34. Either the daughter of Demetrios *Poliorkētēs* who was married first to Seleukos I (ruled 312-281 B.C.) and then to Antiochos I (ruled 280-261 B.C.) or her daughter (by Antiochos) who later married Demetrios II of Macedonia (c. 276-229 B.C.).

however his best-known works, which are now in the buildings of Octavia, are his *Herakles* ascending to heaven by the consent of the gods from Mt. Oeta in Doris after his mortal nature had been purged and [his painting of] the story of Laomedon in connection with Herakles and Poseidon.

Ktesilas

Pliny, N.H. XXXV, 140:   Ktesilas became famous because of his insult to Queen Stratonike,[35] for since he was denied honor by her, he painted a picture of her rolling about with a fisherman, with whom rumor said that she was in love. He put this picture on view in the port of Ephesos and made a hurried escape by ship. But the Queen, [feeling that] the likeness of both figures was marvellously expressed, forbade that the picture be taken down.

Herakleides and Metrodoros

Pliny, N.H. XXXV, 135:   Herakleides of Macedon should also be noted. He started his career by painting ships and after the capture of King Perseus,[36] he migrated to Athens where he was active at the same time as Metrodoros; the latter was both a painter and a philosopher and had a great reputation in both disciplines. Consequently when L. Paullus, after conquering Perseus, made a request to the Athenians that they send him the most respected philosopher available for the education of his children and also a painter to adorn his triumphal procession, the Athenians selected Metrodoros, professing that he was the most outstanding man for both requirements, which turned out to be Paullus' own judgment.

Demetrios the "Topographos"

Diodorus Siculus XXXI, 18, 2:   Ptolemy [VI *Philomētor*] the king of Egypt, after being driven out of his kingdom by his own brother, arrived at Rome in the wretched condition of an ordinary man accompanied by one eunuch and three slave boys, and when he perceived along the road the lodging of Demetrios the topographer, he sought out this man and took lodging with him, since the latter had been entertained by him many times during his residence in Alexandria.

Valerius Maximus V, 1, 1:   Nor indeed was Egypt deprived of the experience of Roman humanity. For when King Ptolemy was robbed of

35. See previous note.
36. Perseus was the last of the kings of Macedonia. He was defeated by the Roman consul and general L. Aemilius Paullus at Pydna in 168 B.C., after which Macedonia became a Roman province.

his throne by his younger brother, he came to Rome in a state of squalor along with a few servants in order to seek allies and found lodging there in the house of an Alexandrian painter.[37]

Timomachos of Byzantium

Pliny, *N.H.* XXXV, 136: Timomachos of Byzantium, in the period when Caesar was dictator [46-44 B.C.], painted an *Ajax* and a *Medea*, which were placed by Caesar, after he bought them for 80 talents, in the temple of Venus *Genetrix*. . . . Works by Timomachos which are equally praised are his *Orestes*, his *Iphigeneia among the Taurians*, his picture of *Lekythion* the trainer in agility, a family portrait of well-known people, and his picture of two men in Greek cloaks, whom he has painted as about to speak, one standing and the other seated. His art seems to have been exceptionally successful, however, in his painting of a *Gorgon*.

The Ajax *and the* Medea *by Timomachos were especially famous. The following poems give an idea of their content.*

Anth. Graec. IV, 181, 299 (Planud. IV, 135), Anonymous: The art of Timomachos has mixed together the hate and love of Medea, as her children are being drawn to their death; for at one moment she was nodding in assent toward the sword,[38] but now she refuses, wishing both to save and to kill the children.

Anth. Graec. IV, 180, 295 (Planud. IV, 83), Anonymous: Ajax, son of Timomachos more than of your father, art has seized upon your nature. The painter saw you raving and painted you. His hand grew mad like the man, and he mixed those blended tears from out of all your pains.[39]

ARCHITECTURE

Hermogenes

Hermogenes was apparently the most influential architectural theoretician of the Hellenistic period. He was the architect of two impos-

---

37. It may be that Demetrios specialized in the type of abbreviated landscape vignettes with Egyptian subject matter which are found on the "Barberini Mosaic" from Praeneste and in the "Nilotic Landscapes." On these monuments cf. G. Gullini, *I Mosaici di Palestrina* (Rome, 1956); G. Bendinelli, "Influssi dell'Egitto Ellenistico sull'Arte Romana," *Bulletin de la Société Royale d'Archéologie d'Alexandrie*, 24 (1929), pp. 21-38 and, "Eléments Alexandrins dans la peinture romaine de l'epoque de l'Empire," *ibid.*, 26 (1931), pp. 227-241.

38. Cf. also *Planudean Anthology*, IV, 136-140.

39. See also Philostratos, *Life of Apollonios of Tyana*, II, 22.

ing late Hellenistic Ionic temples in Asia Minor—that of Dionysos at Teos and that of Artemis Leukophryēnē *at Magnesia on the Meander.*[40] *Both date from c. 130* B.C. *Hermogenes' writings, which Vitruvius cites, were probably commentaries on these temples.*

Vitruvius IV, 3, 1: Some ancient architects maintained that sacred temples should not be made in the Doric order because faulty and ill-fitting proportions used to arise in it. For this reason it was criticized by Arkesias, Pythios,[41] and above all by Hermogenes. For the last-mentioned, when he had prepared a supply of marble to build a temple in the Doric order, changed his plan and made the Ionic temple of Dionysos from the same supply of marble. It is not that the appearance of it [that is, the Doric order] is unlovely or that it lacks order and dignity in its form, but rather that the distribution of the triglyphs and metopes is troublesome and unharmonious.[42]

Vitruvius III, 2, 6: Pseudodipteral temples should be so arranged that there are eight columns in front and behind, with fifteen on the sides including the corners. But the walls of the *cella* are to be lined up with the four middle columns in front and behind. Thus there will be a space all around, between the walls and the outer colonnade, of two intercolumniations plus the diameter of one column. There is no example of this in Rome but at Magnesia there is the temple of Artemis by Hermogenes and at Alabanda there is the temple of Apollo by Menesthes.[43]

Vitruvius III, 3, 6-9 (on the arrangement of temples known as *eustyle* and other arrangements discussed by Hermogenes): "The theory of the *eustyle* arrangement must now be discussed; it is a style which deserves the highest commendation since its theoretical basis takes into account practical use, beauty of appearance, and solidity. For the space in the intervals should be two and one-quarter column diameters, but the middle intercolumniation, one of which shall be in the front, another in the back, shall have a width of three column diameters. Thus the

40. On the Artemis temple see Robertson, *A Handbook of Greek and Roman Architecture,*² pp. 155-157, Figs. 67-68. A plate comparing the Teos temple with the eustyle temple as described by Vitruvius is included in M. H. Morgan's translation of Vitruvius (Cambridge, Mass.: 1914), p. 81.

41. Arkesias wrote on the Corinthian order (see p. 233) and was probably a Hellenistic architect. Pythios, as has been indicated, was one of the architects of the Mausoleum (see p. 184).

42. Vitruvius refers here to the difficulty in the Doric order of placing corner triglyphs over the center of the corner columns and at the same time keeping consistent proportions in both the triglyphs and metopes. On this problem see Robertson, *Handbook of Greek and Roman Architecture,*² pp. 106-113.

43. Menesthes is otherwise unknown.

building shall have beauty of design, its entrance shall be accessible without impediments, and the ambulatory around the cella shall have impressiveness. . . . (Sec. 8) We have no example of this at Rome, but in Asia there is the hexastyle temple of Dionysos at Teos.

These proportions were established by Hermogenes, who also first developed the *exostyle* or pseudodipteral plan. For he removed the inner rows of thirty-four columns from the specifications of the dipteral plan, and by this arrangement he reduced the labor which was needed and made a saving. He produced through this admirable alteration a wider space for walking around the cella but did nothing which would detract from the appearance of the temple, and so, without making one feel the lack of the superfluous parts, he preserved, by this arrangement, the impressiveness of the whole work. (Sec. 9) For this theory of the *pteroma* [ambulatory] and of the disposition of the columns around the temple was devised so that the appearance of the building, owing to the sharp quality of the intercolumniations, would have impressiveness; and if a heavy rainstorm should catch a multitude of people by surprise and force them indoors, there would be a wide and unobstructed space for them to wait in within the temple around the *cella*. These then are the explanations underlying the pseudodipteral plan of temples. It would thus seem that the effect of the works of Hermogenes must have been one of great and acute skill and that he produced and left behind sources, from which later generations could derive the theoretical principles for their own training.

Hermogenes' temple of Artemis is also praised by Strabo.

Strabo XIV, 647: In the city today there is a sanctuary of Artemis *Leukophryēnē*, which, in the size of the temple and in the number of votives falls short of that of Ephesos, but in its harmonious appearance and the artistic skill displayed in the construction of the sacred enclosure, is much superior. In size it surpasses all those in Asia except two, that in Ephesos and that at Didyma.

Cossutius and the Olympieion in Athens

While ancient literature frequently makes mention of Greek artists in the service of Romans, examples of Roman artists in the service of Greeks are almost unknown. One rare example is that of the Roman architect Cossutius, who was hired by the Seleukid king Antiochos IV Epiphanēs (ruled 175-163 B.C.) to supervise the rebuilding of the temple of Olympian Zeus in Athens. This huge temple had been begun in the late sixth century B.C. in the Doric order, but only the foundations were completed before work was abandoned. When Cossutius took up the work again in the mid second century B.C., *he decided to employ the Corinthian order. He too left the temple incomplete,*44 *and it was not finished until the time of the emperor Hadrian (117-138* A.D.*).*45

Vitruvius VII, praef. 15 and 17: For at Athens the architects Antistates, Kallaischros, Antimachides, and Porinos laid the foundations for Peisistratos [governed 560-527 B.C.] when he was making the temple of Zeus *Olympios,* but after his death, because of the interruption resulting from [the establishment of] the republic [510 B.C.], they left it unfinished. Accordingly about four hundred years later, when King Antiochos promised to pay the expenses for the work, a Roman citizen named Cossutius, an architect of the highest skill and learning, designed in a noble fashion the dimensions of the *cella* and the placement of the dipteral colonnade around it and also established symmetrical relationships for the epistyle and the rest of its ornamentation. As a result this work is revered for its magnificence not only by the general public but also by the select few. . . . (Sec. 17) And it is recorded that the building of the *Olympieion* in the city, designed as it was with its ample module and its Corinthian measurements and proportions (as discussed above), was undertaken by Cossutius, by whom, however, there is no commentary extant.

THE MINOR ARTS

The Table by Kolotes at Olympia 46

Pausanias V, 20, 1-3: There are other offerings here . . . [including] a table on which crowns for the victors are laid out beforehand. . . . The table is made of ivory and gold and is the work of Kolotes. They say that this Kolotes was from Herakleia, but those who have devoted considerable attention to the study of sculptors say that he was a Parian and a pupil of Pasiteles, and also that Pasiteles himself was a pupil of

44. Pliny, *N.H.* XXXVI, 45, notes that the temple was still unfinished in his day (mid first century A.D.) and that Sulla carried off some of its columns to Rome (probably in 83 B.C.).

45. Some of its columns still stand in Athens today, cf. Lawrence, *Greek Architecture,* pl. 106-108.

46. Many, if not most, modern scholars have ascribed this table to Kolotes the pupil of Pheidias (see p. 80), and their ascription may be correct. But since Pausanias clearly says that this Kolotes was a pupil of Pasiteles (and the only Pasiteles is the late Hellenistic master from south Italy), he may be a Hellensistic artist from Herakleia in south Italy whom some historians confused with the earlier Kolotes, who was perhaps from Paros.

. . . [lacuna]. Represented on it are Hera, Zeus, the Mother of the Gods, Hermes, and Apollo with Artemis. Behind is a scene representing the games. On one side of it are Asklepios and Hygieia, one of the daughters of Asklepios; also Ares and, by him, Agon ["Contest"]. On the other side are Pluto, Dionysos, and also Persephone and the Nymphs, one of whom carries a ball. As for the key—for Pluto holds a key—they say that the place which is called Hades has been locked up by Pluto and that no one will ever come back from it again.

6

Art History,
Aesthetics,
and Comparative Criticism

Included in this section are passages which treat a sizable number of artists for the purpose either of putting them into historical perspective or of arriving at a relative evaluation of their styles or both. Most of the artists enumerated in them have already been dealt with, but, as will be seen, to break down these passages by author would destroy their effect. Passages which do not deal with specific artists but which express characteristic attitudes toward art in the ancient world are also given here.

GENERAL

Quintilian's History of Greek Art

See Introduction, p. xiv.

Quintilian, *Institutio Oratoria* XII, x, 1-10: [the works produced by any art] differ greatly from one another; for they differ not only by species—as statue differs from statue, picture from picture, and action from action—but also in genus—as statues in the Etruscan style differ from Greek statues, and the Asiatic style of rhetoric differs from the Attic. Moreover just as these different genera of works of which I speak have authors, so too do they have devotees; and the result is that there has not yet been a perfect practitioner of any art, not only because some qualities are more eminent in one artist than in another, but also because one form is never pleasing to everybody; this is partly because of the circumstances of times and places, and partly because of the judgment and point of view of each person.

The first artists, whose works should be inspected not only for the sake of their antiquity [but also for their artistic merit] are said to have been those famous painters Polygnotos and Aglaophon, whose simplicity of color has still such zealous advocates that these almost primitive works, which are like the primordial beginnings of the great art of the future, are preferred to the works of artists who came after them—a judgment prompted, in my opinion, by the urge to appear as a connoisseur. Afterwards Zeuxis and Parrhasios—who were not very far removed from one another in time (for they both were active around the time of the Peloponnesian War, since a conversation of Socrates with Parrhasios is to be found in Xenophon)—contributed much to the art of painting. Of the two, the first discovered the calculation [*ratio*] of lights and shades, while the second is reputed to have concentrated on subtlety of line. For Zeuxis gave more emphasis to the limbs of the body; he thought that this made his art grander and more august, and

219

in this respect, they think, he followed Homer who likes to use the most mighty form in every case, even in the case of a woman. Parrhasios, on the other hand, drew all types of outlines so well that they call him the "proposer of laws," since other artists follow the representations of gods and heroes which have been handed down by him as if there were some sort of necessity to do so. The art of painting flourished primarily, however, from around the time of Philip down to the successors of Alexander, although [different artists were distinguished] for various points of excellence [*virtutes*]. Thus Protogenes was outstanding for laborious care, Pamphilos and Melanthios for theoretical knowledge, Antiphilos for ease of execution,[1] Theon of Samos for imaginary visions which they call *phantasias*,[2] and Apelles for ingenuity and grace, the last of which, he himself boasted, was best revealed in his own art. What makes Euphranor worthy of admiration is that while he was classed among the foremost men in other fields of study, he was also gifted with marvellous skill in both painting and sculpture.

The same differences exist among the sculptors. For Kallon and Hegesias made works which are rather hard and close to the Etruscan style; Kalamis made works which were less rigid and Myron made his even softer than those artists spoken of so far. Precision and appropriateness appeared above all in the art of Polykleitos, to whom the victor's branch is awarded by many critics, although, lest no fault be found in him, they hold that he lacked weightiness [*pondus*]. For while he gave to the human form an appropriateness which surpassed the ordinary,[3] he seems not to have expressed the impressiveness of the gods.

1. "Ease of execution"—*facilitas*. Quintilian elsewhere uses this word to translate the Greek term *hexis* which means a trained habit or skill developed by long practice.

2. Theon's date is not known, but he probably belonged to the early Hellenistic period. Pliny (*N.H.* XXXV, 144) and Plutarch (*De Audiend. Poet.*, 3) attribute to him a painting of Orestes afflicted with insanity after having killed his mother. In later antiquity *phantasia* came to mean something like "imagination" or "spiritual inspiration" (see Introduction, pp. xiv, xvii and also p. 222). Aristotle uses the term to mean "imagination" in a simpler sense, that is, the re-presentation to the mind of images which are based on sense experience but can occur when sense perception is not present (cf. *De Anima* 428a ff.). In a more general sense the word can be used to refer to an "appearance" or "apparition" which is very similar to actual sense perception and hence seems real (for example, Plato, *Theaetetus*, 152c). It is probably this last meaning of the term which applies in the case of Theon. Aelian (*Var. Hist.* II, 44) relates that Theon painted a picture of a young soldier hastening to the aid of his country; in order to make the *phantasia* of the picture more vivid Theon ordered that a military trumpet should be sounded, and that, while the trumpet was sounding, his picture should be unveiled before the public. Theon's *phantasia*, in other words, referred to painted images which were made more persuasive by the use of theatrical side effects.

3. "Surpassed the ordinary"—*supra verum*. The meaning is probably that Polykleitos created ideal forms in which the proportions were more perfect than those found in any living person.

On the contrary it is said that he shied away from representing the more mature age level and did not dare to undertake anything more challenging than smooth cheeks.[4] But those qualities in which Polykleitos was lacking are attributed to Pheidias and Alkamenes. Pheidias, however, is credited with being more skillful at making images of gods than of men, and in working in ivory he is thought to be far beyond any rival and would be so even if he had made nothing besides his Athena in Athens and his Olympian Zeus in Elis, the beauty of which seems to have added something to traditional religion; to such an extent is the majesty of the work equal to the majesty of the god. They affirm that Lysippos and Praxiteles were most successful in achieving realism. Demetrios, however, is criticized because he was too realistic and was hence more fond of verisimilitude than of beauty.

Cicero's History of Greek Art

Cicero, Brutus, 70: Who, of those who pay some attention to the lesser arts, does not appreciate the fact that the statues of Kanachos were more rigid than they ought to have been if they were to imitate reality? The statues of Kalamis are also hard, although they are softer than those of Kanachos. Even the statues of Myron had not yet been brought to a satisfactory representation of reality, although at that stage you would not hesitate to say that they were beautiful. Those of Polykleitos are still more beautiful; in fact, just about perfect, as they usually seem to me. A similar systematic development exists in painting. In the art of Zeuxis, Polygnotos, and Timanthes and the others who did not make use of more than four colors,[5] we praise their forms and their draughtsmanship [*lineamenta*]. But in the art of Aëtion, Nikomachos, Protogenes, and Apelles, everything has come to a stage of perfection.

Late Hellenistic Idealism

As pointed out in the introduction to this volume, one of the principal ideas of the late Hellenistic theory of art history which Quintilian and Cicero preserve in the above passages was that the high point of ancient art was reached in the art of Pheidias. The greatest achievement of Pheidias was thought to have been his ability to visualize and give form to the sublime qualities of the gods; and the supreme examples of this achievement were his Zeus at Olympia and his Athena Parthenos. Although Cicero omits this key idea in the passage above, he develops it fully in the following passage.

4. That is, he represented beardless young men.
5. On the four color painters, see pp. 167, 228.

Cicero, Orator, 8-9: . . . I thus affirm that nothing in any genre is so beautiful that the thing from which it is copied is not more beautiful, as is the case with a mask copied from the face. That which cannot be perceived with the eyes or the ears or with any other sense, we can, however, conceive in the mind through meditation. So in the case of the statues of Pheidias (than which we see nothing more perfect of that kind) and in the case of those paintings which I have named, we are nevertheless able to visualize something even more beautiful. Surely that artist, when he made the form of his Zeus or his Athena, was not contemplating any human model from whom he took a likeness, but rather some extraordinary vision of beauty resided in his own mind, and, fixing his mind on this and intuiting its nature, he directed his hand and his art toward making a likeness from it.

This picture of Pheidias as a contemplative idealist continued to be popular right up to the end of antiquity. It appears briefly, for example, in such diverse authors as the Elder Seneca and Plotinos.

Seneca, Rhetor. Conrov., X, 34: Pheidias did not actually see Zeus, but nevertheless he made [a statue of] him as the thunderer, nor did Athena stand before his eyes, but nevertheless his spirit was equal to the task of conceiving those deities by his art and of representing them.

Plotinos, Enneads, V, 8: When Pheidias carved his Zeus, he did so not by basing it on any model which was perceptible to the senses, but rather by taking from his mind an image which reflected the way Zeus would appear if he did in fact decide to make himself visible to our eyes.

The most thorough presentation of the idea that Pheidias' power of contemplation was a higher power than the ordinary artist's ability to imitate the external world is presented in the following passage.

Philostratos, Life of Apollonios of Tyana, VI, 19: "Did artists like Pheidias and Praxiteles," he said, "after going up to heaven and making mechanical copies of the forms of the gods, then represent them by their art, or was there something else which stood in attendance upon them in making their sculpture?" "There was something else," he [Apollonios] said, "a thing full of wisdom." "What is that?" he asked. "Certainly you would not say that it was anything other than imitation [*mimēsis*]?" "Imagination [*phantasia*]," Apollonios answered, "wrought these, an artificer much wiser [6] than imitation. For imitation will rep-

6. "Wiser"—*sophōtera*. The word can also mean "more skillful," or "cleverer."

resent that which can be seen with the eyes, but imagination will represent that which cannot. The latter will take a reference to reality as its basis, and while terror will often drive back imitation, it will never do so to imagination, for that proceeds undismayed toward the goal which it has set."

Comparison of Rhetoric with the Visual Arts

Dionysios of Halikarnassos, *De Isocrate*, 3: It seems to me that it would not be beside the point if one were to liken the rhetoric of Isocrates to the art of Polykleitos and Pheidias for its holiness, its grandeur, and its dignity; whereas one might liken the rhetoric of Lysias to the art of Kalamis and Kallimachos on account of its subtlety and grace. For just as the latter group was more successful in works which were more modest and on the human level, and the former group was more adept in representing grandiose and divine subjects, so is it with the orators. . . .

Dionysios of Halikarnassos, *De Demosthene*, 50: For sculptors and the apprentices of painters, if they did not have that experience which comes from exercising their power of sight over a long period, would not be able to distinguish easily between the techniques of the different ancient artists, nor would they be able to say with assurance (without having learned it by traditional hearsay) that this work is declared to be by Polykleitos, this one by Pheidias, and this one by Alkamenes; nor with painters that this is by Polygnotos, that by Timanthes, and this by Parrhasios.

Dionysios of Halikarnassos, *De Thucydide*, 4 (illustrating the reason why he presumes to criticize writers who are superior to himself in genius): Certainly because we do not have the ability of Thucydides, and of other men, we are not deprived of our ability to evaluate them. For neither, in the case of Apelles, Zeuxis, Protogenes, and of the other painters, are those who lack the same skill as these artists hindered from judging them, nor do craftsmen of the same ability judge the works of Pheidias, Polykleitos, and Myron.

Dionysios of Halikarnassos, *De Dinarcho*, 7: To sum up, one might identify two ways of distinguishing original works from their imitation. Of these, one is the natural way, which comes from word of mouth information and from a general familiarity with the subject. The other which follows upon the first, comes from first-hand knowledge of the precepts of the art. Concerning the former, what is there that one can say? But concerning the latter one might say something like this: that in the case of original works, there is a certain natural grace, and a fresh quality; while in those works which are made in imitation of them, even though the imitation is of the highest order, there is nevertheless a certain contrived, labored quality which does not arise in a natural way. And on the basis of this first-hand knowledge, not only do rhetoricians evaluate other rhetoricians, but painters distinguish the works of Apelles from those of other artists who imitate him; and modellers do the same with the works of Polykleitos; and those who carve sculpture do the same with the works of Pheidias.

Demetrios, *De Elocutione,* 14:   Therefore the expressive style of the early writers has a certain polished and well-ordered quality, like those ancient images in which the art seemed to have compactness and leanness, while the style of those who came later resembles the works of Pheidias in that it already has a certain grandeur and, at the same time, the quality of precision.[7]

Dionysios of Halikarnassos, *De Isaeo,* 4:   Suppose there were some ancient paintings, executed with simple colors and having none of the variety that comes from the mixing of colors, but precise in their lines and having much in them which was graceful. Then imagine some which were later than these, less excellent in draughtsmanship, but more fully worked out, varied by light and shade, and having their strength in their great number of mixed colors. Lysias would be like the older of these in his simplicity and grace; Isaios would resemble those which were more labored and technically accomplished.

Perfection in the Arts

Diodorus Siculus XXVI, 1:   Neither poet nor prose writer nor any artist in any literary discipline can please all his readers in every respect. It is not possible for human nature, even if it has attained its goal with complete success, to arrive at a state where it is without blame and pleasing to all. It was not possible for Pheidias, who was marvelled at for making images in ivory, nor for Praxiteles, who instilled the very passions of the soul into his marble works, nor for Apelles or Parrhasios, who by their experienced skill in mixing colors brought the art of painting to its highest point—it was not possible even for these men to be so successful in their works that they could put on display a finished product of their skill which was considered completely flawless.

7. Among the "earlier writers" Demetrios mentions specifically Herodotus and Hekataios of Miletos; among the later writers he specifically refers to the rhetoricians Gorgias, Isocrates, and Alkidamas.

SCULPTURE

A Sculptors' Competition in the Fifth Century B.C.

Pliny, N.H. XXXIV, 53: The most highly praised artists have also entered into competition with one another (although they belonged to different age groups) since they all made statues of Amazons; and, when these [Amazons] were dedicated in the temple of Artemis at Ephesos, it was resolved that the most praiseworthy of them was to be selected by the judgment of the artists themselves, who were present. Then it became apparent that there was one which each artist judged to be second to his own [and it became the winner]. This was the one by Polykleitos; next to it came the one by Pheidias, third that of Kresilas, fourth that of Kydon, and fifth that of Phradmon.[8]

Pausanias on the Aeginetan and Attic Schools

Pausanias, as we have noted, was a reticent critic, but there are indications that he had an "eye" for style. One example of this is his frequently demonstrated ability to distinguish at sight between works of the Aeginetan and Attic schools of sculpture.

Pausanias V, 25, 13: . . . This Onatas, even though his images are in the Aeginetan style, I would class as inferior to none of those who are descendants of Daedalus and belong to the Attic school.

X, 17, 12 (in a discussion of the animals found on the island of Sardinia): The he-goats do not exceed those elsewhere in size, but their form resembles that of a wild ram as one would make it in the Aeginetan style of sculpture, except that the hair around their breast is thicker than the way it is represented in Aeginetan art. The horns do not stand out from the head but curl straight back by the ears.

I, 42, 5 (at Megara): The ancient temple of Apollo was made of brick. The emperor Hadrian, however, later rebuilt it in white marble. The image of Apollo called the "Pythian" and the *Dekatēphoros* [tithebringer] is very much like Egyptian carved images, but the one called *Archēgetēs* is similar to Aeginetan works. All of them are made of ebony.

8. Roman copies of some, if not all of these Amazons, have been identified. It has often been suggested that the name "Kydon" is a textual corruption and that the original reference was to "Kydonia," the city of Kresilas. Richter, however, has identified five separate Amazon types and suggests that the text may be correct as it stands. Cf. "Pliny's Five Amazons," *Archaeology,* XII (1959), pp. 111-115.

VII, 5, 5 (on the ancient image from the temple of Athena at Priene): The image is not like those called Aeginetan, nor is it like most ancient images of Attica, but rather, if it is anything, it is distinctly Egyptian.

VIII, 53, 11 (on the road from Tegea to Lakonia): . . . there is a sanctuary of Artemis called *Limnatis* [of the marshes] with an image made of ebony-wood. The style of its workmanship is that which is called "Aeginetan" by the Greeks.

X, 37, 8: . . . The port of Delphi is Kirrha. It possesses a temple dedicated to Apollo, Artemis, and Leto with images of great size done in the Attic style.

The Status of the Sculptor

In view of the many praises showered upon Pheidias and Polykleitos in ancient literature, the following two passages may seem surprising. Perhaps their attitude is more characteristic of the Roman period than of Classical Greece.

Plutarch, *Life of Pericles*, 2: Working with one's own hands on menial tasks calls the labor which is expended on useless things as a witness to one's indifference to finer things. No gifted young man, upon seeing the Zeus of Pheidias at Olympia, ever wanted to be Pheidias nor, upon seeing the Hera at Argos, ever wanted to be Polykleitos. . . . For it does not necessarily follow that, if a work is delightful because of its gracefulness, the man who made it is worthy of our serious regard.

Lucian, Somnium, 6-9 *In this bit of autobiographical reminiscence, Lucian recalls a dream he once had at a time when he was contemplating becoming a sculptor: In the dream two women appeared to him; one was* Hermoglyphikē *["the Art of Statuary"] and the other was* Paideia *["Education"]. The two women fought for possession of him and tried to win him over to their respective sides by speeches. Hermoglyphikē is described as being a rough, manly-looking woman with callused hands and unkempt clothing; Paideia, on the other hand, is described as having a beautiful face and an orderly appearance. The first speech and part of the second follow:* In the end they decided to let me be the judge of which one of them I wanted to go with. The hard and manly-looking one spoke first. "I, my boy, am the Art of Statuary, which you began to learn yesterday. I am one of your relatives and come from the same household. For your grandfather (she was speaking of my mother's father) was a stonecutter and likewise your two uncles earned fine reputations thanks to me. If you decide to put aside the idle chatter and babbling of this one here (and she pointed to the other woman) and to follow me and dwell with me, first you will grow up to be a sturdy fellow, and you'll have broad shoulders; not only that but you will be free of all envy, and you will never go wandering in foreign lands, deserting your homeland and your relatives. Nor will everyone praise you just for your words. Don't feel disgusted at the unkempt condition of my body and the squalid condition of my clothing. After all it was setting out from such beginnings that Pheidias created his Zeus, that Polykleitos made his Hera, that Myron won praise, and that Praxiteles came to be marvelled at. These men are now worshipped along with the gods. If you should become one of these, how could you help but become famous among all men? You will make your father an envied man and bring renown to your homeland." These and many more things the Art of Statuary said to me, stammering at every point in her foreign accent as she strung her words together in an attempt to persuade me. But I no longer remember it all; most of it has already slipped out of my memory.

When she finally stopped, the other woman began as follows: "I, my child, am Education, and am already your intimate acquaintance and friend, even if you have not yet tried to know all about me. Here then are the good benefits which, according to this lady, you will get by being a stonecutter. You will be nothing more than a workman, doing hard physical labor and putting the entire hope of your life into it; you'll be an obscure person, earning a small ignoble wage, a man of low esteem, classified as worthless by public opinion—neither courted by friends, feared by enemies, nor envied by your fellow citizens—but just a common workman, one face in a great crowd, always cowering before the man who is a leader and serving the man who has power over words, living the life of a hare, just a tool to help a better man along. Even if you should become a Pheidias or a Polykleitos and produce many marvellous works, all will praise your art, but not one of those who see your art, if he were in his right mind, would pray to be like you. For this is what you will be: a common workman, a craftsman, one who makes his living with his hands."

PAINTING

The Use of Color

Pliny, N.H. XXXV, 29-30:   We discussed what the single colors used by the first painters were when we treated the question of pigments derived from metals, from which come the different varieties of paintings which are called "monochromes." [9] . . . In the course of time the art differentiated itself and discovered light and shades, with the alternating contrast of colors heightening the effect of one and then the other. Afterwards *splendor* [10] was finally added, which is something different from "light." Those qualities which exist between these [light and *splendor*] and shades is called *tonos* ["tension"], while the joining together and transition of colors is called *harmogē*.[11]

There are moreover "austere colors" and "florid colors." Both types occur naturally and also by mixture.[12]

Pliny, *N.H*. XXXV, 38:   Burnt ceruse [paint made from white lead] was discovered by chance when some of it was burned in some pitchers during a fire in Peiraeus. This was first used by Nikias. . . . Eretrian earth [13] gets its name from that place. Nikomachos and Parrhasios made use of it.

Pliny, *N.H*. XXXV, 42:   Polygnotos and Mikon, those very famous painters, made black paints from grape lees, giving it the name *tryginon*. Apelles invented a way of making black paint by burning ivory, a type which is called *elephantion*.

Pliny, *N.H*. XXXIII, 160:   Polygnotos and Mikon first instituted the practice of painting with yellow ochre, using only that which comes from Attica.

Pliny, *N.H*. XXXV, 50:   These artists made immortal works with only four colors (from the whites they used *Melinum;* from the yellows, Attic ochre; from the reds, *Pontic Sinopis;* and from the blacks, *atramentum*) —Apelles, Aëtion, Melanthios, and Nikomachos, famous painters, seeing that single paintings by them would sell for the value of whole towns.[14]

9. "From which . . . monochromes": the text is corrupt and is translated here in accordance with the editor's idea of what the phrase might have meant. Others take it to mean that the pigments were called "monochromes" after the type of painting in which they were used.

10. *Splendor,* "shine," or "highlight" is perhaps a translation of the Greek *augē,* and may refer to the reflection of highlights from a glossy surface. This was perhaps the quality employed by Pausias in his famous painting of an ox (see p. 170).

11. *Tonos* and *Harmogē* are Greek terms. They probably played an important role in the writings on color by Euphranor and the other painters who wrote on color.

12. Pliny goes on to enumerate the pigments used in each class. Apparently shades of red, blue, purple, and yellow were considered *floridi colores* and the rest were *austeri.*

13. "Eretrian earth" was probably another white pigment with a magnesium base.

14. All these painters belonged to the fourth century, and hence four-color painting belonged to a very sophisticated stage of Greek painting. Cicero (see p. 221) mistakenly assumes that the use of only four colors was a primitive limitation of an early stage of Greek painting. His ascription of Polygnotos to the group is probably erroneous. The original of the Alexander Mosaic in Naples (see p. 175), presumably of the late fourth century and certainly a highly sophisticated work, appears to have been an example of four-color painting.

The Encaustic Technique

Pliny, *N.H.* XXXV, 122-123: There is no agreement as to who first contrived the technique of painting with wax and of doing a picture in encaustic. Some think that it was the invention of Aristeides, and that it was later perfected by Praxiteles. But there were encaustic paintings which were considerably older, such as those of Polygnotos, Nikanor, and Mnasilas of Paros. There was also Elasippos of Aegina who inscribed *enekaën* ["burn in"] on one of his pictures, which he certainly would not have done if encaustic had not been invented.[15]

The Fame of Unfinished Paintings

Pliny, *N.H.* XXXV, 145: Indeed it is an extremely unusual fact and worth remembering that the last works of artists and their unfinished pictures, such as the *Iris* of Aristeides, the *Tyndaridai* of Nikomachos, the *Medea* of Timomachos, and the *Aphrodite* of Apelles, which we have discussed, are held in greater admiration than finished works; for in these the sketch-lines remain and the actual thoughts of the artists are visible; consequently even in the allurement of commendation, there is sadness because the artist's hand was stilled, while he was working on the picture.

Aristotle and Ethos

The term ēthos (see above, pp. 160-161 and p. 174) refers to the inner character of personality of a man (as opposed to his emotions or pathē *which were reactions to experience in the external world). In discussing the role of* ēthos *in Greek drama, Aristotle selects convenient parallels from Greek painting.*

Aristotle, *Poetics*, 1450a23: Further there cannot be a tragedy without action, but there could be one without character. For the tragedies of most of the modern dramatists are without character, and there are, in general, many poets of this sort, who, to use painters as an analogy, are just like Zeuxis when compared to Polygnotos. For Polygnotos was a good *ēthographos* [painter of character], but the painting of Zeuxis has no *ēthos*.

Aristotle, *Poetics*, 1448a1: Since people who are the subject of imitations are represented as being engaged in action, these imitations must of necessity be either of worthy men or inferior men (for characters [*ēthē*] almost always fall into these categories alone, since all characters are differentiated on the basis of evil or virtue), that is to say men who

15. On encaustic see also under Pausias, pp. 170-171.

are better than us, or worse, or of the same sort, as it is with the painters. For Polygnotos represented men as better, Pauson represented them as worse, and Dionysios represented them as they are.

Although ēthos (and the forms derived from it) normally signified "character" in the most general sense—that is, it referred equally to "good character" or "bad character"—there are occasions when, like the English word "character" itself, ēthos could specifically suggest "good character" (as in the English phrase "a man of character"). An example of this usage in connection with painting occurs in Aristotle's politics. Aristotle has been discussing the psychological effects of music, and he brings painting into the discussion to demonstrate how the visual arts are less effective in portraying ēthos than music is.

Aristotle, *Politics,* **1340a33:**   These [visual images] are still not like-nesses of character but rather the poses and colors which result are only signs of character. That is not to say, of course, that there is not some difference which results from our observation of these signs, for the young should not look at the works of Pauson but rather at those of Polygnotos, or any other of the painters or sculptors who is *ēthikos* [concerned with *ēthos*].

Plato and Imitation

In the tenth book of the Republic *Plato presents at length his rea-sons for excluding poetry from his ideal state. The basis of his reasoning, in brief, is that poetry and the mimetic arts in general can only imitate the external world, which is, in itself, merely a weak reflection of the ultimate reality—the world of "ideas" and "forms." By enticing him to become emotionally involved in the "illusion of an illusion," art dis-tracted man from the pursuit of the highest truth.*

This section of the Republic *is really more important in the his-tory of philosophy than in the history of art, since it seems to have had a negligible influence on the latter. But, because it reflects the attitude of one of the great minds of antiquity toward art, an excerpt is included here.*

Plato, *Republic,* **X, 596E:**   (The interlocutors are Socrates and Glaukon. Socrates has just said that there is a sense in which a craftsman, like a cosmic god, can be the creator of all things. When Glaukon asks how that is possible Socrates answers): "You could do it quickly, if you wish, by carrying around a mirror everywhere. For you would quickly make the sun and the heavenly bodies, quickly also the earth, and yourself and the other living creatures, and manufactured objects and plants and all the other things which were spoken of just now."

"Yes," he said, "but these would be appearance, and not things which had any real existence."

"Quite right," I [Socrates] said, "and you are coming to the aid of our argument. For it is to this category of creators that the painter, I think, belongs. Isn't that so?"

"How could it be otherwise?"

"But you will say, I suppose, that the things which he makes are not real. And yet there is a certain sense in which a painter makes a couch, is there not?"

"Yes," he said, "he too makes an appearance of one."

[Sec. 597]: "Well what about the couch-maker? Didn't you just say that he does not actually make the form, which we said is the real couch, but rather that he makes a specific couch?"

"That is what I said."

"Well then if he does not make that which really exists, he should not be looked upon as making something which is real, but only something which is like that which is real but is, in fact, not real. But if anyone should say that reality belongs completely to the product of the couch-maker or of any other artisan, he would not be speaking the truth, would he?"

"That is how it would seem to those who devote time to such arguments."

"We should not marvel then if this turns out to be a kind of dim existence when compared to reality."

"No, we shouldn't."

"Is it agreeable to you," I said, "if we seek to find the true nature of the imitator, whoever he may be, from these examples?"

"If you wish," he said.

"There are then, these three sorts of couches. One of them, which exists in nature, and which we would say, I think, is made by God; or is it someone else?"

"No, no one else, I think."

"And one of them again is made by the craftsman."

"Yes," he said.

"And still another one is made by the painter. Isn't that so?"

"Let it be so."

"The painter, then, and the couch-maker, and God are three commissioners in charge of three types of couches."

"Yes, there are three."

"Now God, either because he did not wish to or because there was some necessity laid upon him not to make more than one couch in nature, accordingly made only one couch which is the real couch. But two or more of this sort were never created in nature by God nor will they be."

"How is that?" he said.

"Because," I answered, "if he should make two, one couch would again appear of which these two would reflect the form, and this would be the real couch, not the other two."

"You're right," he said.

"Knowing this, I think, and wishing to be the maker of the real couch, God, and not just some couch-maker who is the maker of one particular couch, created only one unique couch in nature."

"It seems that way."

"Do you agree then that we should call him its natural creator or something of the sort?"

"Fair enough," he said, "since he has made this and all the other things in nature."

"And what about the human artisan? Is he not the maker of a couch?"

"Yes."

"And as to the painter, is he the creator or maker of something of this sort?"

"Not at all."

"What do you say, then, is his relation to the couch?"

"This," he said, "seems to me to be the most accurate thing to call him—the imitator of that which others create."

"Well then," I said, "would you call him one who produces an imitation which is three stages [16] away from the real existence?"

"Yes, I would indeed," he said.

ARCHITECTURE

Writers on the Theory and Practice of Architecture

Vitruvius VII, praef. 12 and 14:   Afterwards Silenos wrote a volume about the proportions [*symmetriae*] of Doric buildings; Theodoros and Rhoikos wrote one about the Ionic temple of Hera at Samos; Chersiphron and Metagenes about the Ionic temple of Artemis at Ephesos; Pythios about the Ionic temple of Athena at Priene; Iktinos and Karpion about the Doric temple of Athena which is on the Acropolis in Athens; Theo-

---

16. "Three stages" counting the first; in other words, "twice removed."

doros of Phokis about the *Tholos* which is in Delphi; Philon about the proportions of sacred buildings and about the arsenal which was at the harbor in Peiraeus; Hermogenes about the pseudodipteral Ionic temple of Artemis which is in Magnesia and about the monopteral temple of Dionysos at Teos; Arkesias about the proportions of the Corinthian order and about the Ionic temple of Asklepios in Tralles, which [17] it is said he made with his own hand; and Satyros and Pythios wrote about the Mausoleum. (Sec. 14) In addition many less well-known writers have written on *symmetria,* such as Nexaris, Theokydes, Demophilos, Pollis, Leonidas, Silanion, Melampos, Sarnakas, and Euphranor.[18] To no less a degree have there been writers on machinery such as Diades, Archytas, Archimedes, Ktesibios, Nymphodoros, Philon of Byzantium, Diphilos, Demokles, Charias, Polyidos, Pyrrhos, and Agesistratos. As to the things from these commentaries which I have recognized as being useful to our subject, I have collected all these into one body, primarily because I noticed that, while many volumes had been produced on this subject by the Greeks, there were very few indeed by us [the Romans].

THE MINOR ARTS

The Art of Chasing in Silver

Pliny, *N.H.* XXXIII, 154-157: It is a cause for wonder that, in the art of chasing gold, no one has become famous, but in the art of chasing silver many have. The most highly praised, however, is Mentor, of whom we have spoken above. Four pairs [of silver vessels] were all he made, and none of these is now said to be extant owing to the conflagrations of the temple of Artemis at Ephesos [356 B.C.] and of the Capitoline [probably the fire of 83 B.C.]. Varro writes that he possessed a bronze statue by him. Next after Mentor in admiration were Akragas, Boëthos, and Mys. Works by all these artists exist today on the island of Rhodes; by Boëthos [some works] in the temple of Athena at Lindos, by Akragas some drinking cups [*skyphoi*] engraved with centaurs and Bacchantes in the temple of Dionysos in Rhodes itself, and by Mys [goblets with] Sileni and Cupids in the same temple. The representation of hunting scenes on cups by Akragas achieved great fame. After these Kalamis was renowned, and Antipater was said actually to have placed on a bowl a

17. It is not clear whether this "which" refers to the temple or to a statue of Asklepios.

18. Demophilos and Pollis were painters (cf. Pliny, *N.H.* XXXV, 61 and XXV, 91 respectively). Silanion was a sculptor (see p. 138) and Euphranor was both a painter and a sculptor (see p. 139 and p. 172).

satyr who was heavy with sleep rather than simply to have engraved it; [19] subsequently Stratonikos of Kyzikos, Tauriskos, and Ariston and Eunikos are praised,[20] and, around the time of Pompey the Great, Pasiteles, Poseidonios of Ephesos, Hedys, Thrakides,[21] who engraved battles and armed soldiers, and Zopyros, who engraved the court of the Areopagos and the judgment of Orestes on two cups valued at 12,000 sesterces. There was also Pytheas, one of whose works sold at the rate of 10,000 denarii per two ounces: an offering bowl on which the decorated relief represents Odysseus and Diomedes stealing the Palladium. He also made cooks, called the *Magiriskia,* out of small-sized drinking vessels,[22] from which it was even forbidden to make copies by the use of moulds, so subject to injury was its subtlety of detail. Teucer also became famous as an embosser,[23] but suddenly this art degenerated to such an extent that it is now only considered valuable for its age,[24] and esteem is accorded to works which are worn with use, even if the figure cannot be discerned.

19. An epigram in the Greek Anthology (*Anth. Graec* I, 106, 16; *Planud.* IV, 248): "Diodoros actually put this satyr to sleep; he did not simply engrave him. If you prod him, you will wake him. For the silver is overcome with sleep."—suggests that the artist who made the sleeping satyr may have been named Diodoros. Antipater may have been the author of the epigram (although the anthology attributes it to a writer named Plato) or he may have been the client for whom it was made, possibly the poet Antipater of Sidon (late second century B.C.) or Antipater the regent of Macedonia (397-319 B.C.).

20. These were probably all Hellenistic sculptors. The name Stratonikos is connected with the Pergamene school, and Tauriskos with the school of Rhodes.

21. "Hedys" and "Thrakides"—the names were reconstructed by Furtwängler. One of the better manuscripts reads "hedystrachides," which could also be a name. The other manuscripts have less intelligible readings.

22. *Magiriskia* is a Greek word meaning "little chefs." Pytheas probably made little drinking vessels which were in the shape of cooks.

23. "Embosser"—the term used here is *crustarius,* one who works the *crusta* or outer surface of an object by embossing, inlaying, and the like.

24. "For its age"—only in examples which were old.

Appendix

AUTHORS USED IN THIS VOLUME

Greek

Aelian—(Cladius Aelianus, c. 170-235 A.D.) rhetorician and popular historian from Praeneste.

Aeschines—(c. 390-330 B.C.) Athenian orator.

Anthologia Graeca—the name given to a vast collection of short Greek poems—epigrams, epitaphs, love poems, and the like—which range from the seventh century B.C. to the tenth century A.D. The bases of the collection are the *Palatine Anthology* compiled in the tenth century A.D. by Constantine Cephalas and the *Planudean Anthology* collected by the Byzantine monk Maximus Planudes in the fourteenth century A.D. Other poems, not found in either of these collections, are added by modern editors.

In the present volume, references are given to the edition of Brunk and Jacobs (Leipzig, 1793-1814), which was the first complete edition of the anthology and is arranged alphabetically by author. The references given in parentheses are to the original numbering of the poems in the *Palatine* or *Planudean* anthologies; the original numbering is used in the more recent complete edition of Dübner and Cougy (1864-1892).

The poets from the Anthology who are quoted in this volume are Antipater of Sidon (late second century B.C.), Demetrios (date uncertain), Dioskorides (mid second century B.C.), Euenos (date uncertain), Julianus of Egypt (sixth century A.D.?), Philippos of Thessalonica (second century A.D.), Plato (identity and date uncertain, not the philosopher), and Poseidippos (third century B.C.).

Aristophanes—(c. 450-385 B.C.) the comic poet.

Aristotle—(384-322 B.C.).

Arrian—(Flavius Arrianus, second century A.D.) historian from Bithynia.

Athenaeus—(c. 200 A.D.) rhetorician and antiquarian from Naukratis in Egypt.

Clement of Alexandria—(Titus Flavius Clemens, c. 150-216 A.D.) Christian bishop and apologist.

Demetrios—(late first century A.D.?) rhetorician and literary critic.

Demosthenes—(384-322 B.C.) Attic orator.

Dio Chrysostom—(c. 40-112 A.D.) orator from Prousa in Bithynia.

Diodorus Siculus—(late first century B.C.) Greek historian from Sicily.

Diogenes Laertius—(early third century A.D.) biographer and doxographer of the ancient philosophers.

Dionysios of Halikarnassos—(late first century B.C.) rhetorician, literary critic, and historian.

Eustathios—(late twelfth century A.D.) bishop of Thessalonica, author of commentaries on the Homeric epics.

Galen—(c. 129-199 A.D.) Greek physician from Pergamon.

Harpokration, Valerius—(first or second century A.D.) Alexandrian lexicographer.

Herondas—(third century B.C.) Hellenistic mimist.

Herodotus—(c. 485-425 B.C.) Greek historian from Halikarnassos.

Homer—the date of the composition of the *Iliad* and *Odyssey* is usually placed c. 750-700 B.C.

Julian the Apostate—(332-363 A.D.) Roman Emperor 361-363 A.D.

Kedrenos—(eleventh century A.D.) Greek monk, author of a *Synopsis of Histories.*

Kratinos—(fifth century B.C.) Greek comic poet.

Libanios—(c. 314-393 A.D.) rhetorician from Antioch.

Lucian—(c. 120-200 A.D.) Greek rhetorician and satirist from Samosata on the Euphrates.

Niketas Choniates—(late twelfth, early thirteenth centuries A.D.) Byzantine historian.

Pausanias—(middle and late second century A.D.) Greek traveller and antiquarian, author of a *Descriptions of Greece* (see Introduction).

Philo Mechanicus—(second century B.C.) Greek engineer from Byzantium.

Philostratus—three authors, apparently belonging to the same family, bear this name. Flavius Philostratus, author of the *Life of Apollonios of Tyana,* lived in the late second century A.D.

Plato—(427-347 B.C.).

Plotinos—(c. 205-270 A.D.) neo-Platonic philosopher.

Plutarch—(c. 46-120 A.D.) Greek biographer, essayist, and moralist from Chaironea.

Scholiast—the term for a commentator, usually anonymous, who has affixed explanatory notes to the manuscript of an ancient author.

Sextus Empiricus—(late second century A.D.) Greek physician and Sceptic philosopher.

Simonides—(c. 556-486 B.C.) Greek lyric poet from the island of Ceos.

Strabo—(c. 64 B.C.-21 A.D.) geographer and historian from Amaseia in the Pontus region.

Tatian—(Tatianus, second century A.D.) Christian apologist.

Thucydides—(c. 460-400 B.C.) Athenian historian.

Xenophon—(c. 430-354 B.C.) Athenian soldier, historian, essayist, and writer on philosophy.

Zenobios—(second century A.D.) author of a collection of proverbs.

Latin

Ampelius—(third century A.D.?) author of the *Liber Memoralis,* a superficial summary of the most important objects and events in the ancient world.

Cicero, Marcus Tullius—(106-44 B.C.) Roman orator, statesman, and philosopher.

Martial—(Marcus Valerius Martialis, c. 40-104 A.D.) Roman poet born in Spain.

Petronius Arbiter—(died 66 A.D.) author of the satirical, bawdy prose narrative known as the *Satyricon.*

Pliny the Elder—(Gaius Plinius Secundus, c. 27-79 A.D.) Roman encyclopaedist, born near Lake Como (see Introduction).

Propertius—(c. 50 B.C.-16 A.D.) Roman elegiac poet.

Quintilian—(Marcus Fabius Quintilianus, c. 35-95 A.D.) prominent Roman rhetorician.

Seneca the Elder—(c. 55 B.C.-37 A.D.) Roman rhetorician and politician born in Spain.

Statius, Publius Papinus—(c. 45-96 A.D.) Roman poet from Naples.

Valerius Maximus—(early first century A.D.) Roman rhetorician and historian.

Varro, Marcus Terentius—(116-27 B.C.) Roman scholar and antiquarian.

Velleius Paterculus—(c. 19 B.C.-31 A.D.) Roman military officer and amateur historian.

Vitruvius Pollio—(c. second half of the first century B.C.) Roman architect who served under Julius Caesar and Augustus. His *De Architectura* is the sole extant ancient treatise on architecture.

HIPPODAMOS OF MILETUS

Although philosophical prescriptions for the ideal town are given by both Plato (Laws, 778B-779D) and Aristotle (Politics, VII, 10-11), ancient sources preserve relatively little information about the realities of town-planning in antiquity. One ancient town-planner, however, Hippodamos of Miletus, seems to have attained considerable renown. Our sources suggest that he was an eccentric political theoretician who perhaps became interested in town-planning during the time when Miletus was being rebuilt after the sack of the town by the Persians in 494 B.C. Vivid examples of the grid system, which Hippodamos was thought to have invented, have been revealed by the German excavations at Priene and Miletus.[1]

Aristotle, *Politics*, II, v,1-2 (1267b22): Hippodamos, the son of Euryphon, a Milesian (it was he who invented the dividing up of cities and cut up [that is, applies a grid plan to] Peiraeus, and who, in regard to the other aspects of his life, was rather extravagant owing to a need for recognition, to such an extent, in fact, that he seemed to some people, with his mass of hair and expensive jewelry and, along with that, his cheap but warm clothing [which he wore] not only in the winter but also during the warm parts of the year, to live a decidedly peculiar existence; and yet who wished to become learned in the whole of natural science) was the first man of those not actually involved in politics to make proposals about the best form of constitution. He equipped his [ideal] city with a population of ten thousand, divided into three classes. He proposed one class of artisans, another of farmers, and a third to fight for the state in war and to bear arms. He also divided the area of the town into three parts, one of sacred land, one of public land, and another of private land: sacred land on which they

---

1. For a survey of the archaeological evidence, see R. E. Wycherley, *How the Greeks Built Cities* (London, 1949), chapter 2. Excavations at Old Smyrna indicate that the grid plan was used there as early as the seventh century B.C.; cf. J. M. Cook and others, "Old Smyrna, 1948-1951," *Annual of the British School at Athens*, 53-54, 1958-1959, pp. 1-181. Hippodamos, then, did not invent the grid plan, but he may have been the first to write a formal treatise about it.

could make the customary offerings to the gods, public land off of which the military class could live, and private land for farmers. . . .

Aristotle, *Politics* 1330b21: The disposition of private homes [in a city] is thought to be more pleasant and more useful for practical purposes, if it is cut up neatly in the modern manner, that is, according to the Hippodamian system, but, for safety in war, the opposite plan, the type they used to have in early times, is better.

Hesychios, *Lexicon* (c. 5th cent. A.D.), s.v. Hippodamian division: Hippodamos, the son of Euryphon, the astronomer, divided up Peiraeus for the Athenians. This man was a Milesian who participated in the colonization of Thurii.[2]

---

2. Thurii, a Panhellenic colony in South Italy, was settled in 443 B.C. The redesigning of Peiraeus also took place around the middle of the fifth century B.C., which must be taken as Hippodamos' principal period of activity. Strabo, XIV, 654, records but does not affirm a tradition that Hippodamos designed the plan for the new city of Rhodes in 408 B.C.

INDEX OF ARTISTS

GEOGRAPHICAL INDEX

GENERAL SUBJECT INDEX

The abbreviation (R) after an entry signifies "representation(s) of."